DEVELOPMENTAL DISPARITIES: A QUANTITATIVE INSIGHT

DEVELOPMENTAL DISPARITIES: A Quantitative Insight

A.K. AGARWALA
P. HAZARIKA

AKANSHA PUBLISHING HOUSE
NEW DELHI-1100059(INDIA)

AKANSHA PUBLISHING HOUSE
R 37-B, Vani Vihar, Uttam Nagar
New Delhi-110059
Email: ektabooks@yahoo.com
Ph. : 25640621

DEVELOPMENTAL DISPARITIES: A Quantitative Insight

First Edition 2004
ISBN 81–87606–43-6

[The responsibility for the facts stated, conclusions reached etc. is entirely that of the Authors. The publisher is not responsible for them, whatsoever.]

PRINTED IN INDIA

Published by M.P. Misra for Akansha Publishing House, New Delhi and Printed at Mehra Offset Press, Delhi.

To my wife Babita : AKA

To my wife Reeta : P.H.

Preface

At the time of achieving independence, India inherited from the British an economy severely afflicted by regional disparities. The British looked at the problem of regional disparities in the country as a natural manifestation of varying resource endowments of different regions and their geographical location. However, the social scientists and the policy-makers of independent India viewed the problem of regional imbalances differently. According to them inter-regional disparities could by reduced substantially through appropriate government policies. The concern for growing regional disparities was reflected in the Five-Year Plan documents. An objective running through the Five-year plans has been the reduction of regional disparities.

The concept of measuring regional disparities has undergone qualitative changes during the post-independence period. Originally, per capita income was believed to be the most satisfactory measure of regional disparities. Although per capita income can be used as the sole indicator of measuring disparities at inter-state level, it cannot be taken to measure intra-state disparities due to non-availability of requisite data at district, sub-division or block level. Moreover, per capita income may not faithfully reflect the per capita consumption levels. A part of the income earned within the jurisdiction of a state might not be available for consumption within the state, but may get transferred to other states by way of dividend and other remittances. Conversely, income originating within a state might be supplemented by remittances of income from other states. Thus per capita consumption is regarded as a better indicator of measuring regional disparities than per capita income. However, although per capita consumption can be used to measure inter-state disparities, it cannot be used to measure inter-district disparities due to non-availability of such data at district level.

Of late, the researchers have opted for a large number of indicators covering a wide variety of economic activities for measuring regional disparities. Availability of physical infrastructural facilities (such as roads, railways, power, banks, hospitals and dispensaries and soon) helping the growth of the three productive sectors – primary, secondary and tertiary and basic minimum services like primary education, primary health care, drinking water, sanitation etc. also came to be used as the basis for measuring regional disparities.

Our present study which related to the analysis of inter-district development disparities in Assam is carried out on the basis of 25 select indicators out of which seven indicators relate to agriculture, four indicators relate to industry and 14 indicators relate to Basic Infrastructure and Services (BIS). We have analysed inter-district development disparities in the state of Assam on the basis of three composite indices namely - (a) Equal Weightage Index Method, or Indexing Method, (b) Deprivation Method and (c) Principal Comporient Method.

We are inspired in our thoughts by the writings of many well-known authors. The references given at the end of each chapter and the bibliography given at the end been testimony of our indebtedness to these authors.

A.K. AGARWALA
P. HAZARIKA

Contents

1

Introduction

1.1 Besides accelerating the pace of economic development in the country, the main objectives of planning have always aimed at the attainment of an egalitarian socio-economic order with balanced development of regions. The attainment of the objective of reduction of regional development disparities both at the inter-state and intra-state level is very important for a pluralistic and multiethnic society like India. The First-Five Year Plan had two basic objectives – (i) correction of the inequilibrium in the economy caused by the war and the partition of the country, and (ii) initiation of a process of all-round balanced development which would ensure a rising national income and a steady improvement in living standards over time. At the time of the formulation of the Second Five-Year Plan, the objective of socialist pattern of society came to be adopted. This was meant to imply that "the basic criterion for determining the lines of advance must not be private profit but social gain, and that the pattern of development and the structure of socio-economic relations should be so planned that they result not only in appreciable increases in national income and employment but also in greater equality of income and wealth. Major decisions regarding production, distribution, consumption and investment and, in fact, all socio-economic relationships must be made by agencies informed by social purpose. The benefits of economic development must occur more and more to the relatively less privileged classes of society, and there should be a progressive reduction of the concentration of income, wealth and economic power." (Planning Commission, 1956, p 22). This statement has been, in fact, the guiding principle of planning in the country. An objective running through all the nine Five-Year-Plans has been the reduction of regional disparities.

Although the Government of India has given much stress on the removal of regional disparities yet the present trend of economic development in the country has not only led to an increasing level of disparity at the inter-state level but also intra-state and intra-district disparities at the state as welll as district levels. In spite of a significant portion of public sector investment in the backward areas during the planning era prevention of "enclave type" development has not become possible. The policy of development of backward regions has not led to place prosperity with people prosperity. Because of the existance of high magnitude of regional disparities at macro as well as micro level, the country and some states of the country have encountered the problem of regionalism and nativistic tendency, of the ethnic population at various levels. For example, one of the reasons for demand for the formation of different states within the state of Assam is nothing but spatial disparities. Hence, the Central and the various State Governments should be very serious so that the problem of regional disparities can be effectively dealt with.

1.2 PRESENT STUDY

The present study is concerned primarily with the analysis of inter-district development disparities in Assam which is known as one of the backward states of the country. There are, at present, twenty three districts in Assam. An analysis of the disparities in different sectors of the state economy such as agriculture, industry and basic infrastructure and services (BIS) at the inter-district level is attempted through secondary statistics. An overall inter-district disparities has also been analysed taking cognisance of disparities at inter-district level in the three sectors: agriculture, industry and basic infrastructure and services.

1.3 REVIEW OF EXISTING LITERATURE

We have come across several studies made on regional disparities.

These studies may precisely be classified as – (i) disparities in terms of agriculture, (ii) disparities in terms of industry, (iii) disparities in terms of infrastructure, (iv) overall development disparities based on agriculture, industry and infrastructure. We have, of course, come across some works relating to disparities in terms of education, disparities in terms of health facilities and the like. However, health facilities etc. relate to infrastructure. Review of literature relating to regional disparities in agricultural development has been done in the Chapter 3 entitled "Spatial Disparities in Agricultural Development in Assam". Similarly, we have incorporated review of literature relating to regional disparities in industry and basic infrastructure and services in the chapters 4 and 5 entitled "Levels of industrial development in Assam" and "Inter-district developmental disparities in basic infrastructure and services (BIS) in Assam" respectively. Below we have discussed some studies made on overall developmental regional disparities.

Ashok Mitra's Study

Ashok Mitra (1965), the then Registrar General of India conducted a pioneering study on levels of regional development in India using district level data. The indicators used by Mitra were divided by him into the following six blocks and information collected on them for each district of India:

Block I

(A) Geology, Topography, Rainfall, House Type, Language and Scheduled tribes and casts; (B) Soil,Crops and Yield of Rice.

Block II

Agricultural infrastructure which included seven indicators like area under double crop, per cent of net area sown, gross area irrigated per cent of gross area sown, etc.

Block III

Participation rates in trading sector which included five indicators like male participation rate, female participation rate, males working in agriculture per cent of male working population, etc.

Block IV

Potential of human resources which included nine indicators like persons per square mile, females per 1,000 males, rural population per 1,000 of total population, etc.

Block V

Distributive trade, manufacturing and infrastructure which included four indicators like workers in retail trade per 1,000 of population, workers in manufacturing per 1,000 of population, etc.

Block VI

Organized industrial activity in the modern sector which included establishments run on electricity per cent of all industrial establishments, workers in registered factories per cent of all workers and degree of congestion in housing.

Mitra's analysis showed that out of the total of 327 districts in India, 79 were at the lowest level of development and 88 at the second lowest level of development. The number of districts at the highest level of development was 84; 19.66% of the total population of the country lived in districts at the lowest level of development, and 30.72% of the total population in India lived in districts in the highest level of development. *Mitra's study was based on a simple method of "assigning and adding up ranks' to highlight regional disparities.*

Nath's Study

Utilizing the conclusions of Ashok Mitra's study and adopting a similar method of combining ranks (unweighted ranks are simply added up), V. Nath (1970) attempted to highlight disparities between different regions of India. Nath considered data for 14 states and took the following indicators into account: (i) per capita income, (ii) proportion of urban population to total population, (iii) proportion of male workers in manufacturing industry to all male workers, (iv) proportion of population living in districts at the two higher levels of development (data for this indicator were obtained from Ashok Mitra's study), and (v) literacy rate for population in age groups of five years and above.

Nath ranked all the 14 states in respect of each indicator. He then added up the five ranks in respect of five indicators for each state and thus obtained the total rank for each state. The states were then arranged in an ascending order of total rank score, the state having the lowest total rank score being the most developed state and the state having the highest rank score being the least developed one. In Nath's study, Maharastra and Tamil Nadu had the lowest rank score of 14 and thus were considered as the most developed states. Gujarat with rank score of 16 came next. Then came West Bengal, Punjab and Kerala. These six states were considered by Nath as the relatively developed states and the remaining eight states were considered as less developed.

Hemanta Rao's Study

Hemanta Rao's Study (1977) relates to the estimation of regional disparities in India. Rao also made an attempt to answer whether regional disparities reduced over time. He selected 24 variables from the following four specific sectors – agriculture, industry, education and banking. Five indicators related to agriculture, eight to industry, five to education and six to banking.

To form an overall view of regional disparities, Rao combined the indices obtained from the agricultural, industrial, educational and banking sectors into composite index of development. The composite Index showed that West Bengal was the most developed state in all the three years - 1956, 1961 and 1965. The second position was occupied by Maharashtra in all the three years. Tamil Nadu occupied the third position in 1956 and 1961 and Gujarat was fourth in both these years. In 1965, these two states interchanged their places. The agriculturally most developed state of Punjab occupied the fifth position in all the three years. The value of composite index for the nation as a whole was 13.37, in 1956, 14.85 in 1961 and 15.96 in 1965. The index values for the states of Orissa, Rajasthan, Madhya Pradesh, Assam and Bihar were below the national average in all the three years and consequently these states were classified by Hemanta Rao as 'less developed states'. Uttar Pradesh was just around the national average in all the three years.

Rao concluded that regional disparities declined over time. His conclusion was based on the following three observations – (i) there has been a general decline in absolute differentials between the developed and the less developed states, (ii) the national average of composite index has registered an upward trend over time, and (iii) the coefficient of variation of the estimated values of the composite index has declined from 19.70% in 1956 to 13.72% in 1965. While the absolute differential between the first and the last ranked states was 8.8 index points in 1956, it fell to 6.08 index points in 1965. Over the same period, the national average rose from 13.37 to 15.96 index points. The study of Hemanta Rao depends exclusively on the technique of principal component analysis.

Ganguli and Gupta's Study

B. N. Ganguli and Debendra B. Gupta (1976) constructed levels of living indices for 15 states of India. They took into account three periods of time – around 1955, around 1960, and around 1965. The following components of levels of living were considered in the study: nutrition, housing, medical care, education, clothing, leisure, security, and environment. The first five relate to 'primary' components and last three relate to 'secondary' components. Three sets of composite indices were presented. The first covered the 'primary' components, the second covered the 'secondary' components, and the third was an overall index of the level of living which was constructed by taking into account both the 'primary' and the 'secondary' components. As far as the primary aspects of the levels of living were concerned, it was found that in all the three years considered (1955, 1960 and 1965) the states of Punjab, Tamil Nadu, Maharashtra, Kerala and West Bengal showed the highest levels of living. Bihar, Orissa, Uttar Predesh, Madhya Pradesh and Andhra Pradesh showed the lowest levels. Punjab led as the 'highest' state with respect to the nutritional level, Kerala in respect of housing and education and Tamil Nadu and West Bengal in respect of medical care. Examining whether inter-district disparities had reduced over the period 1955-65, Ganguli and Gupta found that in the matter of nutrition and medical care disparities had indeed reduced and in the field of education disparities had widened. As far as the overall primary aspects of living were concerned, it was found that the value of the 'critical minimum distance' had declined from 6.04 in 1955 to 5.61 in 1960 and further to 4.88 in 1965.

By using the method of principal component analysis and taxonomy, Ganguli and Gupta calculated a composite index of the levels of living by combining all primary and secondary indicators. It was found that in 1955, Tamil Nadu, West Bengal, Punjab, Maharastra, and Kerala had the highest levels of living while Orissa, Bihar, Uttar Predesh, Madhya Pradesh, and Assam were at the lowest levels. The same grouping existed in 1960 and 1965 as well, although while Karnataka and Jammu and Kashmir improved their positions considerably, Rajasthan declined to the bottom group. A very important conclusion of the study related to reduction in disparities. It was found that the value of the critical minimum distance declined from 6.04 in 1955 to 5.61 in 1960 and further to 4.88 in 1965 which shows that the disparities in the overall levels of living among the states declined during the period 1955-1965.

Murugaiah's Study

V. Mugugaiah (1997) made a study relating to economic disparities in Karnataka. His study relates to inter and intra-district disparities in economic development of Karnataka at two points of time namely 1980-81 and 1990-91. The districts in the state, based on per capita income, have been classified as highly, moderately and less developed categories. Sectoral composition of output in the districts discloses that tertiary sector exhibits fast growth as well as more contribution for the period of study to district domestic product (DDP) than other two sectors and the contribution of primary sector is slowed down. It resulted to have more number of less developed districts in the state in 1990-91, than in 1980-81.

Dhian Kaur and B. S. Ghuman's Study

Dhian Kaur and B. S. Ghuman (1995) carried out a study for the period 1980-81 to 1988-89 to decompose the prosperity of the state of Punjab over the twelve districts. The study was done on the basis of the indicator 'average per capita income'. Relevant data were collected from the Economic and Statistical Organization, Punjab. Data were analysed by employing techniques such as averages, percentages, growth rates, coefficient of variation and maps.

On the basis of the level of development, various districts of the state were classified into three categories – (i) highly developed, (ii) moderately developed and (iii) less developed. The classification was made for both points of time keeping in view the state average and the behaviour of income across districts.

The study reveals that various districts of Punjab recorded differential rate of growth in their economies during the 1980's. It resulted in both inter and intra-category shifts in their positions. There appeared a notable spatial variation in levels of development in the state by 1988-89. Southern Punjab was more developed than Northern Punjab. It specified that Ludhiana, Sangrur, Ferozpur, Faridkot and Kapurthala districts were highly developed whereas Hoshiarpur and Gurdaspur districts were at a low level of development. The group of remaining districts namely Patiala, Bhatinda, Rupnagar, Amritsar and Jalandhar stood in between the two extremes. It was also found that southern Punjab was more developed in terms of primary activities whereas northern Punjab was more developed in regard to non-primary activities.

Rajkishore Meher's Study

The study made by Rajkishore Meher (1999) was primarily concerned with the issue of inter-district development disparities in Orissa. An attempt was made to detect the number of advance and backward districts by taking key development indicators of agriculture, industry and basic infrastructure and services (BIS) from the state and district level secondary statistics. Meher had chosen *seven indicators of agriculture development (viz.* percentage of cultivable land to total land area, percentage of area sown to total cultivable area, percentage of irrigated area to net sown area, number of electric/diesel pump per 1,000 hectares of area sown, cropping intensity and average yield of food grains per hectare (in tonnes); four indicators of *industrial development* (viz. percentage of secondary sector workers to total workforce, percentage of registered factory workers to total workers, per capita value of industrial output and per capita value added by manufacture) and *sixteen indicators of basic infrastructure and services* (viz. percentage of literate population, percentage of urban population, percentage of tertiary sector workers to total work force, number of primary and middle school per 10,000 population, number of general colleges per 1 lakh population, number of hospitals/ dispensaries per 1 lakh population, number of medical beds per 10,000 population, infant mortality per 1000 births, road length per 100 sq. km area, road length per 1 lakh population, percentage of villages electrified, per capita consumption of electricity (in kWh), number of post offices per 10,000 population, number of banks per 1 lakh population and number of co-operative societies per 10,000 population).

Construction of composite index of development is mainly based on two methods namely, the *Indexing Method* and *Deprivation Method.* An analysis of the disparities trend, especially since 1970s in different sectors of the economy such as agriculture, industry and basic infrastructure and services (BIS) at the inter-district level of the old and undivided 13 districts of Orissa is attempted through secondary statistics. Further, in order to probe deeper into the issue of inter-district level of development disparities and regional backwardness a random sample survey of rural households in four districts of the state, namely, two of the most advanced and two of the most backward, was done.

Jayanta Madhab's Study

Dr. Jayanta Madhab (2001) observes that both foreign investors and all-India financial institutions have shown a bias in favour of the more advanced western region comprising Goa, Gujarat and Maharashtra in financing investment because of their better infrastructure and market-friendly environment resulting in what he calls "viscious circle of prosperity". In contrast, comparative neglect by foreign as well as domestic investors owing to lack of infrastructure, local entrepreneurs and congenial law and order, the north-eastern states, despite their rich resource base, have failed to come out of the "vicious circle of poverty" already in operation there. Consequently, the disparities between the western region and the north-eastern region has got widened during the post-reforms period.

1.4 RATIONALE OF THE STUDY

Because of the glaring regional disparities in India, the planners have accepted the importance of balanced regional planning. In this context the second plan stated: "In any comprehensive plan of development, it is axiomatic that the special needs of the less developed areas should receive due attention. The pattern of investment must be devised as to lead to balanced regional development. The problem is particularly difficult in the early stages when the resources available are very inadequate in relation to needs. But, more and more, as development proceeds and large resources become available for investment, the stress of development programme should be on extending benefits of investment to underdeveloped regions. Only thus a diversified economy be built up." [Government of India, Planning Commission, Second Five-Year Plan, p. 36]

The third plan devoted a separate chapter (Chapter IX) to "Balanced Regional Development." It was once again emphasised that "balanced development of different parts of the country, extension of the benefits of economic progress to the less developed regions and widespread diffusions of industry are among the major aims of planned development." [Government of India, Planning Commission, Third Five Year Plan, p. 142]. The third plan admitted that, on account of technological reasons, it might become necessary to localise production in the large industrial sector. Therefore, it was necessary "to provide for more dispersed advance in sectors like agriculture, small industries, power, communication and social services." The approach in the third plan was to – (i) help the state in reducing intra-state disparities i.e. disparities among different regions of the same state, and (ii) initiate new programmes and extend programmes adopted in previous plans to reduce inter-state inequalities. As far as the first issue is concerned, the programmes included related to – (a) increasing agricultural production, (b) taking steps to ensure "largest feasible" increase in income and employment, (c) developing social services, especially elementary education, water supply and sanitation and health services in rural areas, (d) developing communications and power, and (e) raising the standard of living for less developed areas of the state.

Accepting the importance of district planning in the overall planning process in general, and in the area development approach in particular the Planning Commission prepared a set of guidelines for the formulation of district plans in 1969. The guidelines state, "It has become apparent that plan formulation undertaken exclusively at the state level cannot possibly take fully into account the variety of conditions existing in the different physio-geographical and economic regions of the state." [Planning Commission, Guidelines for the Formulation of District Plans, 1969, pp. 1-2 (U.P. Government Edition)]. The guidelines advocate the adoption of district planning on the following considerations:

(i) The wide disparities which exist between the levels of development attained by different areas and community groups within a state and their full potential for development cannot be narrowed down unless the resources to be provided and the programmes to be taken up in each area or for each community are determined on the basis of a specific local assessment of problems, resources and productive potentials;

(ii) Underutilization of the already available natural resources, infrastructural facilities and productive capabilities in different areas cannot be properly assessed at the state level;

(iii) The uniform application of development schemes formulated at the state level without regard to their suitability to local conditions, leads to inefficient utilization of physical and financial resources;

(iv) Meaningful assessment of on-going schemes cannot be undertaken except at the ground level and with the active participation of local officials and the beneficiaries of schemes;

(v) Without a systematic study and planning of the local infrastructure, a firm and objective basis cannot be provided for the planning of the state;

(vi) Proper phasing to ensure synchornization of the programme with other related programmes cannot be attempted without working out the details of programmmes at the ground level;

(vii) Measures for the mobilization of local resources for development purposes cannot be planned realistically unless the specific context of the needs, aspirations and the economic condition of the people and the level of performance of local institutions are taken into consideration;

(viii) The deliberate steps required to be taken to identify the growth centres and to provide the facilities and services required to meet the growing needs of the villages lying in their hinterlands cannot be taken except at the district level through the analysis of the emerging trends in the economic activities and the pattern of facilities and services already available.

District planning should be properly carried out in conformity with the basic objectives of the state as well as the central plan. Through proper planning at district level, regional disparities in terms of development can be considerably reduced. A state in general may be a developed one in spite of some districts being backward in terms of development. A study of intra-state imbalances will help the planners associated with the state plan to formulate suitable planning policies so as to reduce the regional imbalances to a considerable extent. Our study may help the policy makers, Government and other agencies in formulating future policy decisions in regards to the balanced economic growth of the state of Assam.

The spread of modern education and rapid advancement of modern transport and communication system in an unequal socio-economic set up exacerbates the sense of relative deprivation feeling between the people of various regions, caste and ethnic groups. One of the basic reasons for the demands for the formation of separate states within the state of Assam is spatial disparities. A proper study of regional disparities at district level will help the Central and the State Governments to give due attention to the root cause of separatist movements growing within the state of Assam.

1.5 OBJECTIVES OF THE STUDY

Precisely the main objectives of the study are as follows:

1. To find out the extent of disparity in development among the 23 districts of Assam in respect of agriculture, industry and basic infrastructure and services (BIS) separately;
2. To study an overall inter-district disparities in Assam taking cognisance of disparities at inter-district level in all the three sectors viz. agriculture, industry and BIS;
3. To analyse in relative terms the development of different districts in relation to the development of Assam;
4. To delve into the development problem of backward districts *vis-à-vis* the comparatively advance districts and to explore into the cuses of backwardness;
5. To critically examine the role of various policy measures and decisions taken by the Government to reduce inter district disparities in the state;
6. To devise planning strategy for mitigating disparities on the basis of the findings of the study.

1.6 SCOPE OF THE STUDY

Such study may draw the attention of the government as well as the policy makers to initiate measures to reduce regional disparities which is one of the prime objectives of planning in India. On the basis of such study one may carry out research to know the changing pattern of development of regions over time and to discover the causes of such change.

1.7 INDICATORS OF DEVELOPMENT

Any development oriented study necessarily depends on certain indicators throwing light on living standards and development. Researchers all over the world have tried to define development in terms of certain selected indicators. Although many a researchers advocate per capita income index as singlemost indicator of development yet the use of per capita income as an indicator of development has always been questioned. It has become questionable especially in view of the fact that high income middle east countries are also one of the most backward regions in the world in terms of infrastructure and other facilities. First of all challenge to the use of per capita income as the sole indicator of development came from United Nations Organization as early as in 1954 (Shrivastaba, 1999). The criticism lebelled against the use of per capita income are as follows:

(a) It is an aggregative concept and does not reflect structure and distribution of income. Consequently, while some regions with lower per capita income may attain a better distribution of income because of better income distribution among different sectors of economy and classes of society, some other regions with higher income may not be able to do so. For example, in our country, although Andhra Pradesh, Arunachal Pradesh, Karnataka, Mizoram and Nagaland fall within the same range of income of Rs. 5500 – Rs. 6000 on the basis of per capita income but the backwardness is much more pronounced in case of Arunachal, Mizoram and Nagaland than in Karnataka. Moreover, Mizoram and Nagaland have per capita income level even higher than the national average, but they figure towards the end of the list of states in India ranked in respect of development. Again, regions with lower per capita income may possess better infrastructure and other pre-conditions of development compared with regions with higher per capita income.

(b) Another criticism labelled against the use of per capita income as an index for development is that it does not taken into account the concept, the goods and services which do not enter the market process due to limitations of accounting system. In the present context of development where sustainability of ecology and environment have also assumed equal importance, a very high level per capita income may, in fact, reflect a very poor quality of environment.

(c) Data on the per capita income are collected by states on the basis of prices ruling therein. Since (i) price levels are different in different states, (ii) commodities included in the compilation of price levels by different states are different, and (iii) weights assigned to different commodities in the compilation of price levels are not the same in all the states, per capita income of different states are not comparable.

(d) For comparing inter-district disparities within a state, per capita income cannot be taken into account because per capita income at district level is not available. Per capita income figures, besides concealing differences in intra-state inequalities in distribution, may not truely reflect the per capita consumption levels. A part of the income earned within the jurisdiction of a state might not be available for consumption within the state, but may get transferred to other states by way of dividend and other remittances. Conversely, income originating within state might be supplemented by remittances of income from other states. Per capita consumption levels would reflect the net effect of such transfers. Thus, per capita consumption, rather than per capita income can be regarded as a more reliable measure of inter-state (regional) disparities. However, in our study we cannot consider per capita consumption as a measure of inter-district disparities due to the non-availability of per capita consumption figures at district level. Of late, the researchers have opted for 'component approach' to development using a large number of indicators of development. The component approach was recommended by the UN committee of experts as Measurement of Levels of Living (UNO, 1954). A number of researchers of our country and also the Planning Commission have used different indicators at different points of time. The Committee on Dispersal of Industries (1960) suggested three indicators of backwardness:

(i) Poverty identifiable in terms of low per capita income and consumption;

(ii) High population density in relation to available productive and developmental resources as well as the employment opportunity; and

(iii) Poverty of communication.

As a follow-up of Committee's Report, a working group (1969) was appointed by the Planning Commission in the context of Fourth Five-Year Plan to identify backward areas. The working group classified the backward areas of the country into five categories which were as follows:

(i) Desert areas,

(ii) Chronologically drought affected areas,

(iii) Areas with high concentration of tribal population,

(iv) Hill areas including boarder areas and,

(v) Area with high density of population, low level of income, employment etc.

Most of the states of North-East India fall in the above categories (iii) and (iv). The working group recommended the following 15 indicators of backwardness/development which were accepted by the Planning Commission:

(i) Total population and density of population;

(ii) Cultivable area per cultivator;

(iii) Net area sown per agricultural worker;

(iv) Workers engaged in agriculture sector as percentage of total workers;

(v) Percentage of gross irrigated area to net sown area;

(vi) Intensity of cropping;

(vii) Per capita (rural) gross value of agricultural produce;

(viii) Establishments (manufacturing and repairs) using electricity;

(ix) Number of workers per lakh of population employed in manufacturing sector;

(x) Mileage of surfaced road per 100 sq. km. of area and per lakh of population;

(xi) Number of commercial vehicles registered in a district;

(xii) Percentage of literate population – (a) men and (b) women;

(xiii) Number of seats per million of population for technical training;

(xiv) Percentage of school going children – boys and girls – to the population in the age group of 6-11 and 11-14 years;

(xv) Hospital beds per lakh of population.

The indicators suggested by the working group had major problems despite its exhaustiveness. For data relating to some of the indicators like value of agricultural produce are not available at district level and such data are not available even at the state level in case of state like Assam. Again, in what manner and in what way density of population is related to economic development or backwardness is not clear.

Despite some conceptual problems as well problems arising out of the non availability of data relating to some indicators, the working group's listing of indicators was a definite improvement and most of the researchers afterwards choose indicators from the above list. The list of indicators suggested by later government groups are fairly long and as such while every new classification was an improvement over the earlier ones, the shortcomings will also abound. Pandey Committee (1969) suggested six main indicators for identifying backward areas – (i) per capita income, (ii) per capita income from industry and mining, (iii) number of workers in registered factories, (iv) per capita annual consumption of electricity (v) length of surfaced road in relation to population and area of the state, and (vi) railway route length in relation to population and area of the state. Pandey Committee suggested another set of six indicators for identifying districts within the state (Mahesh Chand and Puri, 1983), most of which are not applicable even today in case of district level study of any state in the north-east region of India due to unavailability of data (Srivastava, 1996). After a careful study of the various secondary sources of information at district level pertaining to the state of Assam and taking note of the various indicators of development/backwardness mentioned above we have finally selected – (i) seven development indicators for agriculture, (ii) four development indicators for industry, and (iii) fourteen development indicators for basic infrastructure and services (BIS) sector. All these indicators are listed in the methodology of study. It is worth mentioning that while selecting these indicators of development we have been greatly influenced by the study made by Rajkishore Meher (1999).

1.8 SOURCES OF DATA

The very nature of investigation is such that it has to be carried out on the secondary sources of information. The data have been collected from *Statistical Hand Book of Assam*, 1997, (Directorate of Economics and Statistics, Assam); *Economic Survey, Assam, 1997-98* (Directorate of Economic and Statistics, Assam); *Development and Planning: Five Year Plan Documents*; Directorate of Information and Public Relations; *Assam Information*, June – 1995, Vol 47; *Census of India – 1991*; *Basic Agricultural Statistics, 1997-98* (Directorate of Agriculture, Government of Assam); *India's Agricultural Sector – A Compendium of Statistics*, September 1995, CMIE Pvt. Ltd. and *List of Registered Factories in Assam* (Published by Office of the Chief Inspector of Factories, Assam, 1996).

1.9 METHODOLOGY OF STUDY

(a) Development Indicators

The study broadly focusses on the development indicators of three sectors at the district level, namely (i) Agriculture, (ii) Industry, and (iii) Basic Infrastructure and Services (BIS) during 1997-98. This involves the choice of appropriate indicators of development or backwardness in these three sectors and the collection and formulation of such indicators for the different districts of the state of Assam. Of course, in a backward state like Assam where the nature of collection and compilation of statistics at the district level is still in rudimentary form, the choice and selection of appropriate development indicators inevitably depend on the availability and accessibility to data. The Third Five-Year Plan document of the country with regard to balanced regional development mentions that for assessing levels of development in different regions, indicators of development based on agricultural production, industrial production, investment, unemployment, electricity consumption, irrigated areas, value of output by commodity producing sectors, level of consumption expenditure, road mileage, primary and secondary education and occupational distribution of population are useful. So in the present study the quantification of disparity between the districts and identification of backward districts and advance districts in Assam for different sectors are mainly based on – (i) seven development indicators for the agriculture, (ii) four development indicators for the industry, and (iii) fourteen development indicators of the BIS.

1. *Indicators of agricultural development*

(i) Percentage of cultivable land to total land area,

(ii) Percentage of area sown to total cultivable area,

(iii) Percentage of irrigation potential created to net sown area,

(iv) Cropping intensity,

(v) Average yield of food grains per hectare (in kg),

(vi) Percentage of high yielding variety area under paddy to net sown area,

(vii) Average consumption of fertilizer per hectare of total cropped area.

2. *Indicators of Industrial Development*

(i) Percentage of secondary sector workers to total work force,

(ii) Percentage of registered factory workers to total workforce,

(iii) Number of registered factories per 1000 sq. km area,

(iv) Maximum horse-power (H.P.) installed per industrial worker in registered factories.

3. ***Basic Infrastructure and Services***

(i) Percentage of literate population,

(ii) Percentage of urban population,

(iii) Percentage of tertiary sector workers to total work force,

(iv) Number of primary and middle schools per 10,000 of population,

(v) Number of high schools per 10,000 of population,

(vi) Number of general colleges per one lakh population,

(vii) Number of hospitals/dispensaries per one lakh population,

(viii) Number of medical beds per 10,000 population,

(ix) Infant mortality per 1,000 births,

(x) Road length per 100 square kilometre area,

(xi) Road length per one lakh population,

(xii) Percentage of villages electrified,

(xiii) Number of post offices per 10,000 population,

(xiv) Number of banks per one lakh population,

(b) Construction of Composite Index

The construction of a composite index is essential for the analysis of regional disparities on the basis of the chosen indicators of development. The selected indicators are to be converted into a single index of overall development, which is known as 'composite index'. Usually most of the 'regional disparity' studies made in the country have followed three methods of aggregating a number of indicators into a single indicator i.e. construction of a composite index. They are (i) Equal Weightage Index Method, (ii) Ranking Method and (iii) Method of Principal Component Analysis. There is another method of construction of a composite index known as 'Deprivation Method'. This method has been used in the construction of Human Development Index (HDI) in Human Development Report (HRD), 1990 published by the United Nations

Development Programme (UNDP, 1990). This type of composite Economic Development Index (EDI) is constructed in three steps. The first step is to define a measure of deprivation that a district suffers with respect to all the chosen variables for Agriculture, Industry, BIS and the total development *vis-à-vis* other districts of the state. A maximum and a minimum value is determined on the basis of the highest and the lowest for each of the 25 variables of the 23 districts of Assam given their actual values. The highest of a particular variable for a particular indicator among the 23 districts of the state is assigned the value one and the lowest is assigned the value zero. The deprivation measure places a district in the range of zero to one. If I_{ij} is the deprivation indicator for the jth district with respect to the ith variable then it is given by:

$$I_{ij} = \frac{(\underset{j}{\text{Max}}\, X_{ij} - X_{ij})}{(\underset{j}{\text{Max}}\, X_{ij} - \underset{j}{\text{Min}}\, X_{ij})}$$

Where X_{ij} indicates the value of the ith indicator with respect to the jth district.

The second step is to define an average indicator (I_j). This is done by taking a simple average of the chosen indicators for different sectors of agriculture, industry and BIS and thus

$$I_j = \frac{\sum_{i=1}^{n} I_{ij}}{n}$$

The third step is to measure the Economic Development Index on the basis of agriculture, industry and BIS development indices for each separate district as one minus the average deprivation index, i.e.

$$(EDI)_j = (1 - I_j)$$

The districts for which the EDI score point is 0.8 and above, is termed as highly developed. If the score point lies between 0.5 and 0.8 (including 0.5 but excluding 0.8) then the district is termed as moderately developed and if the score point is below 0.5 then the district is termed as less developed or backward. *It is to be noted that EDI is an absolute measure of development.*

In Equal Weightage Index Method, the chosen indicators for each of agriculture, industry and BIS are combinely worked out for each district taking the aggregate state value of each indicator as 100. Total index, say for agriculture, is a measure of the level of agricultural development of a district. It provides the value of the sum total of index of seven indicators used in this study for a particular year. The same divided by the number of indicators (here, seven in number) gives the average index of agricultural development in a district.

In ranking method, the individual ranks of a district by the seven indicators are simply to be added up to give a total rank for the district. Then taking the median value as the cut-off point, the district which has a value below the median value is to be considered as backward.

In our study we have refrained from constructing composite indices with the help of ranking method. This is due to the reason that ranking method totally disregards the absolute differences among the values corresponding to an indicator. With the help of ranking method we cannot compare the relative position of a district with respect to the entire state of Assam and also we cannot make inter-district comparison in absolute sense.

We have made our study on the basis of the construction of three composite indices, namely, (i) Equal Weightage Indexing Method or Indexing Method, (ii) Deprivation Method and (iii) Principal Component Method.

Principal Component Method

The method of Principal Component is a special case of the more general method of Factor Analysis. The mathematical formula of Principal Component Analysis was developed by Hotelling (1933). The aim of the method of Principal Component is the construction of a set of new variables P_i, called principal components (i = 1, 2, ..., k) out of a set of variables, X_j's (j = 1, 2, ..., k). Each principal component is a linear combination of the X's:

$$P_1 = a_{11}x_1 + a_{12}x_2 + \ldots + a_{1k}x_k$$

$$P_2 = a_{21}x_1 + a_{22}x_2 + \ldots + a_{2k}x_k$$

.

.

.

$$P_k = a_{k1}x_1 + a_{k2}x_2 + \ldots + a_{kk}x_k$$

The method of principal component can be applied by using the original values of the X_j's or the standardized variables Z_j defined by

$$Z_j = \frac{X_j}{Sx_i}$$

The coefficients a_{ij}'s are called loadings of the factors (principal component) which are so chosen that the newly created variables called principal components satisfy the following two conditions (i) principal component are orthogonal (uncorrelated), ii) the first principal component has a larger variance as possible; the second principal component is then chosen in such a way that it absorbs the maximum of the remaining variations in X's after allowing for the variation accounted by the first principal component and so on. In this procedure the data matrix is transformed to a new set of uncorrelated variates (principal components) which account as much of the variation as possible in descending order. It may be that the first two or three of these variables (principal components) account for substantial variation, say 80 to 90% and the contribution of the remaining variables is very small. In such circumstances it becomes needless to derive the remaining principal components.

The steps in any principal component analysis are:

1. To prepare an inter-correlation matrix R from the variables given in the data matrix.
2. To work out the eigen values of R which imply the variances of various principal components. Let these eigen values arranged in descending order be $\lambda_1, \lambda_2, \ldots, \lambda_p$.

3. To take the first few values of λ s (say r values), and to find out the proportion

$$\frac{\lambda_1 + \lambda_2 + \ldots + \lambda_\rho}{P}$$

If this value is satisfactory, say 70% or more (it may vary from problem to problem) then to find out the eigen vectors corresponding to these eigen values.

4. To convert the original variables into standard scores and using the elements given in the first eigen vector as weights, to get the weighted sum of the standardized scores for each observation. The values so obtained are the scores of the first principal component. Similarly, using the other eigen vectors the scores of 2nd, 3rd, and rth principal components can be worked out.
5. To multiply each eigen vector used above by the square root of their corresponding eigen values and give them as factor loadings.

1.10 HYPOTHESES ENCOUNTERED

We have encountered the following hypotheses against their respective alternatives:

(a) All the districts of the state of Assam are homogeneous with respect to agricultural development.

VIS-À-VIS

All the districts of the state are not homogeneous with respect to agriculture development.

(b) The districts of the state are homogeneous with respect to industrial development.

VIS-À-VIS

The districts are not homogeneous with respect to industrial development.

(c) All the district are homogeneous with respect to development in basic infrastructure and services.

VIS-À-VIS

The districts are not homogeneous with respect to development in basic infrastructure and services.

(d) The districts of Assam are homogeneous with respect to overall development.

VIS-À-VIS

The districts are not homogeneous with respect to overall development.

(e) Variations among the districts in respect of all the select indicators are uniform.

VIS-À-VIS

Variations among the districts in respect of all the select indicators are not uniform.

1.11 LIMITATIONS OF THE STUDY

Our study is based on secondary sources of information. As such, the limitations of secondary data will be applicable to our study. The study would have been more meaningful should we have been able to study inter-district disparities of Assam at two points of time. However, we have failed to make such a study because of the reasons that (i) most of the data are based on census information and there was no census in Assam in 1981, (ii) the data relating to 2001 census are not yet available. Moreover, new districts have come up at different times. Although some sub-divisions of existing districts get the district status yet due to non-availability of most data at sub-divisional level, we donot get data for the newly created districts. Consequently, we had to limit our study on the basis of the information based on 1991 census only. Major portion of the data that we have taken from *Statistical Hand Book of Assam, 1997, Economic Survey, Assam:* 1997-98, are based on 1991 census results. Our failure to study the changing pattern of development disparities among the districts of Assam over time is a severe limitation of our study. However, subsequent researchers may infuse inter-temporal dynamism in similar studies by taking the periodicity of study from 1991 to 2001 when the results of 2001 census would be available.

REFERENCES

Chand, Mahesh and Puri, V.: *Regional Planning in India,* Allied Publishers Pvt. Ltd., 1983.

Ganguli, B. N. and Gupta, Debendra. B. (1976): *Levels of Living in India – An inter-state profile*, S. Chand and Co. Ltd., New Delhi.

Government of India, *Identification of Backward Areas*, Planning Commission, 1969.

Hotteling, H. (1933): Analysis of Complex Statistical Variable into Principal Component, *Journal of Educational Psychology,* 24: 407-441.

Kaur Dhian and Ghuman, B. S. (1995): "Inter district Disparities iin Punjab – Implication for planning," *Indian Journal of Regional Science*, 27: 1-2.

Madhab, Jayanta (2001): New Economic Policy and Regional Disparity, *in:* Atul Goswami (ed), *Regional Disparities in India*, Akansha Publshing House.

Meher, Rajkishore (1999): *"Development Disparities in a Backward Region: A District Level Analysis"*, APH Publishing Corporation, New Delhi.

Mitra, Ashok (1965): *Levels of Regional Development in India,* Government of India.

Murugaiah, V. (1997): "Economic Disparities in Karnataka – A micro level study", *Indian Journal of Regional Science*, Vol. 29(1)

Nath, V. (1970): "Regional Development in Indian Planning", *Economic and Political Weekly*, Annual Number, 242-260.

Planning Commission, Government of India, Second Five Year Plan, 1956, p 22.

Rao, Hemanta (1977): "Identification of Backward Regions and the Trends in Regional Disparities in India", *Artha Vijnana*, 19: 93-112.

Shrivastava, S. C. (1999): *Levels and structure of development – An inter-district study of north-east India*, National Institute of Rural Development, Hyderabad, p 14.

Srivastava, S. C.: *Status of Micro Level Data in North-East India*, NIRD, NERC, 1996.

United Nations Report on International Definitions and Measurement of Standards and Levels of Living, 1954.

2

Eco-geographical Profile of Assam and its Districts

ASSAM
Main Features

CAPITAL	DISPUR (GUWAHATI)
Area	78438 Sq Km
Relief	Hills and Plains
Number of Districts	No of Subdivisions -48
23	No of Blocks 218
	No of Revenue Circles -149
Population	22414322
Male	11657989 (52%)
Female	10756333 (48%)
Rural	19926527 (88.90%)
Urban	2487795 (11.10%)
Decadal growth rate (1991)	24.2%
Density (per sq. km)	286
Sex Ratio (Females per 1000 males)	923
Literacy	52.89%
Male	61.87%
Female	43.02%
Length of road under PWD	33110 km
Important Rivers	Brahmaputra and Barak
Important Industry	Plywood, Tea, Petroleum
Nature of Economy	Agrarian
Important minerals	Coal, limestone, petroleum, natural gas
Important Agricultural Products	Paddy, wheat, jute, tea
Climate	Monsoon type
Important places	Guwahati, Dibrugarh, Tinsukia, Jorhat, Tezpur, Nagaon, Silchar, Barpeta, Nalbari, Bongaigaon, Dhubri
Places of tourist attraction	Kaziranga National Park, Manas Tiger Project, Majuli River Island, Kamakhya Tample, Sankar Dev Kalakhetra etc.

Source: (i) *Statistical Hand Book*, Assam, 1997
(ii) *Economic Survey of Assam*, 1997-98.

2.1 LOCATION AND FOUR BOUNDARIES

The state of Assam is located in North-Eastern part of India. The state is bounded by Bhutan and Arunachal Pradesh on the North, Arunachal Pradesh, Nagaland and Manipur on the East, Mizoram and Meghalaya on the South, and Bangladesh and West Bengal on the West. The state is linked to the country on the West through a narrow corridor of about 35 km width between Bangladesh and Nepal.

2.2 PHYSICAL SETTING

The physiography of Assam is characterised by diverse features such as floodplains, marshes and beels, scattered hillocks, folded hill ranges and old plateaus. On the basis of physiographic characteristics, Assam is broadly divided into three major divisions – the Brahmaputra Valley, the Barak Valley and the Hills of Karbi-Anglong and North-Cachar.

The Assam Valley is built mostly by the aggradational work of the Brahmaputra and its tributaries and is almost a flat level plain with a very little slope from its north-east corner at Sadiya to Dhubri in the West. The valley is characterised by the presence of a good number of isolated hillocks or monadnocks on both the banks of Brahmaputra, right from Tezpur and Mikir hills to as far west as Dhubri, detached from the Meghalaya plateau by the degradational work of the river.

The Brahmaputra has more than 35 tributaries and many of them are large rivers with sizeable catchment area. Major among these tributaries are Manas, Lohit, Sankosh, Dihang, Subansiri, Dhansiri etc. The Brahmaputra with its tributaries carry tremendous volume of water resulting in flood havoc.

Assam falls within the regime of monsoon climate. Its climate is characterised by heavy rainfall in summer and drought in winter, very high per centage of relative humidity and relatively low temperature. Within the state there is significant spatio-temporal variation in the climatic pattern, primarily because of varying terrain conditions.

2.3 NATURAL RESOURCE BASE

Assam is rich in natural vegetation. The vegetation of the region is predominantly characterised by dense mixed semi-evergreen, evergreen and wet deciduous types owing mainly to the impact of heavy monsoonal rainfall, effective temperature and thick fertile soil cover in the valley. The valuable timbers found in the forests of Assam include sal, teak, *sisoo*, *khair*, *gamari*, *bonsum*, *hollong*, *nahar* etc. Lac, gums, resins are other minor forest products. Another important resource in the forests of the state is wildlife. It comprise of the important species of mammals, birds, reptiles and fishes. The one-horned rhino of the valley is an important foreign exchange earner.

Except oil and coal the region has practically no mineral resources worth the name. The upper Assam valley has a large reserve of oil. The oil fields lie around Digboi, Naharkatiya, Moran, Rudrasagar, Lakwa, Geleky and Teok in upper Assam. The coal fields are concentrated in the south-eastern part of the valley. The major coal fields are Ledo-Makum, Jaipur-Dilli and Nazira.

Assam is a land of promise, providing an extensive area for settlements and agricultural land-use. The power resources is rendered more promising with the vast hydro-power potentials, with which the whole flank of the Brahmaputra river valley is endowed within its almost ideal physical conditions, reaching at many points with the conjuncture of promising terrain and huge potential water flow. In essence the land and water resources of the valley promise an extensive, though not so broad based, resource base for economic development.

2.4 THE ECONOMY

(i) Agricultural Economy

Agriculture is, of basic importance to the region because not only provides most of the food requirements and gives employment to a significant portion of population, but also furnishes raw materials such as tea and jute which constitute the backbone of the regional economy in trade and commerce.

Land Use

Though agriculture is the main occupation and primary resource base of the region, the latest provisional estimates of land utilization statistics for Assam available for 1997-98 reveal that Assam has an estimated 39.62 lakh hectares of gross cropped area, of which the net sown area is about 27.81 lakh hecrares which is about 35.43 per cent of the total geographical area of the state. The area sown more than once stood at 11.81 lakh hectares during the year. Thus the ratio of area sown more than once to net sown area was 42.47 per cent in 1997-98.

Amongst the important crops in the state, the area under paddy dominated with a share of 63 per cent of the total cropped area in 1997-98. During the year 1997-98 the area under paddy decreased by 0.1 per cent over 1996-97. Among the commercial crops, rape and mustard accounted for the largest per centage of area covered followed by jute, potato and sugarcane.

Yield Rate

The productivity of some important crops in the state reveals mixed results during 1997-98. The yield rate of autumn rice was 1000 kg/ha during the year 1997-98 as against 853 kg/ha in the previous year. In case of winter rice, the yield rate during 1997-98 was 1439 kg/ha as against 1471 kg/ha in 1996-97. The yield rate of total rice in Assam for the year 1996-97 was only 1334 kg/ha as against 2720 kg/ha for the country as a whole during the same year. The yield rate of wheat decreased from 1332 kg/ha in 1996-97 to 1299 kg/ha in 1997-98. Other important crops which recorded rise in productivity during 1997-98 over 1996-97 were jute, sugarcane, rape and mustard.

Fertilizer Consumption

Chemical fertilizer which is considered as one of the most important inputs for increase in agricultural production, its consumption per hectare of cropped area in the state has in fact been found to be the lowest in the country. However, since 1990-91 the consumption of fertilizer in the state shows rising trend. In 1990-91, the average consumption of fertilizer per hectare of cropped area was 10.9 kg which reached the level 14.6 kg in 1996-97. Figure for the year 1997-98 is 17.98 kg.

AGRICULTURAL PROFILE OF ASSAM, 1997-98

Gross Cropped Area	3962000 hectares
Net Area Sown	2781000 hectares
Area Sown more than Once	1181000 hectares (42.47% of net area sown)
Yield Rate of Rice	
(i) autumn rice	1000 kg/ha
(ii) summer rice	1493 kg/ha
Wheat	1299 kg/ha
Jute	1537 kg/ha
Sugarcane	41109 kg/ha
Rape and Mustard	553 kg/ha
Potato	8927 kg/ha
Fertilizer Consumption	17.98 kg/ha
Irrigation Potential Created up to 31.3.97	480590 hectares (17.28% of net area sown)
Irrigation Potential Utilized (1995-96)	113088.16 hectares
Agricultural Implements	
(i) Ploughs	12.01 lakh nos.
(ii) Carts	51.41 thousand nos.
(iii) Sugarcane Crushers	3225 nos.
(iv) Power Tillers	1342 nos.
(v) Tractors	632 nos.
(vi) Electric Pump Sets	1300 nos.
(vii) Diesel Pump Sets	12904 nos.
(viii) Sprayers and Dusters	4764 nos.
(ix) Seed Drillers	561 nos.
Cropping Intensity	142.47
Percentage of Net Sown Area Under HYV Paddy	45%
Percentage of Cultivable Land to Total Land Area	43.15%
Percentage of Area Sown to Total Cultivable Area	82.11%
Average yield of Food Grains	897.40 kg/ha

Source: (i) *Statistical Hand Book*, Assam, 1997
(ii) *Economic Survey of Assam*, 1997-98.
(iii) *Basic Agricultural Statistics*, 1997-98.

Irrigation

Irrigation facilities are extremely limited in Assam. Although the state has abundant surface and groundwater it is not being effectively utilized for irrigation purposes. Although over the recent years, the state has made some progress in the sphere of creation of additional irrigation potential, much more still remains to be done to bring the situation to a satisfactory level. Out of the total estimated gross cropped area of about 40 lakh hectares, the irrigation potential of Assam utilized during the year 1996-97 was 1.14 lakh hectares as against 1.13 lakh hectares in the previous year. The creation of gross irrigation potential in the state up to 1997-98 was 4.81 lakh hectares under Govt. scheme.

Agricultural Implements

Agricultural implements being used by the cultivators in the state include plough, carts, sugarcane crushers, power tillers, tractors etc. of which the plough is the most commonly used tool. A notable feature observed with regard to agricultural implements is that the number of power tillers, diesel and electric pump sets, sprayers and dusters etc. have recorded a substantial increase in the state over the recent years. This is an indication of increased demand for mechanized cultivation leading to modernization of agriculture in the state.

Tea Plantation

Tea plantation in Assam dates back to 1833 and since then the plantation developed steadily and by the last quarter of the 19th century it became the chief export item of the country as a whole. The tea growing areas are mostly confined to the districts of Lakhimpur, Sibsagar, Darrang, Nowgaon, Dibrugarh and Tinsukia. Out of over 7100 tea estates in India the state alone accounts for more than 1196 estates with 1179 kg average yield per hectare. This oldest and well organised industry of the Assam Valley paved the way for the development of transport and subsequent facilities in the region.

The experience of the other states have proved that Assam is far behind the race in terms of both production and productivity in agriculture thereby pointing to the fact that a realistic policy could only fetch benefits of modern agricultural technology. One must analyse the causes and suggest remedies if the state agriculture has to achieve significant growth in the new millennium. The importance of this sector must be realised by the policy-makers not only as provider of food and fodder but also as a source of employment generation. A growing agriculture ensures consumers demand for industrial goods, provides investible surpluses and gives impetus to rural services sector.

(ii) Industrial Economy

Though the valley appears to be industrially important in the North-East India with its relative industrial supremacy over the adjoining areas in Assam, it would rather appear to be a void on the industrial map of India excepting, however, its tea and petroleum industries.

The region is potentially rich in industrial raw materials but their economic exploitation has been hindered by several factors such as its isolation from the rest of India due to poor transport and communication system, paucity of capital, a very small local market, shortage of cheap labour, lack of entrepreneures and non-availability of cheap power.

The industrial landscape of the state is limited to small pockets around Guwahati in Kamrup district and around Digrugarh and Tinsukia districts in upper Assam. Efforts are being made by introducing new industrial policy of the state i.e. Industrial Policy Resolution, 1997 with a view to creating a strong industrial base and employment opportunities.

Registered Factories

The total number of registered factories in the state decreased from 2601 in 1995 to 2511 in 1996 and again increased to 2526 in 1997. As the latest available results for the year 1994-95 shows that Assam had a total of 1.24 lakh employees engaged in 1514 numbers of registered factories surveyed during the year.

Small Industries

The number of small scale units in the state is increasing steadily due to Government's effort to create a strong industrial base in the state. In Assam, the number of SSI units registered with the Directorate were 33,843 up to 31.12.96 and the number of small scale units registered during 1996 and 1997 were 2468 and 2461 respectively.

INDUSTRIAL PROFILE OF ASSAM

Total No. of Registered Factories	2526 nos. (up to 1997)
No. of Industrial Estates	12 nos.
No. of Growth Centres	6 nos.
Total No. of Medium and Large Scale Industries	179 nos.(up to 1996)
Major Projects of AIDC	
(a) State Sector Projects	1. Assam Petrochemical Ltd. 2. Cachar Sugar Mills Ltd. 3. Assam Syntex Ltd. 4. Assam State Weaving and Manufacturing Corp Ltd. 5. Industrial Papers (Assam) Ltd. 6. Assam State Fertilizers & Chemical Ltd. 7. Fertichem Ltd.
(b) Joint Sector Project	The Prag Bosimi Synthetic Ltd.
(c) On Going Projects	1. Gas Cracker Project at Tengakhat 2. Export Promotion Industrial Park at Amingaon, Guwahati. 3. Growth Centres at Balipara and Matia.
Total No. of Small Scale Industries	33,843 nos. (up to 31.12.96)
Industrial Classification	
(i) Agro Based Industries	Tea, sugar, grain mill products, food processing and Textile Industries.
(ii) Mineral-Based Industries	Steel works, natural gas based, cement and oil industries.
(iii) Forest Based Industries	Plywood, sawing mill, paper, match, leather and hardboard industries
(iv) Other Industries	Power, fertilizer, printing, press, brick, tiles, ice and chemical industries.

Source: Economic Survey of Assam, 1997-98.

Large and Medium Scale Industries

A number of large and medium scale industries have been set up in the state. As per information available, there were 179 numbers of such industries functioning in the state up to the end of 1996. Further, with the completion of some ongoing major projects like Numaligarh Refinary at Numaligarh, Assam Gas Cracker Project at Tengakhat, Export Promotion Park at Amingaon, Industrial Paper (Assam) Ltd. at Dhing, Polyester Filament Yarn Project at Sipajhar etc. the industrial situation of the state will imporve in near future.

In a state like Assam where agricultural performance is still in the hands of vagaries of nature, industrial sector can ensure some sort of stability of growth and employment. Industrial sector remains to be a priority sector for sustained development of the state.

(iii) Infrastructural Facilities in Assam

Infrastructural services such as power, transport, telecommunications, health facilities, literacy etc. improve quality of life and productivity. Major infrastructural failures quickly and radically reduce communities quality of life and productivity. Infrastructure services enhance welfare and foster economic growth. Providing proper infrastructural services to meet the demands of business, industry, households and other users is one of the major challenges for the state of Assam. For the economy of the state to grow at a faster rate it is very important to do something about infrastructure along with agriculture.

Transport and Communication

Assam is served by all modern means of transport viz. roads, railways, waterways and airways. But the existing facilities of transport and communication are not adequate. The total railway route in Assam at the end of the year 1996-97 was 2435.13 km. The proportion of B.G. route length to total railway length is about 22 per cent for the state.

The total length of roads under PWD in Assam was 33110 km for the year 1995-96 including 2070 km under National Highways. Out of total PWD road length only 8572 km (26%)

are surfaced and the rest 24538 km (74%) were unsurfaced roads. The proportion of surfaced roads in Assam is quite lower as compared to the country as a whole.

The most important navigable rivers in the state are the Brahmaputra and the Barak. At present two public sector organizations viz. the state Directorate of Inland Water Transport (IWT) and the Central Inland Water Transport Corporation (CIWTC) are operating water transport services in the state on commercial basis.

The state is well connected with the rest of the country through Air Transport. There are six civil airports in the state.

Postal and Telecommunication Services

The postal and telecommunication facilities in the state have been growing steadily in recent years. Total number of post offices in the state was 3818 in 1996-97. In this year the total number of villages having post offices was 3518 and the average area and population served by each post office were 20.54 sq km and 5870 numbers respectively. The total number of telephone exchanges in the state stood at 299 at the end of 1996-97.

Power

Power is the basic infrastructural requirement for the growth of industries as well as overall economy of the state. Assam accounts for only a small fraction i.e. 0.27 per cent of the total generation of electricity in the country during 1997-98. While the consumption of power in the state has been increasing in absolute term over the recent years, the average per capita consumption of electricity in the state (87.46 kWh) continues to stand at a level much below the all India average. Much has been discussed about the huge hydel power potential in Assam but hardly any strong effort is seen to have been done to exploit this opportunity because of cost and other related factors. Assam must realise that by generating power it may make it a big seller of this essential input to other parts of the country by putting this in National Grid. A comprehensive master plan to develop power sector is the urgent need of the hour.

INFRASTRUCTURAL PROFILE OF ASSAM

Percentage of Literacy	52.89
Percentage of Urban Population	11.09
Percentage of Tertiary Sector Workers	20.40
No. of Primary and Middle Schools	10.86 (per 10,000 population)
No. of High Schools	1.23 (per 10,000 population)
No. of Colleges	0.50 (per lakh population)
No. of Hospitals/Dispensaries	0.48 (per 10,000 population)
No. of medical Beds	5.74 (per lakh population)
Infant Mortality Rate	92 (per 1000 births)
Road Length per 100 sq km Area	42.20 km
Road Length per Lakh Population	148 km
Percentage of Villages Electrified	74.0
No. of Post Offices Per 10,000 Population	1.35
No. of Banks Per Lakh Population	5.45
Length of Total Railway Route	2435.13 km
No. of Universities	4
No. of Agricultural Universities	1
No. of Engineering Colleges	3
No. of IIT	1
No. of Civil Airports	6

Source: (i) Computed from *Statistical Hand Book,* Assam 1997.
(ii) Statement 3.1, Directorate of Census Operations, Assam 1991.

Co-Operative

The co-operative movement in Assam which started in 1904 has passed through several phases of development, is yet to achieve its desired goals. At the end of 1995-96, there were altogether 9136 co-operative societies of various types in the state.

Banking Services

The banking network in the state of Assam has shown some expansion during the recent years. There were only 491 branches of scheduled commercial Banks in the state during 1980 and the same increased to 1217 in 1991 and then further to 1241in 1998. The average population covered by per bank office in the state is, however, much below the all India average.

Infrastructural bottlenecks are serious impediments to economic growth. Whether it is industrial sector, or tourism sector or IT

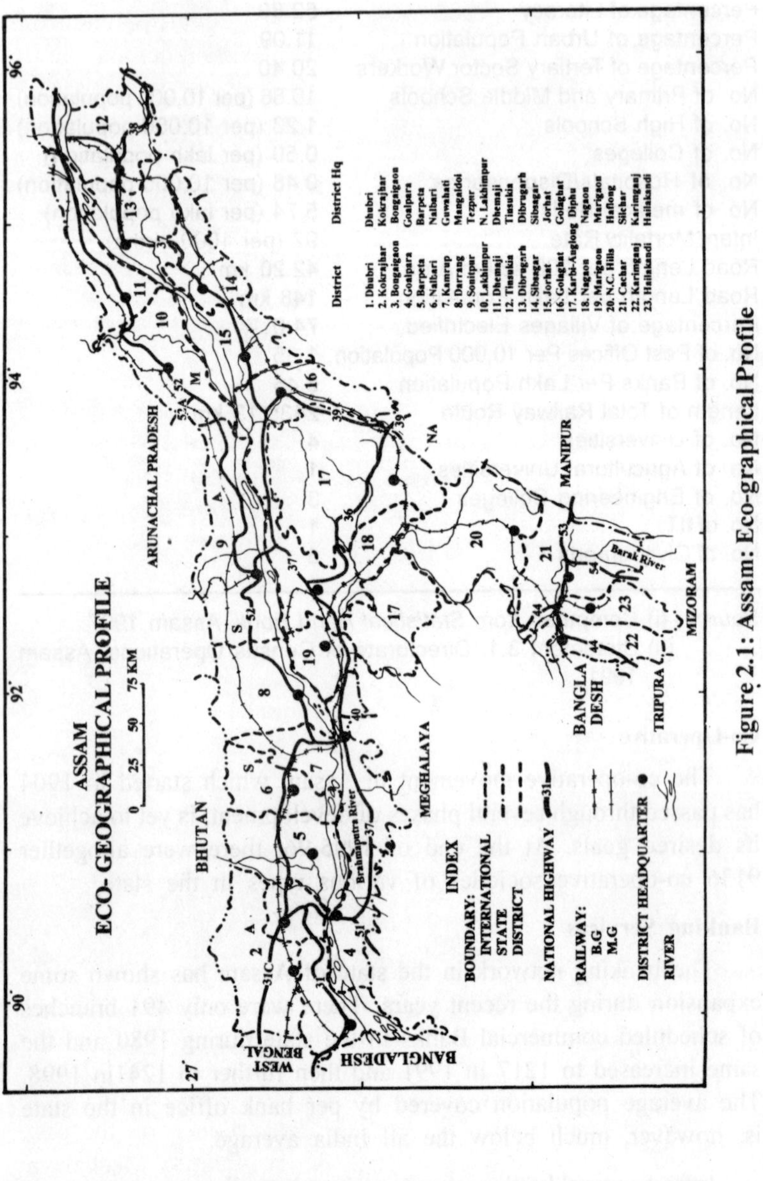

Figure 2.1: Assam: Eco-graphical Profile

areas, growth of infrastructure has its urgency in this state. Construction of roads, bridges connecting important rail transhipment points, riverine ports, development of telecommunication network by using satellites facilities etc. have to be given priority in our state.

(iv) Socio-Economic Environment

The socio-economic environments of the state are to a great extent hindering the pace of development in the state. However, with the spread of education and contact with outside world due to advanced telecommunication network some social factors adversely affecting the development efforts are gradually undergoing changes in a positive direction.

The economic environment is also changing with close contact with the outside market, increasing industrial activities through exploitation of mineral and forest resources, expansion of trade and commerce, awareness of prevalence of improved technology in other regions of the country.

2.5 DISTRICTS PROFILE OF ASSAM

1. Dhubri District

DHUBRI DISTRICT AT A GLANCE

Headquarters	: Dhubri	Literacy Rate	: 38.31%
Population	: 1332475	Male	: 47.32%
Male	: 683298	Female	: 28.75%
Female	: 649177	No Of Subdivisions	: 3
Urban	: 23475	No Of Blocks	: 14
Rural	: 992915	Length of Road Under Pwd	: 1082 km
Area	: 2838 sq km	Population Rank	: 5
Density	: 470 per sq.km.	Literacy Rank	: 23
Sex Ratio	: 950		

Location and Four Boundaries

Dhubri district is located in extreme west of Assam. This district is bound on the north by Kokrajhar district, on the east by Bongaigaon and Goalpara districts, on the south by Meghalaya state and on the west by West Bengal and Bangladesh. Total geographical area of the district is 2838 sq km. Dhubri, Bilasipara and South Salmara and Mankachar are the three sub-divisions of Dhubri District.

Natural Geography

Most of the regions of Dhubri districts are plains. On the northern bank of the Brahmaputra there are small hillocks like Chandar-Dinga, Sonamukh and Mahamaya whereas on the southern bank few hillocks of Garo Hills are visible. The mighty Brahmaputra flows to Dhubri near from Salkocha weaving its way through many char (sand bank) areas and enters Bangladesh. On both sides of the Brahmaputra there are many water-bodies. Among them Dhir-Beel and Dipul-Beel in the extreme east of the district on northern bank are the main.

Population and Habitation

Total population of the district is 13,32,475. There are seven towns and around 1260 villages in Dhubri district. The towns are Dhubri, Gauripur, Bilasipara, Chapar, Sapatgram, Golokganj and Mankachar. Besides these, other important places of the district are Bagaribari, Salkocha, South Salmara and Hatsingimari.

Dhubri is the Headquarter of the district with a population of around 66 thousand. There is a rail-station and a ship-yard in Dhubri.

Natural Resources, Agriculture and Industry

Valuable timbers such as *sal, segun, gomari, azar* are found in the reserved forests of Rupsi, Bagaribari, Mahamaya and Suparighat. These timbers are also found in the foot hills of Garo Hills. Paddy, jute, wheat, gram and masturd are the main agricultural produce of the district. Industrially the district is trailing behind. There is only one match box factory and one plywood factory in Dhubri.

Transportation

National Highway No. 31 coming from West-Bengal passes through Gauripur, Bilasipara and Chapar enters Bongaigaon district. Besides the National Highway there are state highways linking Dhubri with Gauripur and Golokganj, Bilasipara with Kokrajhar. On the Southern bank of Brahmaputra there are road links between Lakhipur to Fakirganj, South-Salmara to Mankachar via Hatsingimari. There is meter-gauge rail-road from Dhubri to Fakiragram via Golokganj. A marine route also exists between Dhubri and Fakirganj.

2. Kokrajhar District

KOKRAJHAR DISTRICT AT A GLANCE

Headquarters	: Kokrajhar	Literacy Rate	: 40.57%
Population	: 800659	Male	: 49.57%
Male	: 412600	Female	: 30.92%
Female	: 388059	No of Subdivisions	: 2
Urban	: 50724	No of Blocks	: 6
Rural	: 749935	Length of Road Under Pwd	: 1038 km.
Area	: 3129 sq km	Population Rank	: 16
Density	: 256 per sq.km.	Literacy Rank	: 22
Sex Ratio	: 941		

Location and Four Boundaries

Kokrajhar district is located on the extreme western part of Assam. This district is bounded on he north by Bhutan, on the east by Bongaigaon and Barpeta districts, on the south by Dhubri and on the west by West Bengal. Kokrajhar and Gosaigaon are the two sub-dibisions of the district.

Natural Geography

Mainly it is a plain district. Nadargiri and Rajshula are the only two hillocks in the district. On the northern part of the district, Kachugaon, Ripu, Guma, Chirang, Bengtal etc. are the forest ranges. There are a number of beels and water bodies in the district. Main rivers of the district are Sonkosh, Gadadhar, Hel, Saralbhanga, Champawati and Aai.

Population and Habitation

The population of the district is 800659. There are three towns and around 975 villages in the district. Main towns are Kokrajhar, Gosaigaon and Basugaon. Kokrajhar town, the head quarters of the district has a rail-station and is the central place of timber business. Other important places of the district are Fakiragram, Dotama, Sarfangguri, Sidli etc.

Natural Resources, Agriculture and Industry

Paddy, greengram and linseed are the main agricultural produce of the district. There are a few tea gardens in the district. The district is industrially backward. There are a few saw-mills and plywood factories in the district. In rural areas cane-work and handloom industries are popular.

Transportation

Transportation system of the district is not so developed due to the presence of dense forests on the northern part of the district. A branch of National Highway No. 31 coming from West-Bengal enters the district through Shreerampur, Kachugaon, Garubhasha and Sidli and passes to Bongaigaon. Besides this, there are state-highways from Kachugaon to West-Bengal via Raimana, Fakiragram and from Sidli to Basugaon. There is a broad-gauge rail-line between Shreerampur to Bongaigaon via Fakiragram and Kokrajhar and a meter-gauge line between Fakiragram to Bongaigaon.

3. Bongaigaon District

BONGAIGAON DISTRICT AT A GLANCE

Headquarters	:	Bongaigaon	Literacy Rate	:	49.06%
Population	:	807523	Male	:	58.67%
Male	:	416216	Female	:	38.72%
Female	:	391307	No of Subdivisions	:	3
Urban	:	73854	No of Blocks	:	6
Rural	:	733669	Length of Road Under Pwd	:	641 km.
Area	:	2510 sq km	Population Rank	:	15
Density	:	322 per sq.km.	Literacy Rank	:	15
Sex Ratio	:	940			

Location and Four Boundaries

This district is situated in lower Assam on the northern bank of Brahmaputra. It is bounded in the north by Bhutan, on the east by Barpeta district, on the south by Goalpara district and on the west by Kokrajhar and Dhubri district. Bongaigaon, Bijni and North-Salmara are the three sub-divisions of the district.

Natural Geography

The northern part of the district is almost plain and the southern part is composed of small hills, char areas and plains. Important hills are Jogighopa, Langtia, Mahadeu, Fagkhat, Dalani, Chipanshila, Bamani, Chakreswar etc. There are many water bodies and beels around Brahmaputra. Main rivers of the district are Brahmaputra, Manah, Aai, Burhi Aai and Kanamakra.

Population and Habitation

The population of the district is 807523. There are five towns and around 877 villages in the district. The towns are Bongaigaon, New-Bongaigaon, Abhayapuri, Bijni and Jogighopa. Other important places are Chapaguri, Srijangram, North-Salmara, Baitamari and Singimari etc.

Natural Resources, Agriculture and Industry

Sal, Titachapa, Banchom, Holok, Khokan are the important timbers available in the forests of the district. Paddy, green gram, linseed, mustard, wheat and tea are the main agricultural product of the district. The district is a little bit advanced in industry. In Jogighopa there is a paper-mill.

Transportation

A branch of National Highway No. 31 coming from chapar of Dhubri district passes to Barpeta district via North-Salmara of the district. Another branch of the same highway coming from Sidli of Kokrajhar district passes to Barpeta district via Bijni. Besides these, from Jogighopa to Bongaigaon and Abhayapuri, there are state highways via North-Salmara. There are rail-road links between New-Bongaigaon to Jogighopa and New Bongaigaon to Bijni town.

4. Goalpara District

Location and Four Boundaries

This district of Lower Assam is situated on the southern bank of Brahmaputra. The district is bounded on the north by Dhubri, Bongaigaon and Barpeta districts, on the east by Kamrup district, on the south by Meghalaya and on the west by Dhubri District. The district is not divided into sub-divisions.

GOALPARA DISTRICT AT A GLANCE

Headquarters	:	Goalpara	Literacy Rate	:	46.81%
Population	:	668138	Male	:	55.47%
Male	:	343154	Female	:	37.58%
Female	:	324984	No Of Subdivisions	:	1
Urban	:	52096	No Of Blocks	:	8
Rural	:	616042	Length Of Road Under Pwd	:	865 km.
Area	:	1828 sq.km	Population Rank	:	18
Density	:	2150 per sq.km.	Literacy Rank	:	18
Sex Ratio	:	947			

Natural Geography

The district is a combination of plains, hills, beels and submerged areas. Main hills of southern part are Dabil, Tukreswari, Ajagar, Deoli etc. whereas Matia, Rendhu, Pancharatna are the hills on the northern part. Suryapahar is situated on the eastern side of Goalpara town. Main rivers of the district are Dudhnoi, Krishnai and Ginjiram.

Population and Habitation

Total population of the district is 668138. The two lone towns of the district are Goalpara and Lakhipur. There are around 975 villages in the district. Goalpara is the main town of the district.

Natural Resources, Agriculture and Industry

In the foothills of Garro Hills valuable timbers such as sal, segun, gomari, khokan etc. are available. Paddy, jute, mustard, gram and linseed are the main agricultural produce of the district. There are a few tea gardens in the district. A good number of cottage industry based on wood and cane are coming up in the district. There are no other major industries.

Transportation

National Highway No. 37 enters Kamrup district via Agia, Dudhnoi and Dhupdhara of Goalpara district. There are state highways from Dudhnoi to Damra and Agia to Mankachar via Lakhipur. National highway No. 37 comes to Pancharatna from Goalpara. National highway No. 51 goes to Tura of Garo Hills from Agia via phulbari. A rail-road link between Pancharanta to Guwahati is on the verge of completion.

5. Barpeta District

BARPETA DISTRICT AT A GLANCE

Headquarters	:	Barpeta	Literacy Rate	: 43.24%
Population	:	1385659	Male	: 52.61%
Male	:	714677	Female	: 33.20%
Female	:	670982	No of Subdivisions	: 2
Urban	:	97318	No of Blocks	: 11
Rural	:	1288341	Length of Road Under Pwd	: 1450 km.
Area	:	3245 sq.km	Population Rank	: 4
Density	:	427 per sq.km.	Literacy Rank	: 20
Sex Ratio	:	939		

Location and Four Boundaries

This district is situated in lower Assam on the northern bank of Brahmaputra. The district is bounded on the north by Bhutan, on the east by Nalbari district, on the south by Kamrup and Goalpara districts, and on the west by Bongaigaon district. Brahmaputra river flows through southern side of the district. Barpeta and Bajali are the two sub-divisions of the district.

Natural Geography

The district varies from low lying plains to elevated land having a small hillock in the south-west corner known as Baghbar. Other hills are Fulara and Chatala. Main rivers are Beki, Chaulkhowa, Palla, Pahumara and Kalidia. There are a number of beels on the southern part of the district. Important reserved forests are Kahitama, Manash National Sacntuary, Kakilbari, Deudhara and Batabari.

Population and Habitation

The population of Barpeta district is 138659. There are seven towns and around 1030 villages in the district. The towns are Barpeta, Barpeta Road, Howley, Sarthebari, Bahari, Pathsala and Sarabhog. Other important places are Bhabanipur, Patacharkuchi, Sarupeta, Chenga, Jania and Kalgachia etc.

Natural Resources, Agriculture and Industry

This district is famous for agricultural produces like paddy, jute, mustard and vegetables. There is a tea garden in the district.

Barpeta town is famous for cottage industry of gold, silver and ivory works. There are no major industries in the district. In the forest of the district valuable timbers like *sal, gomari, titachapa* and medicinal plants are available.

Transportation

National highway no. 31 coming from Bongaigaon district enters Nalbari district via Sarabhog, Howley, Bhabanipur and Pathsala. There are state highways linking Barpeta town and Guwahati via Chenga, Barpeta town and Barpeta Road. There are rail-way lines coming from Bijni and entering Nalbari district via Barpeta Road and Pathsala.

6. Nalbari District

NALBARI DISTRICT AT A GLANCE

Headquarters	: Nalbari	Literacy Rate	: 55.99%
Population	: 1016390	Male	: 66.95%
Male	: 524953	Female	: 44.19%
Female	: 491437	No of Subdivisions	: 1
Urban	: 23475	No of Blocks	: 12
Rural	: 992915	Length of Road Under Pwd	: 1394 km.
Area	: 2257 sq.km	Population Rank	: 9
Density	: 450 per sq.km.	Literacy Rank	: 9
Sex Ratio	: 936		

Location and four Boundaries

This district is situated on the western part of Brahmaputra Valley. It is bounded on the north by Bhutan, on the east by Kamrup district, on the west by Barpeta district, and on the south by Kamrup district. Brahmaputra river flows through the district.

Natural Geography

Topographically, the district forms a great plain comprising a few elevated tracts lying along the Bhutan hills which forms its northern boundary. The district is being traversed from the north to south by two important rivers – the Pagladiya and the Puthimari. Both the rivers originate from Bhutan Hills. It is a flood prone district.

Population and Habitation

The population of the district is 1016390. The middle most part of the district is densely populated. Nalbari town is the head quarters of the district. Other important places are Tihu, Ghagrpara, Morawa, Bijulighat, Mukalmuwa, Belshar and Barama. There are around 824 villages in the district.

Natural Resources, Agriculture and Industry

Natural resources are scarce in Nalbari district. Forest wealths too are limited. Timbers like *Segun, Gomari and Khaira* are available in the reserved forests of Doranga, Suwankhata, Dihira and . Main agricultural produces are paddy, jute, mustard and potato. In char areas vegetables are produced in planty. Traditional cane-work cottage industries are the only industries of the district. No major industries are coming up yet. There is a polyester mill at Nathkuchi near Tihu.

Transportation

National highway no. 31 passes through the district along with rail lines. The length of this highway is 48 km. On both north and south side of this highway there are many important roads. Among them important are Nalbari to Hajo, Nalbari to Dhamdhama, Nalbari to Mukalmuwa, Nalbari to Sarthebari, Borama to Chamata etc. There are four rail-stations in the district.

7. Kamrup District

KAMRUP DISTRICT AT A GLANCE

Headquarters	: Guwahati	Literacy Rate	: 65.04%
Population	: 2000071	Male	: 73.67%
Male	: 1064649	Female	: 55.01%
Female	: 935422	No Of Subdivisions	: 2
Urban	: 655215	No Of Blocks	: 17
Rural	: 1344856	Length Of Road Under Pwd	: 2506 km.
Area	: 4345 sq. km.	Population Rank	: 1
Density	: 460 per sq.km.	Literacy Rank	: 2
Sex Ratio	: 879		

Location and Four Boundaries

This district is situated on the western part of Brahmaputra valley. It is bounded on the north by Nalbari district, on the east by Darrang and Morigaon districts, on the south by Meghalaya and on the west by Barpeta and Goalpara districts. Guwahati and Rangia are the two subdivisions of the district.

Natural Geography

The greater part of Kamrup consists of a wide plain through the lower portion of which Brahmapurta river makes its way, flowing a steady course from east to west. On south of the river, this plain is much broken up by hills. The important hills on the northern bank are Agyathuri, Gaurachal and Hatimura and on the southern bank are Narakasur, Nilachal and hills of Chandrapur area. There are hilly tracts on the south-west part of the district near Boko.

Main rivers of the district are Brahmaputra, Puthimari, Baralia, Barnoi, Digaru, Kulshi and Boko.

Population and Habitation

An area of 4345 sq km bears the load of a population of size 20,00,071. Dispur, the capital of Assam is in the greater city of Guwahati which is densly populated. Important towns of the district are North-Guwahati, Hajo, Rangia, Amingaon, Palashbari, Mirza, Goreswar, Baihata Chariali, Chandrapur, Bijoynagar, Boko and Nagarbera. Guwahati is the central place of not only Assam but whole of north eastern region. Most of the cities and towns of N.E. region are connected with Guwahati by road, rail-road and air-ways.

Natural Resources, Agriculture and Industry

Southern part of the district is rich in forest wealths. Valuable timbers like sal, segun, sonaru etc. are found in planty in Boko, Chaigaon, Bongaon, Luki and Rani areas of south Kamrup.

Paddy, mustard and jute are the main agricultural products of the district. In south Kamrup vegetables and fruits are also produced in large amount. This district is comparatively advanced in industry but most of the industries are concentrated around the city of

Guwahati. Famous among these industries are Nunmati Refinery, India Carbon, Assam Carbon and Steel factories of Amingaon. Brush metal-works Industry of Hajo and industries of Sualkuchi are famous.

Transportation

This district is comparatively better developed with respect to transportation due to Guwahati, the central place of Assam. Natonal highway no. 37 passes through the southern part of the district. Most of the places of south Kamrup are connected with Guwahati through this highway. Head quraters Guwahati is connected by by rail-links with important places of upper and lower Assam. Gopinath Bordoloi Airport near Guwahati is connected with Delhi, Calcutta and important places of north east region.

8. Darrang District

DARRANG DISTRICT AT A GLANCE

Headquarters	: Mangaldoi	Literacy Rate	: 42%
Population	: 1298860	Male	: 50.80%
Male	: 670244	Female	: 32.53%
Female	: 628616	No of Subdivisions	: 2
Urban	: 63984	No of Blocks	: 11
Rural	: 1234876	Length of Road Under Pwd	: 1513 km.
Area	: 3481 sq.km	Population Rank	: 6
Density	: 373 per sq.km.	Literacy Rank	: 21
Sex Ratio	: 938		

Location and Four Boundaries

This district is situated in almost middle part of the Brahmaputra valley. It is bounded on the north by Bhutan and Arunachal Pradesh, on the east by Sonitpur district, on the south by Nowgaon and Marigaon districts and on the west by Kamrup district. Udalguri and Mangaldoi are two sub-divisions of the district.

Natural Geography

This district consists of a narrow strip on the plain lying between the Himalayas and the Brahmaputra. At its eastern-extremity the district is only about 12 miles broad. Though in most part of the district the view on a clear day is bounded on either side by hills, there are no hills or mountains of any size within the actual frontiers of this district. The main rivers of the district are Barnoi, Nanoi, Mangaldoi noi, Dhansiri and Pach noi.

Population and Habitation

Total population of the district is 1298860. There are around 1344 villages. Four main towns are Mongaldoi, Tangla, Udalguri and Kharupetia. Other important places of the district are Sipajhar, Kalaigaon, Khairabari, Paneri, Dalgaon, Routa, Orang and Mazbat.

Natural Resources, Agriculture and Industry

This district is rich in forest wealths. In the reserved forests of the district timbers like cham, makai, khoira, sonaru, gomari and nahar are found. In the Orang sanctuary rhinos and tigers are found.

Sugarcane, paddy, jute and mustard are important agricultural produces. In the char areas various types of vegetables are produced.

There are 28 tea gardens and tea factories in the district. Besides these, at Mangaldoi and Kharupetia, there are a few medium type agro-based industries. Also, at Bijulibari near Sipajhar there is a polyester industry.

Transportation

National highway no. 52 passes through the district. The length of this highway in the district is 79 km. There are state highway links between Mangaldoi to Udalguri via Kalaigaon, Udalguri to Routa, Orang to Mazbat, Kaligaon to Paneri and Sipajhar to Barengajuli. The only railway link of the district comes from Rangia and enters Rangapara.

9. Sonitpur District

Location and Four Boundaries

This district is situated in the middle part of Brahmaputra valley. It is bounded on the north by Arunachal Pradesh, on the east by Lakhimpur district, on the south by Golaghat and Nagaon district and on the west by Darrang district. The tow sub-divisions of the district are Tezpur and Biswanath.

SONITPUR DISTRICT AT A GLANCE

Headquarters	: Tezpur	Literacy Rate	: 48.15%
Population	: 1424287	Male	: 56.70%
Male	: 744778	Female	: 38.60%
Female	: 679509	No of Subdivisions	: 2
Urban	: 103908	No of Blocks	: 14
Rural	: 1320379	Length of Road Under Pwd	: 1963 km.
Area	: 5324 sq.km	Population Rank	: 3
Density	: 268 per sq.km.	Literacy Rank	: 16
Sex Ratio	: 912		

Natural Geography

The northern part of the district is more or less hilly. On the southern bank of Brahmaputra near Biswanath, Tezpur and Singri there are hills of smaller size. Bhamaraguri and Agnigarh are the famous hills. The main rivers of the district are Paachnoi, Belsiri, Gabharu, Jeeya Bharali, Burhigang, Bargang, Burai and Brahmajan etc. There are many beels and marshes in the district.

Population and Habitation

Total population of the district is 14,24,287. The district head quarters Tezpur is an ancient famous town. Rangapara, Dhekiajuli and Biswanath are the main towns of the district. Other important places are Barchala, Singri, Misamari, Balipara, Jamuguri, Chatia, Bargong, Bihali Helem and Gahpur. There are around 1753 villages in the district

Natural Resources, Agriculture and Industry

It is a rich district in forest wealths. There are reserved forests like Balipara, Chariduar, Biswanath and Gahpur where *sal, segun, gomari and simalu* like valuable timbers are found. In the Nameri Sanctuary tigers and birds of rare species are found.

This is an advanced district in agriculture. Paddy, mustard, sugarcane, jute etc. are the main crops of the district. There are around 65 tea gardens in the district.

There is no major industry in the district. Only some agro-based industries are running. In Balipara and Bargong area there are many brick industries.

Transportation

Around 206 km long National highway no. 52 passes through the district. Meter-gauge rail also passes through the district from east to west. A branch of this connects Tezpur with Rangapara. Kaliabhomora bridge on the Brahmaputra near Tezpur makes transportation easier to Nagaon. Salani Airport near Tezpur connects the district by airway with Guwahati and other places.

10. Lakhimpur District

LAKHIMPUR DISTRICT AT A GLANCE

Headquarters	:	North Lakhimpur	Literacy Rate	:	58.96%
Population	:	751517	Male	:	68.28%
Male	:	389125	Female	:	48.85%
Female	:	362392	No of Subdivisions	:	2
Urban	:	702387	No of Blocks	:	9
Rural	:	49130	Length of Road Under Pwd	:	1229 km.
Area	:	2274 sq.km	Population Rank	:	17
Density	:	330 per sq.km.	Literacy Rank	:	5
Sex Ratio	:	931			

Location and Four Boundaries

This district is situated on the north-eastern part of Assam. It is bounded on the north by Arunachal Pradesh, Papun Paro of Himalayas and Lower Suwanshiri district, on the east by Dhemaji district, on the south by Jorhat district with Majuli river island and on the west by Sonitpur district. Dhakuakhana and Lakhimpur are two sub-divisions of the district.

Natural Geography

Mainly the areas of the district are plains. A large portion of the district is covered with forest and the general effect is extremely picturesque. At all seasons of the year the country looks fresh, cool and green. The main rivers of the district are Dikrang, Singra, Ranganoi, Suwanshiri and Karha. A large number of streams and jans flow through the district and create havoc by inundating vast areas during rainy season.

Population and Habitation

Total population of the district is 751,517. There are around 950 villages and two towns in the district. Other important places are Bihupuria, Narayanpur, Banderdewa-Harmati, Laluk, Panigaon and Dhakuakhana.

Natural Resources, Agriculture and Industry

The district is rich in forest wealths. Timbers and animals are found in the forests. There are 10 tea gardens and no major industry exists in the district.

Transportation

Transportation system is not developed in the district. National Highway No. 52 passes through Dhemaji from Hawajan via North-Lakhimpur. Meter-gauge rail line connects Gogamukh with Kathani. From Lakhimpur to Kamalabari and from Gogamukh to Dhakuakhana, there are motorable roads.

11. Dhemaji District

DHEMAJI DISTRICT AT A GLANCE

Headquarters	: Dhemaji	Literacy Rate	: 58.96%
Population	: 478830	Male	: 68.28%
Male	: 248457	Female	: 48.85%
Female	: 230373	No of Subdivisions	: 2
Urban	: 8891	No of Blocks	: 5
Rural	: 469939	Length of Road Under Pwd	: 593 km.
Area	: 3237 sq.km.	Population Rank	: 21
Density	: 148 per sq.km.	Literacy Rank	: 12
Sex Ratio	: 931		

Location and Four Boundaries

Dhemaji district is situated in the north-east part of Assam. On the north it is bounded by Siang district of Arunachal, on the east and south by Brahmaputra river, Tinsukia and Dibrugarh district and on the west by a part of Suwanshiri river and Lakhimpur district.

Natural Geography

It is mostly a plain district of Assam. Main rivers of the district are: Karah, Jiadhal, Gainoi, Dikari, Direng and Burhisuti. There are many streams, jans, beels and water bodies in the district.

Population and Habitation

The district has a population of 478830. There are around 350 villages. Dhemaji and Jonai are two most important places of the district. Other important places are Gogamukh and Chilapathar. From Chilapathar there is a road leading to Arunachal Predesh. On this road an ancient and beautiful place called Malinithan is situated.

Natural Resources, Agriculture and Industry

In this district, main natural resources are forest wealths. Many varieties of soft-wood and rare birds are found here. In agriculture, the district is very backward. And due to bad transportation and communication system no major industries are coming up besides one or two saw mills.

Transportation

Transportation system of the district is not at all developed. National highway no. 52 enters the district from Lakhimpur and passes to Jonai via Gogamukh and Chilapathar. Along with this road a mete-gauge rail line passes from Gogamukh to Jonai. Other important road links are Gogamukh to Dhakuakhana via Bardalani, Dhakuakhana to Dhemaji via Machkhowa and Dhemaji to Sonarighat. In rainy seasons all these roads get damaged and submerged.

12. Marigaon District

MARIGAON DISTRICT AT A GLANCE

Headquarters	: Marigaon	Literacy Rate	: 47.99%
Population	: 639682	Male	: 56.17%
Male	: 329613	Female	: 39.19%
Female	: 310069	No of Subdivisions	: 1
Urban	: 32989	No of Blocks	: 5
Rural	: 606693	Length of Road Under Pwd	: 904 km.
Area	: 1704 sq.km	Population Rank	: 20
Density	: 375 per sq.km.	Literacy Rank	: 17
Sex Ratio	: 941		

Location and Four Boundaries

Marigaon district is situated in middle part of Brahmaputra valley. It is bounded on the north by Darrang district, on the east by Nagaon district, on the south by Karbi-Anglong district and

Meghalaya and on the west by Kamrup district. There is only one sub-division in the district.

Natural Geography

Southern part of the district is hilly and on the northern part flows the mighty Brahmaputra. Mayang region on the north west corner is also more or less hilly. The hills of south-west region are Ghaguwa, Tetelia and Hatimuria. On the southern part of the river Kapili meets the river Kolong and then together they flow to the Brahmaputra trhough western boundary of the district. Other rivers are Sonai and Marasonai. There are many beels and submerged areas in the district.

Population and Habitation

Total population of the district is 639682. Marigaon and Jagiroad are two main towns of the district. Jagiroad is the central business place of the district. Jagiroad is famous for dry-fish market. There are around 593 villages in the district. Other important places are Laharighat, Mikirbheta, Bhurabandha, Dharamtul, Raja Mayang etc.

Natural Resources, Agriculture and Industry

This district has a rich stock of forest wealths. On hills of Southern part sal, segun, sonaru timbers are found. In the dense forests of Pabitara Sanctuary rhinos, tigers and deers are found.

Marigaon district is one of the comparatively advanced district in agriculture. Paddy and jute are the main crops. Besides these, mustard, potato and fruits are also produced. There are few tea gardens in the district.

Main industry of the district is Hindustan Paper Mill situated at Jagiroad. In a few places handloom industries also exist.

Transportation

Transportation system is not so good in the district. National Highway No. 37 passes through southern part of the district. The length of this road is 41 km. in the district. Other important roads are Jagiroad – Marigaon road, Marigaon – Mikirbheta road, Marigaon – Laharighat road and Jagiroad – Rajamayang road. Guwahati – Dimapur broad-gauge rail-line passes through the district.

13. Nagaon District

NAGAON DISTRICT AT A GLANCE

Headquarters	:	Nagaon	Literacy Rate	:	54.74%
Population	:	1893171	Male	:	62.49%
Male	:	981371	Female	:	46.30%
Female	:	911792	No of Subdivisions	:	3
Urban	:	205722	No of Blocks	:	17
Rural	:	1687449	Length of Road Under Pwd	:	2283 km.
Area	:	3831 sq.km	Population Rank	:	2
Density	:	494 per sq. km.	Literacy Rank	:	10
Sex Ratio	:	929			

Location and Four Boundaries

This district is situated in the central part of Brahmaputra valley and is on the south bank of the river. It is bounded on the north by Sonitpur district, on the east by Golaghat district and Karbi-Anglong districts, on the south by Karbi-Anglong and N. C. Hills districts and on the west by Kamrup district and Meghalaya. This district is composed of Nagaon, Kaliabor and Hojai sub-divisions.

Natural Geography

The district may be decribed as tract of level country bounded on the north by the Brahmaputra and surrounded on the three remaining sides by hills. The great part of the district is plain criss-crossed with numerous rivers and waterways and dotted over with beels and marshes. In places like the banks of river Kalang, it is densely populated. The main river of the district is Kapili.

Population and Habitation

The district has a population of 1893171. Nagaon, the head quarters of the district is a central business place. Lamding, Hojai, Lanka, Dhing and Raha are five important towns of the district. Other important places are Jamunamukh, Dabaka, Kampur, Chaparmukh, Kathiatali and Kaliabor etc. There are around 1419 villages in the district.

Natural Resources, Agriculture and Industry

This district is rich in forest products. Laokhowa and Burahchapari are the two wild life sanctuaries. In these sanctuaries rhino, tiger, elephant and various species of birds are found. Sal, segun, simalu, korai, agaru are the timbers found in the district.

Agriculturally this district is advanced. Paddy, jute, mustard, sugarcane and cotton are the main crops. In industry, jute mill of Shilghat, sugar mill of Kampur and agro-based industries of Hojai are famous.

Transportation

Compatatively the transportation system of this district is better. National highway no. 36 and 37 pass through the district. In the district length of these roads is 180 km. The second bridge over the Brahmaputra, the Kalia Bhomora Setu, links the district with Sonitpur district. Other important roads are Nagaon-Dhing road, Nagaon-Laukhowa road, Kampur-Jamunamukh road and Lanka – Dabaka road.

Rail-route is also better here. The main rail route comes from Guwahati and passes to Lamding via Chaparmukh. Other rail routes are Nagaon to Jakhalabandha and Nagaon to Mairabari.

14. Golaghat District

GOLAGHAT DISTRICT AT A GLANCE

Headquarters	:	Golaghat	Literacy Rate	:	58.54%
Population	:	828096	Male	:	66.50%
Male	:	431346	Female	:	49.75%
Female	:	396750	No of Subdivisions	:	3
Urban	:	48838	No of Blocks	:	8
Rural	:	779258	Length of Road Under Pwd	:	1406 km.
Area	:	3502 sq.km.	Population Rank	:	13
Density	:	236 per sq. km.	Literacy Rank	:	6
Sex Ratio	:	920			

Location and Four Boundaries

This district is situated on plains on the eastern part of Assam and on the south of Brahmaputra. The district is bounded on the north by the Brahmaputra with Majuli and parts of Lakhimpur and Sonitpur districts, on the east by Nagaland, Kakdonga river and Jorhat district, on the south by Nagaland and Karbi-Anglong district and on the west by Karbi-Anglong and Nagaon districts. The district is composed of three sub-divisions – Golaghat, Dhansiri and Bokakhat.

Natural Geography

Though mainly it is a plain district, some branches of Naga hills entered the district from south-east side. Likewise from western part, some branches of Karbihills also entered the district. Main rivers of the district are Kakdonga, Ghilamari, Dhansiri, Diphalu and Gelabeel.

Population and Habitation

The district has a population of 828096. It has around 800 villages, three towns and 70 tea gardens. Golaghat, Dergaon and Bokakhat are the main towns. Other important places are Sarupathar, Barpathar, Farkating, Karmarbandha, Kamargaon, Kahara, Numaligarh and Garampani.

Natural Resources, Agriculture and Industry

The district is rich in natural wealth. The famous Kajiranga wildlife sanctuary is situated on the western part of the district where one-horned rhinoes are found. Besides this there are reserved forests like Nambar, Diphu, Rengma etc. Tea industry, oil refinery and sugar factories are main industries of the district.

Transportation

National highway no. 37 passes towards east from west through northern part of the district. From Numaligarh to Nagaland there is National Highway No. 39. From Dergaon and Kamargaon there are separate roads to Golaghat. Broad-gauge rail-line passes towards north-east from Dimapur through the district. There is also a rail line from Farkating to Jorhat and Mariani via Golaghat.

15. Jorhat District

Location and Four Boundaries

This district is situated in the eastern part of Assam. It is composed of the largest river island Majuli and adjacent plain on the south of Brahmaputra. The district is bounded on the north by Lakhimpur district, on the east by a part of the Brahmaputra, the Janjhi river and Sibsagar district. On the south by Nagaland

and on the west by Kakdonga river and Golaghat district. The district has two sub-divisions-Majuli and Jorhat.

JORHAT DISTRICT AT A GLANCE

Headquarters	: Jorhat	Literacy Rate	65.51%
Population	: 871206	Male	: 73.29%
Male	: 455525	Female	: 56.88%
Female	: 415681	No of Subdivisions	: 2
Urban	: 33032	No of Blocks	: 8
Rural	: 738174	Length of Road Under Pwd	: 1653 km.
Area	:	2851 sq.km.	Population
Rank	: 12		
Density	: 306 per sq. km.	Literacy Rank	: 1
Sex Ratio	: 913		

Natural Geography

This is mainly a plain district. Few branches of Naga hills are seen in the southern part of the district. Important rivers of the district are a part of the Brahmaputra, the Tiyak and the Disoi and the Bhogdoi.

Population and Habitation

The district has a population of 871206, around 950 villages and more than 100 tea gardens. Jorhat and Mariani are two important towns of the district. In Jorhat, there is one agricultural University, one regional laboratory and one tea research centre. Other important places are Garmur, Tiyak, Titabar, Na-kachari and Barhola. There are a few famous Satras in Majuli.

Natural Resources, Agriculture and Industry

There are more than 100 tea gardens in the district. Crude oil is produced from places like Barhola and Chengapara. There are plywood factories in Mariani. Kakdonga, Disoibheli, Tiru etc> are the reserved forests of the district. In these forests valuable timbers and animals are found.

Transportation

Transportation system of the district is partially developed. National Highway no. 37 passes through the district towards east. The famous road Dhadar Ali passes towards north-eastern part from Golaghat side via Titabar and Mariani. There are road links between Jorhat to Titabar, Mariani and Nimatighat. Broad-gauge rail line passes through the southern part of the district. Besides this another rail line is there from Mariani towards Golaghat via Jorhat. But the transportation system is in bad shape in Majuli sub division. It is connected to Jorhat sub-division through water ways only.

16. Sibsagar District

Location and Four Boundaries

This district is situated on eastern part of Assam on the south-east bank of the Brahmaputra. The district is bounded on the north by parts of Burhidihing and Dishang rivers and Dibrugarh district, on the east by Arunachal Pradesh, on the south by Nagaland and on the west by the Janjhi river, the Brahmaputra river and Jorhat district. It is composed of Sibsagar, Charaideu and Nazira sub-divisions.

SIBSAGAR DISTRICT AT A GLANCE

Headquarters	Sibsagar	Literacy Rate	64.46%
Population	907983	Male	71.91%
Male	476009	Female	56.14%
Female	431974	No of Subdivisions	3
Urban	65689	No of Blocks	9
Rural	842294	Length of Road Under Pwd	1778 km.
Area	2668 sq.km.	Population Rank	11
Density	340 per sq. km.	Literacy Rank	3
Sex Ratio	907		

Natural Geography

Mainly this is a plain district. But on the south-eastern part of the district some branches of Arunachal and Nagaland Hills entered. Main rivers of the district are Dimau, Tiphuk, Dishang, Darika, Dikhau, Namdang and Janjhi. On the banks of Dikhau and Brahmaputra there are many beels and marshes. Sibsagar, like the rest of upper Assam enjoys a cold winter and a cool and pleasant spring.

Population and Habitation

The district has a population of 907983. In the district there are 873 villages, 87 tea gardens and 5 towns. The main towns of the district are: Sibsagar, Nazira, Amguri, Moranhat and Sonari. Other important places are Janjhi, Charing, Namati Ali, Nitai Pukhuri, Barhat, Simaluguri and Charaideu.

Natural Resources, Agriculture and Industry

It is an advanced district in natural resources and industry. There are 87 large tea gardens. In Lakuwa, Geleki, Rudrasagar and Longsai, crude oil and natural gases are found. There are some reserved forests in the district where valuable trees and animals are found.

Transportation

Transport and communication system is comparatively developed in the district. National highway no. 37 enters the district from Jorhat side and passes to Dibrugarh via Sibsagar and Maran. There are roads linking Sibsagar to Disangmukh, Namati Ali and Nazira. Broadgauge rail line passes through the southern part of the district. From Simaluguri junction to Maranhat and Bihubar, there are rail lines.

17. Dibrugarh District

DIBRUGARH DISTRICT AT A GLANCE

Headquarters	:	Dibrugarh	Literacy Rate	:	58.32%
Population	:	1042457	Male	:	66.72%
Male	:	547266	Female	:	48.49%
Female	:	495191	No of Subdivisions	:	1
Urban	:	183580	No of Blocks	:	7
Rural	:	858874	Length of Road Under Pwd	:	1309 km.
Area	:	3381 sq.km.	Population Rank	:	8
Density	:	308 per sq. km.	Literacy Rank	:	7
Sex Ratio	:	905			

Location and Four Boundaries

This district is situated in the north-east part of Assam. It is bounded on the north and west by the river Brahmaputra and

Dhemaj district respectively, on the east by Tinsukia district and on the south by Sibsagar district and a part of Tirap district of Arunachal.

Natural Geography

This is totally a plain district. Only in south-east near Jaypur few small hillocks entering from Tirap district are visible. The main rivers of the district are Dibru, Checha and Burhidihing.

Population and Habitation

The population size of the district is 1042457. There are around 1200 villages, 120 tea gardens and five main towns in the district. The headquarters Dibrugarh town is the biggest place next to Guwahati. It is an ancient place and is the heart of tea industry and commercial activities. Other important places of the district are Namrup, Duliajan, Naharkatia, Chabua and Maran.

Natural Resources, Agriculture and Industry

The district is comparatively advanced in industry. There are more than hundred tea gardens in the district. Crude oil is available in places like Maran, Tengakhat, Duliajan, Naharkatia and Hugrijan. Coals are found near Jaypur.

Transportation

The transportation network is slightly developed in the district. The first rail-line in Assam – the Dibru-Sadia rail line was constructed here. Now it is converted to broad-gauge line and it connects Dibrugarh with the rest of the state and the country. This line is also extended to the south-eastern part of the district. National Highway no. 37 passes towards Tinsukia from Maran via Dibrugarh. There are road links from Dibrugarh to Namrup via Tengakhat and Maran to Chabua via Tengakhat. There is a air port near Chabua which connects the district with Guwahati and rest of the country.

18. Tinsukla District

Location and Four Boundaries

This district is situated in the extreme north-east corner of Assam. This district is bounded on the north by Brahmaputra, a part of Dhemaji district and Arunachal Pradesh, on the east by a portion Na-Dihing river and Arunachal Pradesh, on the south by a part of Arunachal and on the west by Dibrugarh district. Sadia, Margharita and Tinsukia are the three sub-divisions of the district.

TINSUKIA DISTRICT AT A GLANCE

Headquarters	:	Tinsukia	Literacy Rate	:	50.28%
Population	:	962298	Male	:	59.27%
Male	:	508948	Female	:	39.99%
Female	:	453350	No of Subdivisions	:	3
Urban	:	158674	No of Blocks	:	7
Rural	:	803654	Length of Road Under Pwd	:	1326 km.
Area	:	3790 sq.km.	Population Rank	:	10
Density	:	254 per sq. km.	Literacy Rank	:	14
Sex Ratio	:	891			

Natural Geography

This district is composed of plains created by Lohit, Dibang and Brahmaputra. On the south-east corner some branches of Patkai hills of Arunachal are seen. The main rivers of the district are the Dibang, the Lohit, the Brahmaputra, the Laikajan, the Dangari, the Dumduma, the Dibru and the Bruhidihing. There are many water bodies in the north-west part of the district.

Population and Habitation

The district has a population of 962298, around 1200 villages, 120 tea gardens and five towns. Tinsukia, the head quarters of the district is the central place of administration, transportation, trade and commerce. Other important places are Digboi, Margherita, Dumduma, Makum, Chepakhoa, Sadia, Panitola, Talap and Lido.

Natural Resources, Agriculture and Industry

Tea industry of the district is world famous. Moreover there are coal mines in Lido-Lekhapari area. There is a Oil-refinery at Digboi. Plywood industry of Margherita is also well known. Forests of the district are rich in animals. Dihing reserved forest is a evergreen rain forest.

Transportation

Transportation and communication network is developed in this district. National Highway no. 37 passes to Dangari from

Digrugarh via Panitola and Tinsukia. National highway no. 38 goes towards Arunachal Pradesh from Tinsukia via Digboi and Lido. Also there are road links between Dumduma and Arunachal Pradesh via Kakopathar; Tinsukia and Namrup via Bardubi. Tinsukia and Makum are rail-junctions. There are rail lines from Naharkatia to Dibrugarh via Tinsukia and from Tinsukia to Dangari and Lido.

19. Karbi-Anglong District

KARBI-ANGLONG DISTRICT AT A GLANCE

Headquarters	:	Diphu	Literacy Rate	:	45.57%
Population	:	662723	Male	:	55.55%
Male	:	347607	Female	:	34.35%
Female	:	315116	No of Subdivisions	:	3
Urban	:	70466	No of Blocks	:	11
Rural	:	592257	Length of Road Under Pwd	:	700 km.
Area	:	10434sq. km	Population Rank	:	19
Density	:	64 per sq. km.	Literacy Rank	:	19
Sex Ratio	:	907			

Location and Four Boundaries

This district is situated between Karbi and Meghalaya hills. This district is divided into two detached parts by the partition of Nagaon district, jutting into it the contiguity of it as a whole has been maintained only by the N.C. Hills linking up this gap between the eastern and western parts of Karbi-Anglong. The district is composed of three sub-divisions – Diphu, Bokajan and Hamren. Diphu and Bokajan form one part of the district. This part is bounded on the north by Nagaon and Golaghat districts, on the east by Golaghat district, on the south-east by Nagaland, on the south-west by N.C. Hills and on the west by Nagaon district. Another part of the district is the Hamren sub-division. This part is bounded on the north and north east by Nagaon district, on the south-east by N. C. Hills district, on the south and west by Meghalaya.

Natural Geography

Both parts of Karbi-Anglong are full of hills. These hills are 300 metres to 1300 metres high. Dambukosha is the highest peak of these hills with a height of 1363 metres. The Dhansiri river flows through the eastern boundary of the district. The Jamuna river flows towards west through Diphu sub-division. The Diyang is another big river in the south-western boundary. The Kapili is the main river of Harren district. Other important rivers are Barapani and Kiling.

Population and Habitation

Population of the district is 662723. There are around 1000 villages and six towns in the district. The headquarters Diphu is the central place of administration, business and education. Other important places are Bokajan, Dakmaka, Howraghat, Bakaliaghat, Manja, Hamran, Dankamokam, Baithlangshu and Kalanga.

Natural Resources, Agriculture and Industry

Coal is found in Longloi, Koilajan, Kaliyani, Disama and Silbheta. Lime stone is found in south-eastern part of Hamren sub-division, Silbheta and Dilai. In industry, Bokajan's cement factory is famous. Coffee and rubber plantation are coming up in the district.

Transportation

Transportation system is not developed in the district. National Highway no. 36 passes to Dimapur from Nagaon via Diphu and Bokajan sub-divisions. National highway no. 39, which comes from Numaligarh touches the eastern part of the district. There is a road from Lanka to Hamren. From Lumding of Nagaon district to Dimapur there is a broad-gauge rail line which passes via Diphu.

20. N.C. Hills District

N.C. HILLS DISTRICT AT A GLANCE

Headquarters	:	Haflong	Literacy Rate	:	57.76%
Population	:	150801	Male	:	66.39%
Male	:	81196	Female	:	47.34%
Female	:	69605	No of Subdivisions	:	2
Urban	:	34486	No of Blocks	:	5
Rural	:	116315	Length of Road Under Pwd	:	1131 km.
Area	:	4883 sq. km	Population Rank	:	23
Density	:	31 per sq. km.	Literacy Rank	:	8
Sex Ratio	:	857			

Location and Four Boundaries

This hills district is situated in the middle part of Assam. It is bounded on the north by Karbi-Anglong, on the east by Nagaland, on the south by Cachar district and on the west by Meghalaya. This district is surrounded on the north, east and west by hills. Only on the south there are plains of the river Barak.

Natural Geography

This district is full of hills. Barail hills range passes through the district from south-west towards north-east. On this hills range, highest peacks of Assam are situated. The highest among them are Mahdeu (1756 meters), the peak on the east of Indulong (1881 meters) and the peak on north-east of Thenbung (1972 metres). The Dhansiri river flows through the north-east boundary of the district. The Diyung is another main river of northern part. The Kapili flows through north-west Boundary. Jatinga, Langting, Mahur and Langlai are other important rivers of the district.

Population and Habitation

The district has the lowest population of 150801 in Assam. It is composed of Haflong and Maibong sub-divisions. The density of population per sq. km. in these districts is the lowest in the state. There are around 300 villages and 3 main towns in the district. These towns are Haflong, Maibong and Mahur. Other important places are Umrangshu, Jatinga and Ditakchara. Umrangshu is famous for Kapili Hydel Project. Jatinga is a beautiful place near Haflong which is famous for bird-watching.

Natural Resources, Agriculture and Industry

It is a rich district in forest wealths. Valuable timbers, bamboo and animals are found in the forests. Limestone is found in Umrangshu area. Coffee and rubber plantations are coming up in the district. Fruits like orange and apple are grown in Jainga area. There are a few fruit based industries in the district.

Transportation

Transportation system is in bad shape in the district. There is a road from Lanka to Haflong via Umrangshu. From Lumding to the plains of Barak, there is a meter-gauge rail line through this district. There are 37 tunnels on this line.

21. Karimganj District

Location and Four Boundaries

This district is situated in Barak valley on the southern part of Assam. It is bounded on the north by Cachar district and Bangladesh, on the east by Cachar district, on the south by Mizoram and Tripura and on the west by Tripura and Bangladesh.

KARIMGANJ DISTRICT AT A GLANCE

Headquarters	:	Karimganj	Literacy Rate	:	54.71%
Population	:	827063	Male	:	64.05%
Male	:	425018	Female	:	44.76%
Female	:	402045	No Of Subdivisions	:	1
Urban	:	60381	No Of Blocks	:	7
Rural	:	766682	Length Of Road Under Pwd	:	700 km.
Area	:	1809 sq. km.	Population Rank	:	13
Density	:	457 per sq. km.	Literacy Rank	:	11
Sex Ratio	:	956			

Natural Geography

The south and south-western parts of the district are hilly tracts. Some hillocks are also seen in the plains of the district. The Barak river flows from the northern boundary. The Longai and the Singla river flow through the district from south to north and ultimately merge with the Barak. There are many beels and marshes in the district. Sonbeel is the largest among them.

Population and Habitation

Population of the district is 827063. Karimganj and Badarpur are two important places of the district. Other important places are Patharkandi, Ratabari, Baraigram and Durlabhchara. There are around 933 villages in the district.

Natural Resources, Agriculture and Industry

It is a rich district in forest wealth. Singla, Badshah Tila and Langai are the reserved forests where sonaru, nahar, segun, cham etc. timbers are found with bamboo and cane.

Paddy, mustard, gram and tea are main agricultural products of the district. There are 24 tea gardens in the district. In industry only Panchagram's Paper mill and Chargola's sugar mill need mentioning.

Transportation

National highway no. 44 passes to Tripura from Badarpur via Karimganj. A branch of this highway enters Hailakandi district via Ratabari and Krishnanagar. The main rail line passes to Tripura via Patharkandi from Badarpur. Another rail line connects Baraigram with Durlabhchara via Ratabari. Southern part of the district is in poor state in regard to transportation.

22. Hailakandi District

HAILAKANDI DISTRICT AT A GLANCE

Headquarters	:	Hailakandi	Literacy Rate	.	53.07%
Population	:	449048	Male	:	64.08%
Male	:	232735	Female	:	41.06%
Female	:	216313	No Of Subdivisions	:	1
Urban	:	34138	No Of Blocks	:	7
Rural	:	414910	Length Of Road Under Pwd	:	461 km.
Area	:	1327 sq. km.	Population Rank	:	22
Density	:	338 per sq. km.	Literacy Rank	:	13
Sex Ratio	:	929			

Location and Four Boundaries

This district is situated on the middle part of the Barak-valley on the southern part of Assam. It is bounded on the north by Cachar district, on the east by Cachar district and Mizoram and on the west by Karimganj district. The district has only one sub-division.

Natural Geography

Southern part of the district is full of hills. Branches of Luchai Hills of Mizoram entered the district. On the plains of the district there are some hillocks. The Barak river flows through the northern boundary of the district. Other rivers coming from south are Katakhal, Bhairabi and Dhaleswari which ultimately merge with the mighty Barak.

Population and Habitation

Population of the district is 449048. The headquarters Hailakandi is situated on the bank of the river Dhaleswari. Lala is an important place nest to Hailakandi. Other important places are Katakhal, Algapur, Kalibari, Manchara, Katlichara etc. There are around 330 villages in the district.

Natural Resources, Agriculture and Industry

The southern hilly part of the district is full of forests. Inner line and Katakhal are the reserved forests. In the forests Azara, Sonaru, Nahar and Khaire timbers and bamboo and cane are found.

The economy of the district is mainly agrarian in nature. Paddy, mustard, maize and gram are the main crops. There are no major industries in the district baring a few cottage industries based on bamboo and cane works.

Transportation

This district is not developed in regard to transport network. There is no national highway in the district. The main road coming from Silchar passes towards south via Hailakandi and Katlichara. Another road links Hailakandi with Lala. Silchar–Karimganj rail line passes through the northern part of the district. Another rail-line connects Katakhal with Lalaghat via Hailakandi.

23. Cachar District

CACHAR DISTRICT AT A GLANCE

Headquarters	:	Silchar	Literacy Rate	: 59.19%
Population	:	1215385	Male	: 68.79%
Male	:	629196	Female	: 48.76%
Female	:	586189	No of Subdivisions	: 2
Urban	:	1096161	No of Blocks	: 14
Rural	:	119224	Length of Road Under Pwd	: 1130 km.
Area	:	3786 sq. km	Population Rank	: 7
Density	:	321 per sq. km.	Literacy Rank	: 4
Sex Ratio	:	932		

Location and Four Boundaries

This district is situated in the Barak valley on the southern part of Assam. It is bounded on the north by N.C. Hills district, on the east by Manipur, on the south by Mizoram and on the west by Hailakandi and Karinganj district and Meghalaya. Silchar and Lakhipur are the two sub-divisions of the district.

Natural Geography

The areas on the north, east and south boundaries of this district are hilly tracts. There are many hillocks of small sizes situated on the plains of the district. The Barak river flows through the district from east to west. Other important rivers of the district are Larang, Jatinga, Madhura, Labak, Rukni, Sonai. There are many beels and marshes in the district.

Population and Habitation

The district has a population of 1215385. There are around 1050 villages in the district. The headquarters Silchar is situated on the bank of the Barak river and is the central place of administration, business and education. Other important places are Lakhipur, Katigara, Barkhola, Udarband, Sonai, Bashkandi, Dhalai etc.

Natural Resources, Agriculture and Industry

North Cachar, Barail, Jiri, Barak, Sonai and Innerline are the main reserved forests of the district. In these forests Narar, Azar, Sonaru etc. valuable timbers are found. In agriculture the district is comparatively developed. Paddy, jute, sugarcane, cotton are the main agricultural produce of the district. There are around 80 tea gardens in the district. There is a natural reservoir of crude oil and natural gas in Mashimpur. In industry, bamboo and cane-work based cottage industries are prominent.

Transportation

Transportation network is better in the district. National highway nos. 44, 53 and 54 pass through the district. The headquarter Silchar is connected with Shillong, Imphal and Aizal. Meter-gauge rail line coming from Haflong passes to Jiribum of Manipur through the district. Silchar is connected with Tripura by rail lines. Near Silchar, there is an airport in Kumbhirgram. Boundary areas are less developed with respect to transportation.

REFERENCES

Deka Phani and Bhagabati Abani: *"Geography – Economic and Regional"*, Wiley Eastern Ltd. 1992.

Economic Survey of Assam, 1997-98.

Singh, R. L. (ed): *"India – A Regional Geography"* , National Geographical Society of India, Varanasi. 1999.

Statistical Hand Book of Assam, 1997.

Taher, Md. and Ahmed, P: *"Geography of North-East India"*, El-Dorado Publications, Guwahati, 1998

3

Spatial Disparities in Agricultural Development in Assam

3.1 INTRODUCTION

The State of Assam, the green beauty of the North Eastern region of the country, has vast fertile land and enough natural resources providing immense potentiality for the development of agriculture. Agriculture is the backbone of the State economy. Approximately 70 per cent of the total working force are being engaged in agriculture and allied activities. The share of this sector in the SDP of Assam at constant (1980-81) prices was 37.6 per cent in 1991-92 which decreased to 35.3 per cent in 1996-97 (*Economic Survey of Assam*, 1997-98). Keeping in view the importance of this sector, agricultural programmes have always been assigned high priority in each successive Five-Year Plans. But compared to many other counterparts in the country, the pace of development of this sector in the state has not been up to expectation.

The importance of agriculture in economic development has not only been theoretically established but also empirically found when we look into the history of development of a number of countries of the word as well as a number of states of our country. We find that it is agriculture that played the pivotal role in initiating and sustaining the process of economic growth in those economies. Assam too needs a sound agricultural sector. Although the sectoral share of agriculture in state SDP has been declining over the years, the primacy of agrarian sector has been more or less stable when viewed in terms of its support base for the vast rural populace. Agriculture can still provide Assam with a "bargain sector" – a sector with large un-exploited potential which can produce the requisite surplus with relatively low investment in a comparatively short time period. That agriculture is the sine-qua-non for the economic emancipation of the state of Assam is beyond any doubt.

3.2 STATE OF AGRICULTURE IN ASSAM

Agriculture in Assam is extremely backward and poverty stricken. Despite having most fertile soil and plentiful water, agriculture in Assam is being plagued with backwardness. Land under cultivation remains extremely limited compared to land potential for farming. The cultivable land area in the state is around 43 per cent of total land area. Whatever lands are used for farming remain again highly underutilised since multicropping in the state is yet to gain momentum. Only about 43 per cent of the cultivable area in the state come under multicropping compared to very high percentages in Punjab, Haryana and West Bengal. Mono-cropping is the prevailing mode of agriculture in the state with poor yield rate and extremely low return per hectare. The methods of cultivation still remains primitive. Consumption of fertilizer per hectare is extremely low being 18 kg per hectare against national average of 75 kg per hectare. The packages of agricultural practices are dominated by traditional concepts. And as a result of these factors the level of marketable agricultural surplus in the state is very poor. Ours is a food deficit state and this has made the state a net importer of food products. This has adverse impact in the growth of income and savings of the state.

3.3 AGRO-CLIMATIC SUB-ZONES OF ASSAM

In order to tackle problems associated with rainfed agriculture and to formulate suitable production plan, the entire state is delineated into eight broad agro-climatic sub-zones based primarily on rainfall pattern, moisture regime, temperature, cropping pattern, cropping intensity etc. Below we give a brief profile of these eight sub-zones:

1. Upper Brahmaputra Valley (North)

It consists of Dhemaji, Lakhimpur and Sonitpur districts and located in the north bank of the river Brahmaputra. This sub-zone falls in humid and per humid climatic belt with rainfall varying around 2741 mm per year. This sub-zone has different physiographic characters consisting flood plain areas, younger alluvial soils and structural hills. Groundwater is available at shallow depth in flood plain and younger alluvial plain areas whereas it is poor in structural hill areas.

2. Upper Brahmaputra Valley (South)

This sub-zone consists of Tinsukia, Dibrugarh, Sibsagar, Jorhat and Golaghat district and falls in the humid and per humid climatic belt with an annual average rainfall varying from 2040 mm to 2740 mm. The physiography has different characters and geomorphic units like active flood plain, younger alluvial plain, older alluvial plain and structural valley and hills. Groundwater is available at shallow depth in flood plain and younger alluvial plain areas and greater depth at older alluvial areas.

3. Central Brahmaputra Valley

This sub-zone consists of Nagoan and Marigoan districts and falls under humid and sub-humid climatic belt with annual rainfall varying from 1129 mm to 1795 mm. About 30 per cent of the area of this sub-zone comes under rain shadow belt where rainfall is around 600 mm. The maximum temperature rises to 37°c and minimum falls to 8°C. This sub-zone is characterised by varied physiographic situations having different geomorphic units like active flood plain, younger alluvial plain, older alluvial plain and structural hill areas. Groundwater is available at shallow depth in active flood plain and younger alluvial plain areas whereas at greater depth in older alluvial plain areas.

4. Lower Brahmaputra Valley (North West)

This sub-zone comprising Nalbari, Barpeta and Darrang districts falls under the humid climatic belt with annual average rainfall varying around 2072 mm. The geomorphic units are mostly flood plain areas and younger alluvial plain areas. Groundwater is available at shallow depth in flood plain and younger alluvial plain areas.

5. Lower Brahmaputra Valley (North)

This sub-zone comprising Dhubri, Kokrajhar and Bongaigoan districts and falls in the humid climatic belt and average annual rainfall varies from 2464 mm to 3000 mm. The geomorphic units are active flood plain areas and younger alluvial plain areas and hill areas. Groundwater is available at shallow depth in active flood plain and younger alluvial plain areas.

6. Lower Brahmaputra Valley (South)

This sub-zone comprising Kamrup and Goalpara districts falls in the humid climatic belt. Annual rainfall varies from 1616 mm to 2504 mm. Geomorphic units are active flood plain, younger alluvial plain areas, old alluvial plain areas and hilly areas. Groundwater is available at shallow depth in active flood plain areas and younger alluvial plain areas.

7. Barak Valley

This sub-zone comprising Silchar, Karimganj and Hailakandi districts falls under humid climatic belt. Annual average rainfall varies from 3227 mm to 3500 mm. The relative humidity varies from 58 per cent to 91 per cent. Physiographically the sub-zone is uneven and its different units are active flood plain areas, younger alluvial plain areas and undulating plain areas. Groundwater is available at shallow depth in active flood plain areas but in younger alluvial plain areas Groundwater is available at a deep level. Groundwater is available at moderate to greater depth in undulating plain areas.

8. Hills Sub-Zone

This sub-zone comprising Karbi-Anglong and N.C. Hills districts falls in the sub-humid and humid climatic belt. Annual average rainfall varies from 1200 mm to 1622 mm. Relative humidity varies from 62 per cent to 92 per cent. The different geomorphic units are active flood plain, younger alluvial plain areas, structural valley areas and structural hilly areas. Groundwater is available at shallow depth in flood plain areas and younger alluvial plain areas. In structural valley areas, Groundwater is available at moderate to greater depth.

3.4 AGRICULTURAL DEVELOPMENT IN CROP PRODUCTION IN ASSAM

Agricultural production as a whole plays an important role in economic development. Also production of food-grains is of special importance in terms of the quality of life of agricultural workforce constituting the bulk of Assamese humanity. *"Food that we eat, water that we drink and the air that we breathe constitute elements that we are made of. Food production is, therefore, not only an economic parameter"* (Raza and Singh).

The major crops grown in the state are rice, wheat, pulses, oilseeds, jute and mesta and horticultural crops like fruits, vegetables and spices.

(i) **Rice:** Rice is the most important cereal crop grown over an area of about 26 lakh hectares annually occupying around 80 per cent of annual cropped area. About 90 per cent of the population of the state are rice eaters. Production and productivity of autumn rice, winter rice and summer rice have registered an upward trend. In 1991-92 total production of rice was 31.97 lakh tonne which increased to 33.83 lakh tonne in 1997-98. Average yield of rice was 1261 kg per hectare in 1991-92, which gradually increased to 1359 kg. per hectare in 1997-98. The increase in total rice production and productivity can be attributed to the successful implementation of Integrated Programme for Rice Development - a central sector scheme and gradual saturation of high yielding paddy areas.

(ii) **Wheat:** Wheat is another important crop grown in the state to stabilize food-grain production. In 1991-92, average yield of wheat was 1455 kg per hectare and during 1997-98 the productivity decreased to 1299 kg per hectare. Over this time period total production of wheat in the state remains more or less the same being 1.11 lakh tonnes.

(iii) **Pulses:** Assam has around 0.6 per cent of area under pulses in the country and produces 0.5 per cent of the pulses produced in our country. The major pulses in the state are *tur*, summer green gram and black gram during

Kharif season and green gram, black gram, pea, lentil, *rajmah* etc. are grown during *Rabi* season. Pulses production in the state is far below than the requirement. During 1997-98 the productivity of pulses was recorded to be 547 kg per hectare as compared to 480 kg per hectare during 1991-92. Total production of pulses during 1997-98 was 64,464 tonne against 60,000 tonne in 1991-92.

(iv) **Oil Seeds:** Assam contributes little over one per cent of the total production of oilseeds in the country. Rape and mustard are the major oilseeds grown in the state and accounts for more than 90 per cent of the total oilseed production in the state. With the large scale introduction of groundnut and sunflower and adoption of improved technology and input services to farmers, spectacular results in the production of oilseeds are expected. However, during the period from 1991-92 to 1997-98 total production of oilseeds decreased from 2.06 lakh tonne to 2.04 lakh tonne.

(v) **Jute and Mesta:** Among the fibre crops, jute plays an important position in fibre production. It is generally grown as rainfed crop in Assam and mostly concentrated in districts of Nagaon, Marigaon, Darrang, Kamrup, Nalbari, Barpeta, Kokrajhar and Dhubri. The area and production of mesta is negligible. Productivity of jute increased to 1720 kg per hectare during 1997-98 as compared to 1537 kg per hectare during 1991-92.

(vi) **Sugarcane:** Sugarcane is grown mostly in Kharif season. The per hectare yield is much below the national average. Over the period from 1991-92 to 1997-98, total production of sugarcane decreased from 15.37 lakh tonne to 12.87 lakh tonne but productivity increased from 38,461 kg. per hectare to 41,109 kg. per hectare.

(vii) **Potato:** The production of potato has been increased significantly over the years in the state. During 1997-98 total production increased to 6.72 lakh tonne from 4.73 lakh tonne in 1991-92. Productivity during 1991-92 was 7,704 kg per hectare which increased to 8,927 kg per hectare during 1997-98.

(viii) **Spices:** Spices includes chilies, onion and turmeric. During 1997-98 total production of spices was recorded as 34,392 tonnes and productivity was 1216 kg per hectare.

(ix) **Fruits:** Major fruits grown in the state are banana, pineapple, orange, lemon, jackfruit, guava, mango etc. Total production during 1991-92 was 10.48 lakh tonne which increased to 25.04 lakh tonne during 1997-98.

3.5 REVIEW OF SOME WORKS DONE ON DISPARITIES IN AGRICULTURAL DEVELOPMENT

Several researchers have worked on regional disparities in agricultural development. Below we discuss some of such works.

We have come across the study done by Tyagi (1994) to measure the levels of agricultural development in Aligarh distreict at block level in terms of technological factors such as fertilizer, irrigation, HYV of seeds and implements etc. using the methodology of standard scores (Z-scores). The general conclusion derived from the study is that levels of agricultural development is not uniform in all the blocks of Aligarh district and lowly developed blocks need special attention on a priority basis for technological transformation so that their level of agricultural development can be raised.

Mahanty (1999) carried out a study relating to inter-district disparities in agriclutural development in Andhra Pradesh using 32 indicators of development and five commonly used methods of indexing for evaluating inter-district disparities in levels of development at three points of time. He concluded from the estimated results that there was a strong regional cohesion-spread effect and government intervention had benefited some of the poorer districts in catching up the pace of development. The five methods used in this study were: (i) Ranking, (ii) Indexing, (iii) Standard Score, (iv) Deprivation method and (v) Principal Component Method.

Kaur and Sethi (1995), in the backdrop of the phenomenal increase in agricultural production in Punjab since 1966 undertook a study to analyse the nature and degree of inter-district variations of crop yield in the state during 1966-67 to 1988-89. The findings show that although there has been a high degree of variation in yields among different districts of the state, the degree of inter-district variation has shown a declining trend for all crops taken together. For cash crops, however, the variation has increased over the period. Average productivity of most principal crops in the state has increased over the period under study.

Verma and Das (1995) attempted to analyse and explain the process and performance of agricultural development in India in a regional framework, during the different decades in the pre- and post-independence periods. It is shown that the colonial pattern of spatially lopsided agricultural development still persists largely because of the inability of the planners to overcome certain institutional and structural constraints. Though the growth pole strategy of Indian planners has yielded good results in terms of overall agricultural output, the agricultural policy has failed to bring about more or less balanced agricultural development over the different regions. The historical legacy of land tenure system still persists in terms of its impact upon agricultural development.

3.6 THE PRESENT STUDY

In this section we are primarily concerned with the analysis of inter-district development disparities in agricultural sector in Assam with secondary data collected from different sources. The objectives of the study are as follows:

(1) To find out the extent of disparities in agricultural development among the 23 districts of the state,

(2) To analyse in relative terms the development of agriculture in different districts in relation to the agricultural development in Assam,

(3) To study the variability in respect of select indicators of agricultural development.

We have chosen the following indicators of agricultural development subject to availability of data at district level:

X_1 = Percentage of cultivable land to total land area,

X_2 = Percentage of area sown to total cultivable area,

X_3 = Percentage of irrigation potential created to net sown area,

X_4 = Cropping intensity,

X_5 = Average yield of foodgrains per hectare,

X_6 = Percentage of high yielding variety area under paddy to net sown area,

X_7 = Consumption of fertilizer per hectare of total cropped area.

In the following section we give an analysis of the above indicators of agricultural development in districts of Assam wherein we rank each district with respect to each select indicator. Afterwards, we have classified all the 23 districts in terms of agricultural development on the basis of composite indices constructed by Indexing Method and Deprivation Method based on all the 7 chosen indicators.

3.6.1 Land Use Efficiency

Two important indicators to measure the land use efficiency in agriculture are the gross cropped and net sown areas. Table – 3.1 shows that in Assam the percentage of cultivable land to total land area is approximately 43 per cent, whereas 82 per cent of cultivable land is actually sown. The percentage of cultivable land to total land area is the highest in Jorhat district (89%) followed by Nalbari (approx. 80%) and Darrang (approx. 73%). N.C. Hills and Karbi-Anglong districts have minimum percentage of cultivable land to total land area. But percentage of area sown to total cultivable area is the highest in these two districts (100% in each) indicating the highest land use efficiency. In case of Jorhat the situation is just reverse. Its rank is 19 with respect to percentage of area sown to cultivable area indicating lower efficiency in land use. Nalbari is the exception with higher percentage of cultivable land (80% approx), and higher percentage of area sown to cultivable land (90% approx), and it is next to N.C. Hills and Karbi-Anglong in terms of land use efficiency. Next to Nalbari is Barpeta district (89%). The least efficient districts are Tinsukia (46% approx), Dhemaji (54% approx) and Karimganj (69%). Also out of 23 districts 11 districts namely Dhubri, Goalpara, Barpeta, Nalbari, Sonitpur, Lakhimpur, Marigaon, Nagaon, Karbi-Anglong, N.C. Hills and

Hailakandi are having higher percentages than the state's. All other districts have lower percentage of area sown to cultivable land than the state percentage (82%) indicating low efficiency in land use than the state's performance.

Table 3.1
Percentages of Cultivable land to total land area and area sown to cultivable land in districts of Assam

Sl. No.	*District*	*% of cultivable land to total land area*	*Rank*	*% of area sown to total cultivable area*	*Rank*
1.	Dhubri	60.573	8	86.982	8
2.	Kokrajhar	34.505	21	79.630	15
3.	Bongaigaon	48.400	14	80.165	14
4.	Goalpara	49.457	12	86.813	9
5.	Barpeta	62.424	7	89.320	5
6.	Nalbari	79.808	2	90.361	3
7.	Kamrup	54.036	10	74.689	16
8.	Darrang	72.989	3	81.890	11
9.	Sonitpur	35.526	20	88.888	6
10.	Lakhimpur	45.957	16	87.963	7
11.	Dhemaji	39.198	19	53.543	22
12.	Marigaon	72.327	4	83.478	10
13.	Nagaon	64.964	6	89.513	4
14.	Golaghat	46.045	15	73.619	17
15.	Jorhat	89.123	1	70.857	20
16.	Sibsagar	67.308	5	80.571	13
17.	Dibrugarh	51.622	11	72.000	19
18.	Tinsukia	55.409	9	45.714	23
19.	Karbi-Anglong	12.585	22	100.000	1.5
20.	N.C. Hills	5.726	23	100.000	1.5
21.	Karimganj	48.619	13	69.318	21
22.	Hailakandi	42.857	17	80.370	12
23.	Cachar	40.476	18	73.203	18
	Assam	43.146		82.108	
	C.V.	37.14		15.63	

Note: *C.V. Stands for coefficeint of variations*
Source: *Computed from "Statistical Handbook of Assam 1997".*

The C.V. (Co-efficient of variation) value for percentage of cultivable land to total land area being greater than that of percentage of area sown to total cultivable area indicates greater variability in the former than in the later.

3.6.2 Irrigation Scenario

The irrigation scenario in the state is not satisfactory. Table 3.2 shows that the percentage of irrigation potential created to net sown area in respect of Assam is only 17.28 per cent.

Table 3.2
Percentage of Irrigation potential created to net sown area in districts of Assam

Sl. No.	*District*	*% of irrigation potential created to net sown area*	*Rank*
1.	Dhubri	9.524	17
2.	Kokrajhar	24.483	4
3.	Bongaigaon	10.109	15
4.	Goalpara	14.480	10
5.	Barpeta	30.166	3
6.	Nalbari	11.870	12
7.	Kamrup	18.156	6
8.	Darrang	24.192	5
9.	Sonitpur	30.428	2
0.	Lakhimpur	10.902	14
11.	Dhemaji	7.751	20
12.	Marigaon	16.339	9
13.	Nagaon	36.195	1
14.	Golaghat	13.387	11
15.	Jorhat	9.775	16
16.	Sibsagar	11.099	13
17.	Dibrugarh	8.880	18
18.	Tinsukia	5.483	21
19.	Karbi-Anglong	16.823	8
20.	N.C. Hills	17.843	7
21.	Karimganj	4.741	23
22.	Hailakandi	7.872	19
23.	Cachar	4.801	22
	Assam	17.281	
	C.V.	56.95	

Source: Computed from Statistical Hand Book Assam, 1997.

Only in seven districts namely, Kokrajhar, Barpeta, Kamrup, Darrang, Sonitpur, Nagaon and N.C. Hills the percentage of irrigation potential created to net sown area is higher than the state percentage. In this regard Nagaon district occupies first position (36%) followed by Sonitpur (30%), Barpeta (30%), Kokrajhar (24%), Darrang (24%), Kamrup (18%) and N.C. Hills (18%). In Karimganj, Cachar, Tinsukia and Dhemaji this percentage is very low in comparison to the state percentage. In other districts also the scenario is not encouraging. Benefits from irrigation potential created have not been adequate due to lack of on-farm development works.

The C.V value indicates a significant inequality of around 57 per cent in creating irrigation potential in districts of the state.

3.6.3 Cropping Intensity

One way to measure the utilisation of land in agricultural sector is through the cropping intensity which is the ratio of gross cropped area to net area sown expressed in percentage. Higher cropping intensity implies higher multiple cropping. From Table 3.3 it is seen that cropping intensity of Assam is approximately 142 which means multiple cropping is done in 42 per cent of cultivable land in Assam. Out of 23 districts of Assam, seven districts have higher cropping intensity than that of the state. Multiple cropping is the highest in Barpeta district (75%) followed by Karimganj (74%), Lakhimpur (73%), Kokrajhar (67%), Nagaon (61%), Bongaigaon (56%) and Dhubri (53%). Multiple cropping is least practiced in the district of Sibsagar (13% only). Districts with low cropping intensity are Kamrup (23%), Cachar (24%), Goalpara (29%) and Darrang (29%). Sonitpur, Dhemaji, Marigaon, Golaghat, Tinsukia and Karbi-Anglong districts exhibit more or less similar cropping intensity as that of the state.

"The pattern of agriculture in the plain districts and adjoining hills districts are diametrically opposite, in so far as there is settled cultivation with plough and mud culture in the former, and shifting (Jhum) and/or terrace cultivation in the latter. The former permits technological reform and investment while the latter defies it. While **crop rotation** is possible in the plain districts during different seasons, in the hill districts it is the **plot rotation** rather than crop rotation, with mixed cropping." (Goswami, 1988).

The significant point that this analysis reveals is that the two hill districts – N.C. Hills and Karbi-Anglong accustomed in plot-rotation culture are doing much better in multiple cropping than some of their counterpart districts.

The C.V. value of nearly 12 per cent indicates not so significant variation in regard to multiple cropping in the districts of the state.

Table 3.3
Cropping intensity in districts of Assam

Sl No	District	Cropping intensity	Rank
1.	Dhubri	153.061	7
2.	Kokrajhar	168.600	4
3.	Bongaigaon	155.670	6
4.	Goalpara	129.114	20
5.	Barpeta	175.543	1
6.	Nalbari	132.000	17
7.	Kamrup	123.333	22
8.	Darrang	129.327	19
9.	Sonitpur	139.881	10
10.	Lakhimpur	172.632	3
11.	Dhemaji	141.176	8
12.	Marigaon	137.500	13
13.	Nagaon	160.669	5
14.	Golaghat	140.000	9
15.	Jorhat	130.645	18
16.	Sibsagar	113.475	23
17.	Dibrugarh	132.539	16
18.	Tinsukia	138.541	12
19.	Karbi-Anglong	139.231	11
20.	N.C. Hills	135.714	14
21.	Karimganj	173.770	2
22.	Hailakandi	134.783	15
23.	Cachar	124.107	21
	Assam	142.462	
	C.V.	11.95	

Source: Computed from *"Statistical Handbook of Assam, 1997"*.

3.6.4 Production of Foodgrains in Assam

Yield rate of foodgrains is an indicator of agricultural development. The major foodgrains of Assam include - rice, wheat, maize, small millets and other cereals and pulses. Pulses include tur, gram, black gram, green gram, lentil, peas and other Rabi pulses. In average yield of rice/hectare as shown in Table 3.4, the leading districts are Golaghat, Dibrugarh, N.C. Hills and Karimganj. Rice production per hectare is minimum in Dhubri district (832 kg/ha). Goalpara tops the list in per hectare production of wheat (1636 kg/ha). Maize productivity is highest in Dhemaji (936 kg/ ha) followed by Karbi-Anglong and N.C. Hills. In pulses, the districts with high productivity in descending order are Golaghat (717 kg/ ha), Nagaon (688 kg/ha), Barpeta (657 kg/ha). And in case of small millets and other cereals, productivity is highest in Darrang (656 kg/ha).

The overall food productivity of foodgrains is highest in Sibsagar district (1000.25 kg/hect) followed by Karbi-Anglong (954.60 kg/ ha) and Karimganj (927 kg/ha). Average food productivity per hectare is minimum in Lakhimpur district. Except Nalbari, Golaghat, Sibsagar, Karbi-Anglong and Karimganj all other districts have lower average productivity of foodgrains than the state average (897.40 kg/ha).

The C.V. of average yield of foodgrains suggests only a variation of about 7 per cent in overall foodgrain productivity in the districts of Assam. The variation in pulse productivity is the highest being 30 per cent. The variation in productivity in case of rice (C.V. 21%), and maize (C.V. 20%) are also relatively higher. In regards to wheat productivity the variation is the least (C.V. 16.50%).

3.6.5 Area under HYV Paddy

Good quality seeds act as a catalyst for realizing the potential of all other inputs in agriculture. There has been continuous increase in cultivable areas with high yielding and improved varieties of seeds under different crops in India with no exception to Assam. Paddy, the basic food crop of Assam is historically known to have been discovered in Assam itself first in the world. Till now many high yielding varieties (HYV) of paddy have been developed by

Table 3.4

Average yield of food grains in districts of Assam – 1997-98 (kg/ha)

Sl No	*District*	*Rice*	*Wheat*	*Maize*	*Small millets & other cereals*	*Pulses*	*Total*	*Average yield*	*Rank*
1.	Dhubri	832	1374	6cereals00	553	578	3937	787.40	21
2.	Kokrajhar	1061	1446	520	569	522	4118	823.60	16
3.	Bongaigaon	994	1197	609	549	523	3872	774.40	22
4.	Goalpara	1256	1636	580	393	483	4348	869.60	11
5.	Barpeta	966	1234	650	500	657	4007	801.40	19
6.	Nalbari	1178	1598	750	420	634	4580	916.00	5
7.	Kamrup	1491	1182	620	514	201	3494	873.50	9
8.	Darrang	1073	1097	610	656	514	3950	790.00	20
9.	Sonitpur	1536	1043	582	442	626	4229	845.80	14
10.	Lakhimpur	1253	853	599	552	374	3631	726.20	23
11.	Dhemaji	1180	1275	936	469	522	4382	876.40	8
12.	Marigaon	1435	1536	400	429	643	4443	888.60	6
13.	Nagaon	1568	982	665	367	686	4270	854.00	13

14.	Golaghat	1930	906	540	488	717	4581	916.20	4
15.	Jorhat	1560	1209	520	367	411	4067	813.40	17
16.	Sibsagar	1534	1299	682	514	486	4001	1000.25	1
17.	Dibrugarh	1777	1173	535	443	460	4388	877.60	7
18.	Tinsukia	1221	1299	600	504	502	4126	825.20	15
19.	Karbi-Anglong	1498	1506	871	341	557	4773	954.60	2
20.	N.C. Hills	1729	1299	750	452	54	4284	856.80	12
21.	Karimganj	1720	1299	650	514	411	2781	927.00	3
22.	Hailakandi	1613	1299	403	670	564	3250	812.50	18
23.	Cachar	1618	1299	500	410	533	4360	872.00	10
	C.V.	20.66	16.51	20.08	18.60	29.73	-	7.23	
	Assam	1359	1299	766	514	547	4487	897.40	

Source: Computed from Basic *Agricultural Statistics, Assam*, 1997-98. Directorate of Agriculture, Govt. of Assam.

national and local scientists of agricultural universities and our farmers have shown a positive gesture to these varieties. The HYV crops are high value added, short duration and hence quick yielding.

In Assam about 45 per cent of net sown area is under HYV paddy cultivation as shown in Table 3.5.

Table 3.5
Percentage of High Yielding Variety (HYV) area under paddy to net sown area in districts of Assam

Sl. No.	*District*	*% of HYV area under paddy to net sown area*	*Rank*
1.	Dhubri	36.34	14
2.	Kokrajhar	30.86	18
3.	Bongaigaon	39.63	13
4.	Goalpara	41.30	9
5.	Barpeta	41.26	10
6.	Nalbari	54.83	7
7.	Kamrup	42.73	8
8.	Darrang	79.02	1
9.	Sonitpur	29.22	20
10.	Lakhimpur	30.21	19
11.	Dhemaji	24.52	22
12.	Marigaon	60.36	4
13.	Nagaon	65.18	2
14.	Golaghat	40.90	11
15.	Jorhat	36.38	15
16.	Sibsagar	27.50	21
17.	Dibrugarh	31.72	17
18.	Tinsukia	31.97	16
19.	Karbi-Anglong	56.62	6
20.	N.C. Hills	21.75	23
21.	Karimganj	63.77	3
22.	Hailakandi	57.26	5
23.	Cachar	39.84	12
	Assam	45.05	
	C.V.	34.32	

Source: Computed from *Basic Agricultural Statistics*, Assam, 1997-98, Directorate of Agriculture, Govternment of Assam.

Out of 23 districts of the state only seven districts have higher percentage of area under HYV paddy than the state percentage. Among those seven districts leading positions are occupied respectively by Darrang (79%), Nagaon (65%), Karimganj (64%) and Marigaon (60%). N.C. Hills (21.75%), Dhemaji (24.52%), Sibsagar (27.50%) etc. are the districts with lower percentage of area under HYV paddy. Goalpara, Barpeta, Kamrup, Golaghat and Cachar are the few districts where the area under HYV paddy is more or less at par with the state percentage figures.

It is observed that the use of HYV paddy has not received the desired attention of the farmers in most of the districts of the state. Once this improved agricultural input gets due attention of farmers of the state, the deficit in food grains will be wiped out but also the state will attain the status of surplus state in respect of rice production.

The C.V. value shows a variation of 34 per cent in area under HYV paddy in districts of the state.

3.6.7 Consumption of Fertilizer in Assam

In modern times, chemical fertilizers are used to increase agricultural output though there are other factors which determine agricultural development in a region. However, it is found that agricultural output increases along with the increase of chemical fertilizers. In India, the consumption of chemical fertilizers has shown a rising trend leading to increasing production of foodgrains. But sadly enough, there has been very little increase in agricultural out put in Assam. The use of chemical fertilizers has also not increased significantly in this state in comparison to states like Punjab, Haryana and Uttar Pradesh. The use of chemical fertilizers has been and continues to be low priority due to inundation of most of the agricultural fields in rainy season and lack of irrigation in winter and summer season. So far as agricultural statistics are concerned, Table 3.6 shows that during 1997-98 fertilizer consumption per hectare (both for Rabi and Kharif crops) was only 18 kg (approx) which was very low in comparison to the figures of agriculturally developed states of India.

Table 3.6
Consumption of fertilizer per hectare of total cropped area in districts of Assam

Sl. No.	*District*	*(Kharif & Rabi) Consumption of fertilizer per ha of total cropped area (in kg)*	*Rank*
1.	Dhubri	19.448	8
2.	Kokrajhar	8.655	19
3.	Bongaigaon	16.847	13
4.	Goalpara	20.853	5
5.	Barpeta	14.606	15
6.	Nalbari	18.868	11
7.	Kamrup	27.810	2
8.	Darrang	20.877	4
9.	Sonitpur	12.127	17
10.	Lakhimpur	1.317	23
11.	Dhemaji	1.833	21
12.	Marigaon	69.977	1
13.	Nagaon	25.419	3
14.	Golaghat	10.404	18
15.	Jorhat	17.327	12
16.	Sibsagar	15.125	14
17.	Dibrugarh	19.059	10
18.	Tinsukia	20.766	6]
19.	Karbi-Anglong	1.397	22
20.	N.C. Hills	1.894	20
21.	Karimganj	19.367	9
22.	Hailakandi	20.225	7
23.	Cachar	13.661	16
	Assam	17.980	
	C.V.	77.85	

Source: Computed from *Basic Agricultural Statistics*, Assam, 1997-98, Directorate of Agriculture, Govt. of Assam.

Among the 23 districts of Assam, Marigaon district has the highest consumption of fertilizer (70 kg/ha) followed by Kamrup (28 kg/ha) and Nagaon (25 kg/ha). Lakhimpur (1.32 kg/ha), Karbi-Anglong (1.40 kg/ha) and Dehmaji (1.8 kg/ha) are the lowest fertilizer consuming districts of the state. Only 11 districts out of

23 in the state have higher consumption of fertilizer than the state's consumption. It is seen that the districts with higher level of consumption of chemical fertilizes are among the comparatively developed districts of Assam in respect of agriculture. The low consumption level of fertilizer is an indication of backwardness of agriculture in Assam than the cause of this backwardness. Because the use of fertilizers can increase agricultural output only when other factors like irrigation, high yielding seeds, crop protection measures etc. are also used simultaneously.

The C.V. value shows a very high disparity of around 78 per cent in use of fertilizers in the districts of Assam.

3.7 Extent of Agricultural Development Disparities

Table 3.7 shows that Indexing Method has classified seven districts of the state out of 23 as relatively developed (RD). In descending order they are Marigaon, Nagaon, Darrang, Barpeta, Nalbari, Kamrup and Jorhat. The rest 16 districts are reported to be backward (B) by this method. Dhemaji ranks 23rd in respect of agricultural development succeeded respectively by N.C. Hills, Lakhimpur, Cachar, Karbi-Anglong, Tinsukia, Golaghat etc. The C.V. of ADI values by Indexing Method reveals a variation of 20.40 per cent.

Deprivation Method, on the other hand, also has classified 7 districts of the state as moderately developed (MD) and rest 16 as backward (B) with slight variation to Indexing Method. The seven moderately developed districts are respectively Nagaon, Marigaon, Barpeta, Darrang, Nalbari, Karimganj and Sibsagar. Dhemaji is also placed in 23rd rank by this method in agreement with Indexing Method. The C.V. of ADI values by Deprivation Method shows a variation of 25.43%.

We observe that both the methods place Nagaon, Marigaon, Darrang, Nalbari, and Barpeta as developed relatively or moderately. Therefore these five districts should be regarded as developed relatively or moderately in agricultural sector.

We also observe from Table 3.8 that out of eight agro-climatic sub-zones, only two sub-zones namely "Central Brahmaputra Valley"

Table 3.7
Agricultural Ranking of Districts of Assam by Indexing Method and Deprivation Method.

Sl.No.	District	Indexing Method			Deprivation Method		
		ADI Value	Rank	Status	ADI Value	Rank	Status
1.	Dhubri	97.921	11	B	.422	13	B
2.	Kokrajhar	92.198	14	B	.445	9	B
3.	Bongaigaon	92.178	15	B	.388	16	B
4.	Goalpara	99.904	8	B	.428	12	B
5.	Barpeta	116.193	4	RD	.587	3	MD
6.	Nalbari	112.150	5	RD	.538	5	MD
7.	Kamrup	107.812	6	RD	.429	11	B
8.	Darrang	125.604	3	RD	.553	4	MD
9.	Sonitpur	98.773	10	B	.443	10	B
10.	Lakhimpur	79.030	21	B	.366	18	B
11.	Dhemaji	66.040	23	B	.243	23	B
12.	Marigaon	154.651	1	RD	.646	2	MD
13.	Nagaon	137.576	2	RD	.694	1	MD
14.	Golaghat	88.979	17	B	.410	14	B
15.	Jorhat	101.269	7	RD	.387	17	B
16.	Sibsagar	93.519	13	B	.510	7	MD
17.	Dibrugarh	89.421	16	B	.352	19	B

18.	Tinsukia	84.498	18	B	.265	22	B
19.	Karbi Anglong	83.692	19	B	.476	8	B
20.	N.C. Hills	69.695	22	B	.323	20	B
21.	Karimganj	99.867	9	B	.522	6	MD
22.	Hailakandi	97.415	12	B	.392	15	B
23.	Cachar	79.927	20	B	.304	21	B

N.B. : (i) ADI Implies Agricultural Development Index.
(ii) ADI values are taken from table 3.9 & 3.10 .
(iii) B refers to Backward, RD refers to Relatively Developed & MD refers to Moderately Developed .
(iv) While Indexing Method is a relative measure of development, Deprivation Method is an absolute measure of Development.

and "Lower Brahmaputra Valley" are classified as developed relatively or moderately by both the methods we have applied in our analysis.

REFERENCES

Chowdhury, B.: (1994). "Spatio – Temporal Dynamism in the Agricultural Development in Assam" – An Econometric Approach", Ph.D. thesis submitted in Gauhati University, (Unpublished).

Goswami, P. C.: (1988). *"Land Utilisation and its Economic Implictions (With special reference to Assam)"* in: Thakur, K (ed) – *Profile of a Development Strategy for India's North-East*, SPAN Publications Pvt. Ltd., Guwahati, p. 25.

Kaur, P. and **Sethi, K.**: (1995). Inter district variation in agricultural productivity in Punjab – *Indian Journal of Regional Scie nce*, 27(1 & 2).

Mahanty, G. (1999). *"Regional Development in Andhra Pradesh: A District Level Analysis"* – Indian Journal of Regional Science, 31(2).

Raza, M and **Singh, J.**:(nd) Food Production in India: The Regional Dimension – in *Contributions to Indian Geography*, pp. 258-259.

Tyagi Sadhna: (1994). Levels of Agricultural Development in Aligarh District" – *Indian Journal of Regional Science*, 26(1).

Verma, B. N. and **Das H.C.L.**: (1995). "Regional Pattern of Agriclutural Development in India (1891-1976): An Institutional Approach" – *Indian Journal of Regional Science*, 27(1 & 2).

Table 3.8

Classification of Agro-Climatic Sub-zones of Assam with Respect to Agricultural Development

Sl.No.	Agro Climatic sub-zones of Assam	Districts in the sub zone	Status as per Indexing Method	Status as per Deprivation Method	Observation on sub zones
1.	Upper Brahmaputra valley (North)	i) Lakhimpur	B	B	Backward sub-zone
		ii) Dhemaji	B	B	
		iii) Sonitpur	B	B	
2.	Upper Brahmaputra valley (South)	i) Tinsukia	B	B	Backward sub-zone
		ii) Dibrugarh	B	B	
		iii) Sibsagar	B	MD	
		iv) Jorhat	RD	B	
		v) Golaghat	B	B	
3.	Central Brahmaputra valley	i) Nagaon	RD	MD	Relatively or Moderately Developed sub-zone
		ii) Marigaon	RD	MD	
4.	Lower Brahmaputra valley (North-West)	i) Nalbari	RD	MD	Relatively or Moderately Developed sub-zone
		ii) Barpeta	RD	MD	
		iii) Darrang	RD	MD	

(contd...)

Table 3.8 Contd...

Sl.No.	*Agro Climatic sub-zones of Assam*	*Districts in the sub zone*	*Status as per*		*Observation on sub zones*
			Indexing Method	*Deprivation Method*	
5.	Lower Brahmaputra valley (North)	i) Dhubri	B	B	Backward sub-zone
		ii) Kokrajhar	B	B	
		iii) Bongaigaon	B	B	
6.	Lower Brahmaputra valley (South)	i) Kamrup	RD	B	Backward sub-zone
		ii) Goalpara	B	B	
7.	Barak valley	i) Cachar	B	B	Backward sub-zone
		ii) Karimganj	B	MD	
		iii) Hailakandi	B	B	
8.	Hills zone	i) Karbi Anglong	B	B	Backward sub-zone
		ii) N.C. Hills	B	B	

Table 3.9
Indicators and Indices of Agricultural Development in Districts of Assam (By Indexing Method)

Sl. No. Districts	% of Cultivable land to total land area	% of area sown to total cultivable area	% of irrigation potential created to net sown area	Cropping intensity	Average yield of food grains area (kg/Hec)	% of high yield variety under paddy to net sown area	Consumption of Fertiliser per hectare of total cropped area (kg)	Total Index	Average Index of Agricultural Development	Rank
	X1	X2	X3	X4	X5	X6	X7			
1	2	3	4	5	6	7	8	9	10	11
01 Dhubri	60.573 (140.390)	86.982 (105.936)	9.524 (55.112)	153.061 (107.436)	787.400 (87.742)	34.341 (80.668)	19.448 (108.164)	685.448	97.921	11
02 Kokrajhar	34.505 (79.972)	79.630 (96.982)	94.483 (141.675)	168.600 (118.343	823.600 (91.776)	30.863 (68.508)	8.655 (48.136)	645.392	92.198	14
03 Bongaigaon	48.400 (112.177)	80.165 (97.633)	10.109 (58.497)	155.670 (109.267)	774.400 (86.293)	39.626 (87.960)	16.847 (93.698)	645.525	92.178	15
04 Goalpara	49.457 (114.627)	86.813 (105.730)	14.48 (83.791)	129.114 (90.627)	869.600 (96.902)	41.299 (91.673)	20.853 (115.328)	699.328	99.904	8
05 Barpeta	62.424 (144.680)	89.320 (108.783)	30.166 (174.561)	175.543 (123.216)	801.400 (89.302)	41.257 (91.580)	14.606 (82.234)	813.356	116.193	4
06 Nalbari	79.808 (184.971)	90.361 (110.051)	11.87 (68.688)	132.000 (92.653)	716.000 (102 .072)	54.827 (121.702)	18.868 (104.916)	785.053	112.150	5

(contd...)

Table 3.9 Contd...

1	2	3	4	5	6	7	8	9	10	11
07 Kamrup	54.036	74.689	18.156	123.333	873.500	42.729	27.810	754.688	107.812	6
	(125.239)	(90.964)	(105.063	(86.568)	(97.336)	(94.847)	(154.671)			
08 Darrang	72.989	81.890	24.192	129.327	790.000	79.025	20.877	879.228	125.604	3
	(169.167)	(99.734)	(139.991)	(90.776)	(88.032)	(175.416)	(116.112)			
09 Sonitpur	35.526	88.888	30.428	139.881	845.800	29.221	12.127	691.417	98.773	10
	(82.339)	(108.257)	(176.077)	(98.184)	(94.250)	(64.863)	(67.447)			
10 Lakhimpur	45.957	87.963	10.902	172.632	726.200	30.211	1.317	553.211	79.030	21
	(106.515)	(107.130)	(63.086)	(121.173)	(80.922)	(67.061)	(7.324)			
11 Dhemaji	39.198	53.543	7.751	141.176	876.400	24.518	1.833	462.28	66.040	23
	(90.849)	(65.210)	(44.852)	(99.093)	(97.659)	(54.423)	(10.194)			
12 Marigaon	72.327	83.478	16.339	137.500	888.600	60.362	69.977	1082.562	154.651	1
	(167.633)	(101.668)	(94.548)	(96.513)	(99.019)	(133.988)	(389.193)			
13 Nagaon	64.964	89.513	36.195	160.669	854.000	65.184	25.419	963.038	137.576	2
	(150.567)	(109.018)	(209.449)	(112.776)	(95.163)	(144.692)	(141.373)			
14 Golaghat	46.045	73.619	13.387	140.000	916.200	40.899	10.404	622.857	88.979	17
	(106.719)	(89.661)	(77.466)	(98.268)	(102.094)	(90.785)	(57.864)			
15 Jorhat	89.123	70.857	9.775	130.645	813.400	36.381	17.327	708.887	101.269	7
	(206.561)	(86.297)	(56.565)	(91.701)	(90.639)	(80.756)	(96.368)			
16 Sibsagar	67.308	80.571	11.099	113.475	1000.250	27.505	15.125	654.639	93.519	13
	(156.000)	(98.128)	(64.226)	(79.650)	(111.460)	(61.054)	(84.121)			
17 Dibrugarh	51.622	72.000	8.880	132.539	877.600	31.720	19.059	625.953	89.421	16
	(119.644)	(87.689)	(51.385)	(93.031)	(97.793)	(70.410)	(106.001)			

18 Tinsukia	55.409 (128.422)	45.714 (55.675)	5.483 (31.728)	138.541 (97.244)	825.200 (91.954)	31.973 (70.972)	20.766 (115.494)	591.489	84.498	18
19 Karbi Anglong	12.585 (29.168)	100.000 (121.790)	16.823 (97.349)	139.231 (97.728)	954.600 (106.373)	56.615 (125.671)	1.397 (7.769)	585.848	83.692	19
20 N.C. Hills	5.726 (13.271)	100 (121.790)	17.843 (103.252)	135.714 (95.259)	856.800 (95.475)	21.753 (48.286)	1.894 (10.533)	487.866	69.695	22
21 Karimganj	48.619 (112.684)	69.318 (84.422)	4.741 (27.434)	173.770 (121.972)	972.000 (103.298)	63.768 (141.549)	19.367 (107.714)	690.073	99.867	9
22 Hailakandi	42.857 (99.330)	80.702 (98.287)	7.827 (45.552)	134.783 (94.606)	812.500 (90.539)	57.263 (127.109)	20.225 (112.486)	667.909	95.415	12
23 Cachar	40.476 (93.811)	73.203 (89.154)	4.801 27.781	124.107 (87.112)	872.000 (97.169)	39.865 (88.490)	13.661 (75.978)	559.495	79.927	20
Assam	43.146 (100)	82.108 (100)	17.281 (100)	142.467 (100)	897.4 (100)	45.05 (100)	17.98 (100)			
C.V.	37.14	15.63	56.95	11.95	7.18	34.32	77.85			

N.B.: Figures in Parentheses refer to the value of indices computed on the basis of state average as 100.

Source :: (i) Statistical Hand Book, Assam 1997, Directorate of Economics and statistics , Govt. of Assam.

(ii) Basic Agricultural statistics, 1997-1998, Directorate of Agriculture, Govt. of Assam.

Table 3.10
Indices of Agricultural Development by Deprivation Method

Sl. No.	District	X1	X2	X3	X4	X5	X6	X7	Deprivation Indicator (Ij)	Average Deprivation Indicator	Agri. Development Index Value =1-Ij	Rank
01	Dhubri	.342	.239	.847	.362	.776	.745	.735	4.046	.578	.422	13
02	Kokrajhar	.654	.375	.372	.111	.644	.840	.893	3.889	.555	.445	9
03	Bongaigaon	.488	.365	.829	.320	.824	.687	.773	4.286	.612	.388	16
04	Goalpara	.475	.242	.690	.748	.476	.658	.715	4.004	.572	.428	12
05	Barpeta	.320	.196	.191	0	.725	.659	.806	2.897	.413	.587	3
06	Nalbari	.111	.177	.773	.701	.307	.422	.744	3.235	.462	.538	5
07	Kamrup	.420	.466	.573	.841	.462	.633	.613	4.008	.571	.429	11
08	Darrang	.193	.333	.381	.744	.767	0	.714	3.132	.447	.553	4
09	Sonitpur	.642	.204	.183	.574	.563	.869	.842	3.904	.557	.443	10
10	Lakhimpur	.517	.221	.804	.046	1.0	.852	1.0	4.440	.634	.366	18
11	Dhemaji	.598	.855	.904	.553	.451	.951	.992	5.304	.757	.243	23
12	Marigaon	.201	.304	.631	.612	.407	.325	0	2.480	.354	.646	2
13	Nagaon	.289	.193	0	.239	.533	.241	.648	2.143	.306	.694	1
14	Golaghat	.516	.485	.725	.572	.306	.665	.867	4.136	.590	.410	14
15	Jorhat	0	.536	.839	.723	.681	.744	.766	4.289	.613	.387	17
16	Sibsagar	.261	.357	.797	1.0	0	.899	.117	3.431	.490	.510	7

17	Dibrugarh	.449	.515	.868	.692	.447	.825	.741	4.537	.648	.352	19
18	Tinsukia	.404	1.0	.976	.596	.638	.821	.716	5.151	.735	.265.	22
19	Karbi Anglong	.917	0	.615	.585	.166	.391	.998	3.672	.524	.476	8
20	N.C. Hills	1.0	0	.583	.641	.523	1.0	.991	4.738	.677	.323	20
21	Karimganj	.485	.565	1.0	.028	.267	.266	.736	3.347	.478	.522	6
22	Hailakandi	.554	.355	.900	.656	.685	.379	.724	4.253	.608	.392	15
23	Cacnar	.583	.493	.998	.828	.467	.683	.820	4.872	.696	.304	21

N.B.: Calculated from the values of 7 agricultural indicators given in table-3.9, using the formula for Deprivation Method.

4

Levels of Industrial Development in Assam

4.1 INTRODUCTION

The development of modern materialistic world rests on the growth of industries run by inanimated sources of energy and machines under the factory-based production system. Industrialization is a world-wide phenomenon in today's world. Despite fairly rich resource endowments providing the base for a high rate of economic development, Assam suffers from the underdevelopment syndrome of industrial backwardness. Assam's pace in industrial development is painfully slow. The major industries of the state namely. Tea, Oil and Plywood have extremely feeble linkages with the state's economic aspirations. The sectoral shift from the primary sector to the secondary sector has been marginal during the planning period. The state has a very old historical background with regard to its industrial development. Industrialization of the state started during the nineteenth century when the country's first Oil Refinery was set up at Digboi and Tea plantation was taken up by the British in the Upper Assam area. But the state is yet to find a proper place in the country's industrial map.

In the state the problems faced by industrial sector are very complicated in nature. Partitioning of India created a major setback for the entire North-Eastern Region by geographically isolating it from the rest of the country. "While foreign colonial interest in taking up new industrial ventures in Assam waned after independence, there was no significant step up of investment by domestic private or public sector for sustaining growth of industry during the first three Five-Year Plans". (Sarmah, 1996)

In the next ten years or so there was a revival of the industrialization process led by establishment of a number of public sector units. This process received a jolt in the early 1980s from which it has not fully recovered even today. The recent schemes of special fiscal incentives are yet to have any perceptible impact.

4.2 INDUSTRIAL FEATURES OF ASSAM

The two major industries of Assam are *Oil and Natural Gas* and *Tea,* which account for the maximum value addition. The Oil and Natural Gas industry is controlled by the government and operates under the Ministry of Oil and Natural Gas. The Tea industry in Assam, which accounts for around 50% of the country's total tea production, is mainly controlled by large private companies. Both of these sectors have made considerable progress over the years and are way ahead of other industries in the state. Another important industry in Assam is mining. Coal and limestone are mined in considerable quantities in the state.

"The food product sector accounts for bulk of the industrial production in the state. There is a large scope for establishment of large and medium scale industries in this sector. Another significant sector of the state is Petroleum, Plastics and Rubber sector. This sector accounts for 30% of the total output value for the state's manufacturing industries." [Report on Environment Analysis, **Tata Consultancy Service,** Feb. 1996, p.4]

4.3 INDUSTRIAL POTENTIAL OF ASSAM

An analysis of the current status of industries incorporated in the *Report of Environment Analysis* prepared by T.C.S (1996) reveals that the potential of industries is much higher in Assam as compared to other states of North-East. Assam derives its advantage because it already has an established industrial culture and also has the most developed infrastructure in the entire North-Eastern Region. This is supported by a diverse resource base which can form the basis of many industries. Assam also has a much higher surplus generation than the other north-eastern states.

This can support a host of demand-based industries in the state. In the state there is plenty of scope for value addition in the mineral based downstream and ancillary units. The crude that is extracted can be further value added through refineries and also many down stream projects can come up to these refineries.

Despite the adoption of a number of policy resolutions since 1956 for industrial development and its decentralisation thereof, regional disparities in industrial development persists. The pace of industrial development in the backward state like Assam is slow compared to that of the developed states like Gujarat and Maharastra. The industrial sector is more diversified in the developed states than in the lagging state like ours despite being provided many incentives for industrial development. *"Regional imbalance are inherent in the process of development and its degree goes on changing with the change in the stage of development"* (Anuradha, and Rao, 1995). Prof. Hirschman (1961) correctly observes that *"inter regional inequality of growth is an inevitable concomitant and condition of growth itself."* But one of the important dimensions of "Economic Sustainability" is an even industrial development in all parts of the nation (Joshi, 1997). Industrial development in a state may not survive if it is not spread in the districts which are lagging industrially. The consequences of imbalanced industrial development are manifold. For instance, the concentration of labour force in large urban centres may result in negative externalities. It may cause overload on the urban infrastructure, which leads to underloading and jeoparadising the maintenance of rural infrastructure.

4.4 REVIEW OF SOME WORKS DONE RELATING TO INDUSTRIAL DISPARITIES

Many studies are available on disparities in industrial development in India. Here, we shall discuss some important studies made. In his study Joshi (1997) had come to the conclusion that industrial development of traditionally industrially lagging states has remained stagnant with a poor degree of industrial diversification. His study supports the hypothesis that the benefits in the form of incentives and concession to faster industrial development of industrially lagging states which were introduced in Five-Year Plans and corresponding industrial resolutions, in fact, favoured industrially developed states.

Reddy, and Reddy, (1994) conducted a study in Andhra Pradesh using five indicators of industrial development namely – (i) number of industrial units per 10,000 population, (ii) investment per 10,000 population, (iii) industrial workers per 10,000 population, (iv) percentage of industrial workers to total workers and (v) per capita power consumption. They used the methodology of factor analysis and derived the conclusion that industrial development in Andhra Pradesh is very poor and unbalanced. The backward districts have very few types of industries. They also observed that the higher the level of development the greater is the tendency of diversification of industries. They identified out of 23 districts of the state, 10 to be backward and 6 very backward.

Another impressive study was conducted in Gujarat by Sidhu, (1995). Her study reveals that industrialization in Gujrat has been taking place in and around the already industrialized regions while the distantly located districts, having poor infrastructure, particularly railway network, have remained dismal.

Chowdhury (1993) conducted a study on industrial development in Assam using 6 indicators not for all the 23 districts but for 10 districts only. He used the methodology of principal component analysis and catagorised Dibrugarh, Kamrup and Sibsagar as industrially advanced districts; Goalpara, Darrang and Cachar as developing districts and Lakhimpur, Nagaon, Karbi-Anglong and N.C. Hills as backward districts.

We are also influenced greatly by the studies done by Pradhan, (1984), Kumar, (1999), Dutta, and Mukhopadhayay, (1999), Sahoo, (1995) and a few others.

Our study is primarily aimed at the analysis of inter-district disparities in industrial development in the state of Assam. Constrained by non-availability of secondary data relating to industry at district level in Assam, we were compelled to select only four indicators of industrial development namely –

X_1 = percentage of secondary secotor workers to total workforce,

X_2 = percentage of registered factory workers to total workforce,

X_3 = number of registered factories per 1000 sq. km. area and

X_4 = Maximum Horse-Power (H.P.) installed per industrial worker in registered factories.

We have employed Indexing Method and Deprivation Method to find the indices of industrial development in all the 23 districts of the state. In the subsequent section an attempt is being made to analyse development scenario of these four key indicators of industrial development in detail.

4.5 We have first of all ranked the districts in respect of each of the indicators selected for studying industrial development disparities at district level. Afterwards, we have categorized all the 23 districts in terms of industrial development on the basis of composite indices, based on all the four chosen indicators, by Indexing Method and Deprivation Method.

4.5.1 Industrial Workforce in Assam

With a predominantly rural economy and with relatively few landless cultivators, the people of Assam are strongly attached to their lands even when the land holdings of most cultivators are tiny and uneconomic. A subsistence economy and more or less village self-sufficiency generally discourage labour emigration from rural areas, even when there is large scale rural-under-employment. *"A labour class willing to become factory workers has not yet developed in Assam; most of the factory workers in the state are immigrants from other states".* [**Goswami, 1988: 192**] This observation of Prof. Goswami is valid even today.

Table 4.1 shows that only 6.1% of total workforce of Assam are workers in secondary sector which includes manufacturing, processing, servicing, repairs in household and non-household industry, construction, mining and quarrying. Out of 23 district of the state, 9 districts have higher percentage of secondary sector workers than the state percentage. Among these nine districts Kamrup tops the list with 12.2% followed by Tinsukia (9.9%), Dibrugarh (8.3%), N.C. Hills (7.7%), Karimganj (7.6%), Sibsagar (7%), Jorhat (6.9%), Nalbari (6.5%) and Cachar (6.4%). On the other hand, the percentage of secondary sector workers is the least in Dhemaji being 2.3% only.

Table 4.1
Percentage of Secondary Sector Workers to Total Workforce in Districts of Assam

Sl No	*District*	*% of Secondary Sector Workers to Total Workforce*	*Rank*
1.	Dhubri	5.9	10
2.	Kokrajhar	3.0	22
3.	Bongaigaon	4.6	16
4.	Goalpara	5.0	14
5.	Barpeta	5.2	13
6.	Nalbari	6.5	8
7.	Kamrup	12.2	1
8.	Darrang	3.2	21
9.	Sonitpur	3.9	18
10.	Lakhimpur	3.3	20
11.	Dhemaji	2.3	23
12.	Marigaon	4.7	15
13.	Nagaon	5.7	11
14.	Golaghat	4.2	17
15.	Jorhat	6.9	7
16.	Sibsagar	7.0	6
17.	Dibrugarh	8.3	3
18.	Tinsukia	9.9	2
19.	Karbi-Anglong	3.6	19
20.	N.C. Hills	7.7	4
21.	Karimganj	7.6	5
22.	Hailakandi	5.3	12
23.	Cachar	6.4	9
	C.V.	40.067	
	Assam	6.1	

Source:: Calculated from: *Assam State District Profile, 1991, Census of India 1991.*

The coefficient of variation (C.V) of percentage of secondary sector workers to total workforce for the districts of Assam has been worked out to be around 40% indicating significant variation in the distribution of secondary sector workers all over the state.

4.5.2 Registered Factory Workers

Table 4.2 shows that in Assam the share of total workforce of the state in registered factories is only 3.11%. In Tinsukia district this share is 13.12%, in Dibrugarh 10.61%, in Sibsagar almost 6%, in Jorhat 5.63% in Bongaigaon 4.64% and in Kamrup 3.83%.

Table 4.2
Percentage of Registered Factory Workers to Total Workforce in Districts of Assam

Sl No	*District*	*% of Registered Factory Workers to Total Wokforce*	*Rank*
1.	Dhubri	1.108	17
2.	Kokrajhar	1.412	13
3.	Bongaigaon	4.639	5
4.	Goalpara	0.372	21
5.	Barpeta	0.312	22
6.	Nalbari	0.579	20
7.	Kamrup	3.833	6
8.	Darrang	1.275	16
9.	Sonitpur	2.703	10
10.	Lakhimpur	0.952	19
11.	Dhemaji	0.122	23
12.	Marigaon	1.659	13
13.	Nagaon	1.289	15
14.	Golaghat	3.390	7
15.	Jorhat	5.632	4
16.	Sibsagar	5.978	3
17.	Dibrugarh	10.612	2
18.	Tinsukia	13.122	1
19.	Karbi-Anglong	1.107	18
20.	N.C. Hills	1.892	12
21.	Karimganj	2.998	8
22.	Hailakandi	2.982	9
23.	Cachar	2.487	11
	C.V.	99.736	
	Assam	3.112	

Source: Calculated from :

(i) List of Registered factories in Assam (1996), Published by Office of the Chief Inspector of Factories, Assam.

(ii) Assam State District Profile 1991, Census of India, 1991.

(iii) Statistical Hand-Book, Assam, 1997.

The district of Dhemaji bottoms the list, the percentage being only 0.12. We observe that each of Barpeta (0.31%), Goalpara (0.37%), Nalbari (0.58%) and Lakhimpur (0.95%) district is having less than one per cent share of total workforce in registered factory sector. All the three districts of Barak Valley namely Karimganj, Hailakandi and Cachar have relatively better share of workforce in registered factories than some of their counterparts with more than two per cent share. Most of the districts of lower Assam baring Bongaigaon and Kamrup are having lesser share in registered factory sector than the state of Assam as a whole.

The coefficient of variation (C.V.) value for percentage of registered factory workers to total workforce shows almost hundred per cent variation in this regard indicating alarming disparities in employment opportunities in registered factory sector.

4.5.3. Registered Factories in Assam

Total number of registered factories in Assam is an important indicator for the progress of industrialization in the state. The *Table 4.4* reveals that over the past few years there has been a steady increase in the number of registered factories in Assam, though this increase is insignificant in comparison to the developed states of our country.

In *Table 4.3* we have presented the number of registered factories per thousand sq. km, of area districtwise. In Assam there are on the average approximately 31 registered factories per thousand sq. km. of area. Out of 23 districts of Assam only 6 districts have higher number of factories per thousand sq. km. of area than the state average. The leading among them is Kamrup (105) followed by Tinsukia (88), Dibrugarh (87), Sibsagar (68), Jorhat (64) and Golaghat (44) respectively. Darrang, Dhemaji, N.C. Hills, Karbi-Anglong, Marigaon, etc. are the districts having least number of registered factories. In other districts also the industrialization scenario is disappointing. All the three districts of Barak Valley too registered lower figures than that of the state.

The coefficient of variation (C.V.) for the number of registered factories per thousand sq. km area shows around 99 per cent variation in establishment of factories in districts of Assam. This is due to the fact that in the districts of Kamrup, Tinsukia, Dibrugarh and Jorhat most of the factories are located. In our study relating to infrastructural disparities at district level in Assam we find that these districts have good infrastructural base barring Tinsukia.

Table 4.3
Number of Registered Factories per Thousand sq. km Area in Districts of Assam

Sl No	*District*	*% of Registered Factories per thousands sq. km. area*	*Rank*
1.	Dhubri	20.436	11
2.	Kokrajhar	15.659	14
3.	Bongaigaon	13.147	15
4.	Goalpara	16.474	13
5.	Barpeta	9.553	17
6.	Nalbari	8.418	18
7.	Kamrup	104.718	1
8.	Darrang	2.125	23
9.	Sonitpur	25.544	9
10.	Lakhimpur	12.296	16
11.	Dhemaji	2.780	22
12.	Marigaon	5.281	19
13.	Nagaon	27.066	7
14.	Golaghat	43.689	6
15.	Jorhat	63.837	5
16.	Sibsagar	68.215	4
17.	Dibrugarh	86.956	3
18.	Tinsukia	87.862	2
19.	Karbi-Anglong	3.641	20
20.	N.C. Hills	3.273	21
21.	Karimganj	22.111	10
22.	Hailakandi	18.085	12
23.	Cachar	28.262	8
	C.V.	**98.747**	
	Assam	**31.134**	

Source: Calculated from "List of Registered Factories in Assam, 1996, Published by Office of the Chief inspector of factories, Assam.

Table 4.4
Number of Registered Factories in Assam

Year	*No. of Registered Factries*
1971	1604
1975	1715
1980	1987
1985	2462
1986	2503
1987	2604
1988	2523
1989	2567
1990	2677
1991	2670
1992	2442

Source: Chief Inspector of Factories, Assam.

4.5.4. Electricity Consumption in Registered Factories

In Assam, on the average, approximately 6 H.P. is installed per registered factory worker which is very low. The coefficient of variation (C.V.) for power installed per registered factory worker, as shown in *Table 4.5* in districts of Assam is very high with a value of 162 per cent showing wider disparity in installation of power in factories in the districts of the state.

Table 4.5 shows that maximum H.P. installed per worker is the highest in Bongaigaon district (38.21) followed by Sonitpur (18.70), N.C. Hills (12.31), Kamrup (8.13) and Dibrugarh (5.63). Kokrajhar (1.00), Dhubri (1.12) and Jorhat (1.25) are some of the districts occupying lower ranks. Out of 23 districts of the state only 4 districts have more installed H.P. than the state figure and the rest of the districts except Dibrugarh are having less H.P. installed than that in the state.

Out of the 4 indicators of industrial development we have selected, the widest disparity is registered by this indicator.

Table 4.5
Maximum Horse-Power Installed per Industrial Worker in Registered Factories in Districts of Assam

Sl No	*District*	*Maximum H.P. installed per industrial worker in registered factories*	*Rank*
1.	Dhubri	1.116	19
2.	Kokrajhar	0.828	23
3.	Bongaigaon	38.208	1
4.	Goalpara	2.380	10
5.	Barpeta	1.452	16
6.	Nalbari	3.283	6
7.	Kamrup	8.130	4
8.	Darrang	2.266	12
9.	Sonitpur	18.696	2
10.	Lakhimpur	1.702	13
11.	Dhemaji	3.252	7
12.	Marigaon	2.737	9
13.	Nagaon	2.144	14
14.	Golaghat	1.453	15
15.	Jorhat	1.251	18
16.	Sibsagar	0.869	22
17.	Dibrugarh	5.625	5
18.	Tinsukia	2.298	11
19.	Karbi-Anglong	2.822	8
20.	N.C. Hills	12.314	3
21.	Karimganj	1.009	20
22.	Hailakandi	0.981	21
23.	Cachar	1.451	17
	C.V.	162.076	
	Assam	5.963	

Source: Calculated from "List of Registered Factories in Assam, 1996, published by Office of the Chief inspector of factories, Assam.

4.5.5. Magnitude of Industrial Disparity

From *Table 4.6* we see that the Indexing Method shows 8 districts out of 23 in Assam as relatively developed (R.D.) while the rest 15 are shown as backward (B) districts. In relatively developed districts Bongaigaon ranked first followed by Tinsukia,

Table 4.6
Industrial Ranking of Districts of Assam by Indexing Method and Deprivation Method

Sl. No.	*District*	*Indexing Method*			*Deprivation Method*		
		IDI Value	*Rank*	*Status*	*IDI Value*	*Rank*	*Status*
01	Dhubri	54.170	14	B	.157	15	B
02	Kokrajhar	39.683	18	B	.326	7	B
03	Bongaigaon	226.864	1	RD	.422	4	B
04	Goalpara	46.686	17	B	.119	17	B
05	Barpeta	37.576	21	B	.099	19	B
06	Nalbari	51.814	15	B	.147	16	B
07	Kamrup	198.964	4	RD	.620	2	MD
08	Darrang	22.108	23	B	.055	22	B
09	Sonitpur	136.592	5	RD	.267	8	B
10	Lakhimpur	38.181	20	B	.072	20	B
11	Dhemaji	26.272	22	B	.018	23	B
12	Marigaon	48.305	16	B	.111	18	B
13	Nagaon	72.468	12	B	.202	13	B
14	Golaghat	85.620	9	B	.216	12	B
15	Jorhat	130.027	7	RD	.378	6	B

(contd...)

Table 4.6 Contd...

Sl. No.	District	Indexing Method			Deprivation Method		
		IDI Value	*Rank*	*Status*	*IDI Value*	*Rank*	*Status*
16	Sibsagar	135.131	6	RD	.393	5	B
17	Dibrugarh	212.674	3	RD	.592	3	MD
18	Tinsukia	226.174	2	RD	.728	1	MD
19	Karbi Anglong	38.402	19	B	.062	21	B
20	N.C. Hills	101.029	8	RD	.250	9	B
21	Karimganj	77.216	10	B	.239	10	B
22	Hailakandi	64.311	13	B	.171	14	B
23	Cachar	74.990	11	B	.217	11	B
	C.V	70%			73%		

N.B. :: (i) IDI implies Industrial Development Index.
(ii) IDI values are taken from table 4.7 & 4.8.
(iii) B refers to Backward, RD refers to Relatively Developed and MDrefers to Moderately Developed.
(iv) While Indexing Method is a relative measure of development,DeprivationMethod is an absolute measure of development.

Dibrugarh, Kamrup, Sonitpur, Sibsagar, Jorhat and N.C. Hills respectively. This method ranks Darrang as the Most backward district. Dhemaji, Barpeta, Lakhimpur, Karbi-Anglong and Kokrajhar are placed just above Darrang. The C.V. for IDI values by Indexing Method is found to be around 70 per cent indicating significant imbalance in industrial development scenario of the state.

Deprivation Method, on the other hand, places only 3 districts as moderately developed. These are Tinsukia, Karmrup and Dibrugarh respectively. The rest 20 districts are catagorised as backward by this method. Bongaigaon being judged first by Indexing Method is ranked 4th and termed backward by the Deprivation Method. Kamrup, ranked 4th by Indexing Method but ranked 2nd by Deprivation Method.

The C.V. of IDI values by Deprivation Method comes out to be approximately 73 per cent indicating again significant disparity in industrialization in the state.

We also observe that only three districts namely Kamrup, Tinsukia and Dibrugarh are being adjudged developed either relatively or moderately by both the methods. Thus we consider only these 3 districts in the state as leaders in industrial development and the rest 20 as lagging industrially so far as our 4 indicators are concerned.

We also note that the results earlier obtained by Chowdhury M. K. are in conformity to our findings up to a great extent.

REFERENCES

Anuradha, A and Rao, A.V.V.S.K, (1995). "An Analysis of Inter-State Industrial Disparities in India, 1970-71 – 1985-86" *Indian Journal of Regional Science,* 29(1).

Choudhury, M. K (1993). "Inter-District Disparity in Industrial Development of Assam: An Econometric Approach" – Unpublished Ph. D. thesis submitted to Guwahati University.

Dutta, S. K. and Mukhopadhyay, F. (1999). "Industrial Disparity in India: A Test of Convergence" – *Indian Journal of Regional Science*, 31(1)1.

Goswami, P. C. (1988). The Economic Development of Assam, - Kalyani Publishers, New Delhi.

Hirschman, A. O. (1961). "The Strategy of Economic Development", Yale University Press, New Haven.

Joshi, S. (1997). "Regional Disparities in Industrial Development in India" – *Indian Jurnal of Regional Science*, 29(1).

Kumar, S. (1999). *"Inter-State Variations in Productivity in Indian Manufacturing Sector: A Translog Index Approch." - Indian Journal of Regional Science*, 31(2)

Pradhan, G. (1984). "Inter-District Analysis of Orissa: Industrial Estates" – *The Economic Times*, Aug 24.

Reddy, G. J. and Reddy, N. B. K. (1994). "Regional Disparities in Industrial Development in Andhra Pradesh" – *Indian Journal of Regional Science*, 26(1).

Report on Environment Analysis (Comprehensive Business Plan for NEDFI – Vol. 1), Prepared by: Tata Consultancy Services, Feb, 1996.

Sahoo, S. (1995). "Determinants of Regional Productivity Disparities in Organised Factory Sector in Oirssa: An Econometric Analysis" – *Indian Journal of Regional Science*, 27(1&2).

Sarmah, J. N. (1996). "Problems of Economic Development in Assam", *Economic and Political Weekly*, 1(7).

Sidhu, Hina (1995). "Industrial Development in Gujaraj: Inter District Variation" *Indian Journal of Regional Science*, 29(1 & 2).

Table 4.7
Indicators and Indices of Industrial Development in Districts of Assam (by Indexing Method)

Sl. No.	Districts	% of Secondary sector workers to total workforce	% of Registered factory workers to total workforce	No. of Registered factories per thousand sq. km	Max Horse Power (H.P.) installed per industrial worker	Average Index of Industrial Development	Rank
		Y1	Y2	Y3	Y4		
1	2	3	4	5	6	7	8
01	Dhubri	5.900 (96.721)	1.108 (35.604)	20.436 (65.638)	1.116 (18.715)	54.170	14
02	Kokrajhar	3.000 (49.180)	1.412 (45.372)	15.659 (50.295)	.828 (13.885)	39.683	18
03	Bongaigaon	4.600 (75.409)	4.639 (149.068)	13.147 (42.227)	38.208 (640.751)	226.864	1
04	Goalpara	5.000 (81.967)	0.372 (11.953)	16.474 (52.913)	2.380 (39.912)	46.686	17
05	Barpeta	5.200 (85.245)	0.312 (10.025)	9.553 (30.683)	1.452 (24.350)	37.576	21
06	Nalbari	6.500 (106.557)	0.579 (18.605)	8.418 (27.037)	3.283 (55.056)	51.814	15
07	Kamrup	12.200 (199.999)	3.833 (123.168)	104.718 (336.346)	8.130 (136.341)	198.964	4
08	Darrang	3.200 (52.459)	1.275 (40.970)	2.125 (6.825)	2.266 (38.001)	22.108	23

(contd...)

Table 4.7 Contd...

1	2	3	4	5	6	7	8
09	Sonitpur	3.900	2.703	25.544	18.696	136.592	5
		(63.934)	(86.857)	(82.045)	(313.533)		
10	Lakhimpur	3.300	0.952	12.296	1.702	38.181	20
		(54.098)	(30.591)	(39.493)	(28.543)		
11	Dhemaji	2.300	0.122	2.780	3.525	26.272	22
		(37.704)	(3.920)	(8.929)	(54.536)		
12	Marigaon	4.700	1.659	5.281	2.737	48.305	16
		(77.049)	(53.309)	(16.962)	(45.900)		
13	Nagaon	5.700	1.289	37.066	2.144	72.468	12
		(93.442)	(41.420)	(119.053)	(35.955)		
14	Golaghat	4.200	3.390	43.689	1.453	85.620	9
		(68.852)	(108.933)	(140.325)	(24.367)		
15	Jorhat	6.900	5.632	63.837	1.251	130.027	7
		(113.114)	(180.976)	(205.039)	(20.979)		
16	Sibsagar	7.000	5.978	68.215	.869	135.131	6
		(114.754)	(192.095)	(219.101)	(14.573)		
17	Dibrugarh	8.300	10.612	86.956	5.625	212.674	3
		(136.065)	(341.002)	(279.295)	(94.332)		
18	Tinsukia	9.900	13.122	87.862	2.298	226.174	2
		(162.295)	(421.658)	(282.205)	(38.538)		
19	Karbi Anglong	3.600	1.107	3.641	2.822	38.402	19
		(59.016)	(35.571)	(11.694)	(47.325)		
20	N.C. Hills	7.700	1.892	3.273	12.314	101.029	8
		(126.229)	(60.796)	(10.512)	(206.507)		

21	Karimganj	7.600 (124.590)	2.998 (96.396)	22.111 (71.018)	1.009 (16.921)	77.216	10
22	Hailakandi	5.300 (86.885)	2.982 (95.822)	18.085 (58.087)	.981 (16.451)	64.311	13
23	Cachar	6.400 (104.918)	2.487 (79.916)	28.262 (90.775)	1.451 (24.351)	74.990	11
	Assam	6.100 (100.00)	3.112 (100.00)	31.134 (100.00)	5.963 (100.00)		
	C.V.	40.067	99.736	98.747	162.076		

N.B.: Figures in Parentheses refer to the values of indices computed on the basis of state average as 100.

Source : (i) "List of Registered Factories in Assam", Published by Office of the Chief Inspector of Factories, Assam.
(ii) *Assam State District Profile* ,1991, Census of India, 1991.
(iii) *Statistical Hand Book of Assam 1997-98*, Directorate of Economics and statistics, Govt. of Assam.

Table 4.8

Indices of Industrial Development in Districts of Assam (by Deprivation Method)

Sl. No.	District	Y1	Y2	Y3	Y4	Total	Average (Ij)	Industrial Dev. Index Value =1-Ij	Rank
01	Dhubri	.636	.924	.822	.992	3.374	.8431	.1565	15
02	Kokrajhar	.929	.900	.868	1.000	2.697	.6742	0.3257	7
03	Bongaigaon	.768	.653	.893	0	2.314	.5785	.4215	4
04	Goalpara	.727	.981	.860	.958	3.526	.8815	.1185	17
05	Barpeta	.707	.985	.928	.983	3.603	.9008	.0992	19
06	Nalbari	.576	.965	.937	.934	3.412	.8530	.1470	16
07	Kamrup	0	.715	0	.805	1.520	.3800	.6200	2
08	Darrang	.909	.911	1.000	.962	3.782	.9455	.0545	22
09	Sonitpur	.838	.801	.772	.522	2.933	.7333	.2668	8
10	Lakhimpur	.899	.936	.901	.977	3.713	.9283	.0718	20
11	Dhemaji	1.000	1.000	.994	.935	3.929	.9823	0.0177	23
12	Marigaon	.758	.882	.969	.949	3.558	.8895	.1105	18
13	Nagaon	.657	.910	.659	.965	3.191	.7978	.2022	13
14	Golaghat	.808	.749	.595	.983	3.135	.7838	.2162	12
15	Jorhat	.535	.576	.398	.989	2.498	.6245	.3755	6
16	Sibsagar	.525	.550	.356	.998	2.429	.6073	.3927	5

17	Dibrugarh	.394	.193	.173	.872	1.632	.4080	.5920	3
18	Tinsukia	.232	0	.164	.961	1.087	.2718	.7282	1
19	Karbi Anglong	.869	.924	.985	.947	3.754	.9385	.0615	21
20	N.C. Hills	.455	.864	.989	.693	3.001	.7503	.2497	9
21	Karimganj	.465	.779	.805	.995	3.044	.7610	.2390	10
22	Hailakandi	.697	.780	.844	.996	3.317	.8293	.1707	14
23	Cachar	.586	.818	.745	.983	3.132	.7830	.2170	11

N.B.: Calculated from the values of 4 Industrial Indicators given in Table-4.7 using the formula for Deprivation Method.

5

Inter-District Developmental Disparities in Basic Infrastructure and Services (BIS) in Assam

5.1 INTRODUCTION

Infrastructural services like power, transport, health facilities, educational facilities, roads and railways, postal and bank services, telecommunications etc. improved quality of life and productivity. Major failure in these services quickly and radically reduce quality of human life and their productivity. On the other hand, improvement in infrastructural services boosts walfare and fosters economic growth. One of the major challenges faced by most of the developing regions is to provide proper and state of the art infrastructural services to meet demands of industry, business, households and other users. **Medhi, (1978)** righly puts:

> *Today efforts have been made to explain regional imbalance in terms of infrastructure. . . . Infrastructure aids income generation and production in the rest of the economy rather than income generation and production within the infrastructure enterprises themselves."*

Though the availability of infrastructure has increased up to some extent in our state over the last few decades, it is far from being up to the mark resulting in loss of economic opportunities. The root cause for this is inadequate incentives embodied in the institutional arrangements for providing infrastructural services.

In our country, public sector held a monopoly in provision of most of the infrastructural services for almost five decades of planning. In 1991, when the current period of reforms started, electricity, railways, ports, roads and telecommunications were among the sectors reserved for the public sector. Now, virtually all parts of the economy - including infrastructure are open to private investments. What more is required is a better infrastructural policy to improve productivity of our industries and human resources. Creating right atmosphere for private sector participation in infrastructure projects and encouraging foreign investment in them is the need of the hours (Prasad, 2000).

Lack of developed infrastructure is one of the weakest links in the process of economic reforms, which is holding up the economic growth of Assam. After more than 50 years of development we have not been able to ensure uninterrupted supply of power, continuous supply of safe drinking water to our citizens. The roads are in bad shape, there are no express highways, the local and inter-city transport is in shambles, even the private transport system is backward not to say by world standard but by standards of some of our counterparts in India. How then we expect our remote villages and towns to grow in economic terms unless they are linked with proper roads and the communication system? 'We should take a lesson from what the development of infrastructure has done to the economy of South Korea. After the partition of Korea into North Korea and South Korea all the industries went to North Korea while the agricultural land came to South Korea. South Korea taking some tips from Germany concentrated on the development of power as well as express highways. Today, South Korea is not only self-sufficient in agriculture but also highly industrialised while North-Korea stands not only deindustrialised but also has been an agricultural disaster.' (Mehta, 2000)

Therefore development of infrastructure needs serious attention from us and our statesmen in the helm of affairs. The significant role of infrastructural facilities in the process of regional development has been recognised by economsts and planners. The pace of regional development cannot be accelerated without adequate infrastructural facilities.

5.2 REVIEW OF SOME WORKS DONE ON DEVELOPMENTAL DISPARITIES IN BIS

Some studies are already done on the role of infrastructure on economic development. Saxena and Sahoo (1998) made an attempt to examine the importance of major infrastructure viz. transport, electricity, gas and water supply on the output, income and employment generation of the Kanpur economy through input-output technique. They found that infrastructure services have low output and low income generating capabilities but high employment generating effects.

In another study made by Shukla and Dhagat (1999) the existence of inter-regional differences in the level of infrastructural facilities in India had been highlighted. They found that availability of infrastructure motivated the farmers for wide-spread use of new agricultural practices leading to higher level to modern agriculture and therefore a suitable policy for infrastructure development with a rural bias is needed for economic development of the agriculturally based backward economies like Orissa and Rajasthan.

Meher (1999) conducted a study relating to district level disparities in Orissa on the basis of secondary source of information. So far as infrastructural disparities are concerned, this study used 16 indicators of infrastructural development. For construction of composite index of development this study used the methodology of Equal Weightage Indexing Method and Deprivation Method. The study reveals that unlike the case of agriculture and industry, the districts of the state have much lesser variation in the development of infrastructure. It was found that the planning machinery of the state is putting efforts to bridge the inter-district level gap in the availability of BIS facilities.

5.3 INDICATORS OF BIS DEVELOPMENT

We found the methodology and indicators of the study done by Meher fascinating. Moreover, in case of Assam Secondary data relating to most of the indicators are available at district level based on 1991 census. Following Meher, in this chapter an attempt has been made to analyse the inter-district disparities, construct composite indices of infrastructural development and identify the backward and moderately or relatively developed districts in Assam with respect to development in infrastructure. To determine the level of infrastructural development and disparities in the districts of Assam, secondary data relating to 14 infrastructural indicators have been used. These indicators are:

X_1 = Percentage of literarcy,

X_2 = Percentage of urban population,

X_3 = Percentage of tertiary sector workers,

X_4 = Number of primary and middle schools per 10,000 population,

X_5 = Number of High Schools per 10,000 population,

X_6 = Number of colleges per lakh population,

X_7 = Number of hospitals/dispensaries per 10,000 population,

X_8 = Number of medical beds per 10,000 population,

X_9 = Infant mortality per 1000 births,

X_{10} = Road length per 100 sq. km area,

X_{11} = Road length per lakh population,

X_{12} = Percentage of villages electrified,

X_{13} = Number of post offices per 10,000 population,

X_{14} = Number of banks per lakh population.

We now proceed to analyse the desparities with respect to these 14 infrastructural variables one by one in all the 23 districts of Assam.

5.3.1 Literacy

Illiteracy and poverty are the two major problems that we are facing with. Even the generally inflated statistics provided by various agencies revealed that enrolment in primary schools is very low. The dropout rate is so high that even half of those enrolled failed to reach the fourth standard. The limited literacy that they acquire is soon lost adding to the ocean of illiterates. Although literacy is not same as education, this is the most important entry point into the world of education. The principal concern today is to find out how more and more people can become literate and how these new converts can sustain their literacy.

Assam, ranks 16th in literacy among all the states in India. We observe from Table 5.1 that 52.89 per cent of our state population is literate.

Table 5.1
Literacy Rate In Districts of Assam

Sl No	District	% of Literacy	Rank
1.	Dhubri	38.31	23
2.	Kokrajhar	40.57	22
3.	Bongaigaon	49.06	15
4.	Goalpara	46.81	18
5.	Barpeta	43.24	20
6.	Nalbari	55.99	9
7.	Kamrup	65.04	2
8.	Darrang	42.00	21
9.	Sonitpur	48.14	16
10.	Lakhimpur	58.96	5
11.	Dhemaji	53.84	12
12.	Marigaon	47.99	17
13.	Nagaon	54.74	10
14.	Golaghat	58.54	6
15.	Jorhat	65.51	1
16.	Sibsagar	64.46	3
17.	Dibrugarh	58.32	7
18.	Tinsukia	50.28	14
19.	Karbi-Anglong	45.57	19
20.	N.C. Hills	57.76	8
21.	Karimganj	54.71	11
22.	Hailakandi	53.07	13
23.	Cachar	59.19	4
	Assam	52.89	–
	C.V.	14.58	–

Source: Calculated from Statistical Hand Book of Assam, 1997, Directorate of Economics and Statistics, Govt. of Assam.

Out of 23 districts 11 have lower literacy rate than that of the state while 12 districts register higher literacy rate than the state. Jorhat district ranks first with 65.51% literacy followed by Kamrup (65.04%) and Sibsagar (64.46%). Nalbari, Lakhimpur, Dhemaji, Nagaon, Golaghat, Dibrugarh, N.C. Hills, Karimganj, Hailakandi and Cachar districts also have higher literacy rate than that of the state. Dhubri ranks 23rd with the lowest literacy rate of only 38.31%, succeeded respectively by Kokrajhar (40.57%), Darrang (42%) and Karbi-Anglong (45.57%). The districts of Bongaigaon, Barpeta, Sonitpur, Marigaon and Tinsukia register lower literarcy rate than that of Assam as a whole.

The coefficient of variation (C.V.) for literacy in 23 districts of the state shows 14.58% average disparity.

We will observe later on that low literacy is one of the major factors contributing towards backwardness of economy of some districts like Dhubri, Kokrajhar, Marigaon, Karbi-Anglong etc. whereas higher literacy boosts economic development as is apparent in case of Jorhat, Kamrup, Dibrugarh etc.

5.3.2 Urbanization

Urbanization is one of the common features of economic development. The attainment of high rate of economic development paves the way for growing urbanization. Assam has predominantly rural population with majority of the total population living in the rural areas. Due to slow pace of urbanization as well as industrialization migration of people from rural to urban areas was insignificant earlier but an increasing trend of urbanization is being observed over the past few decades.

According to 1991 census as shown in *Table 5.2,* 11.10 per cent of total population of Assam live in urban areas against 26.73 per cent of urban population in India. The range of urbanization in districts of Assam varies from the lowest of 1.86 per cent in Marigaon to the highest of 32.76 per cent in Kamrup district. There are 17 districts in the state where urbanization took place at lower pace in comparison to the state itself whereas in 6 districts namely Kamrup, Jorhat, Dibrugarh, Tinsukia, N.C. Hills and Dhubri urbanization is higher. We also observe from *Table 5.2* that the coefficient of variation (C.V.) for urbanization is pretty high being almost 67 per cent.

Table 5.2
Distribution of Urban Population in districts of Assam

Sl No	*District*	*% of Urban Population*	*Rank*
1.	Dhubri	12.16	6
2.	Kokrajhar	6.34	18
3.	Bongaigaon	9.15	10
4.	Goalpara	7.80	11
5.	Barpeta	7.02	16
6.	Nalbari	2.31	22
7.	Kamrup	32.76	1
8.	Darrang	4.93	21
9.	Sonitpur	7.30	13.5
10.	Lakhimpur	6.54	17
11.	Dhemaji	1.86	23
12.	Marigaon	5.16	20
13.	Nagaon	10.87	7
14.	Golaghat	5.90	19
15.	Jorhat	15.27	5
16.	Sibsagar	7.23	15
17.	Dibrugarh	17.61	3
18.	Tinsukia	16.49	4
19.	Karbi-Anglong	10.63	8
20.	N.C. Hills	22.87	2
21.	Karimganj	7.30	13.5
22.	Hailakandi	7.60	12
23.	Cachar	9.81	9
	Assam	11.10	–
	C.V.	66.95	–

Source: Computed from *Statistical Hand Book of Assam*, 1997.

Factors like change in administrative set up of certain units and consequent enlargement of government expenditure and employment potentialities along with expansion of educational facilities etc. are responsible for higher urbanization in some districts of Assam.

5.3.3. Tertiary Sector Wrokforce

The pattern and level of economic development in a region is reflected more or less by work participation rate of workforce in the tertiary sector economy. Moreover, percentage distribution of workers in the tertiary sector is an important indicator of development and state of basic infrastructure and services available in a district.

As seen from *Table 5.3*, Assam has a low percentage of workforce of only 20.40 in tertiary sector. In the state only 7 districts have higher percentage of workforce in tertiary sector. Of these 7 districts four are in Brahmaputra valley, two are in Barak valley and one in hills district. Kamrup district with 42.50% ranks first in the state with regard to tertiary sector workers followed by N.C. Hills (29.40%), Cachar (24.60%), Jorhat (24.30%), Karimganj (23.60%), Dibrugarh (23%) and Nalbari (22%). Lower per centages of tertiary sector workforce are registered by Karbi-Anglong (11.60%), Dhemaji (12.20%), Darrang (12.90%), Kokrajhar (13%) and Marigaon (13.10%). Other districts also show percentage below the state figure. The coefficient of variation (C.V.) of percentage distribution of tertiary sector workers in districts of Assam shows substantial variation in opportunities of employment in tertiary sector, being 33.48, which is very high.

5.3.4. Primary and Middle School Education

Primary education in Assam has made rapid strides in the past five decades. The number of schools as well as the number of students have gone up. There have been attempts to extend infrastructural facilities to a large number of schools. Yet the state of primary and middle education cannot be considered to be satisfactory.

According to the Sixth All India Education Survey, more than 4 children for every 100 persons in Assam do not have access to primary school within a radius of 2 km In the state, according to 1991 census data, there are almost 11 primary and middle schools per 10,000 population. *Table 5.4* shows that out of 23 districts in the state 14 have relatively higher number of such schools per 10,000 population and 9 districts have lower number of schools than that in the state. N.C. Hills district ranks first with around 34 primary and middle schools per 10,000 population followed by Dhemaji (19), Lakhimpur (18), Marigaon (17) and Nagaon (14). Kamrup district ranks 23rd in this regard with only 7 such schools per 10,000 population. Cachar, Darrang, Sonitpur, Barpeta and Nalbari each has around 9 such schools per 10,000 population.

Table 5.3
Percentage Distribution of Tertiary Sector Workers in Districts of Assam

Sl No	*District*	*% of Tertiary Sector Workers*	*Rank*
1.	Dhubri	18.30	12.5
2.	Kokrajhar	13.00	20
3.	Bongaigaon	20.40	8
4.	Goalpara	19.90	9.5
5.	Barpeta	18.40	11
6.	Nalbari	22.00	7
7.	Kamrup	42.50	1
8.	Darrang	12.90	21
9.	Sonitpur	18.30	12.5
10.	Lakhimpur	16.20	17
11.	Dhemaji	12.20	22
12.	Marigaon	13.10	19
13.	Nagaon	19.90	9.5
14.	Golaghat	15.10	18
15.	Jorhat	24.30	4
16.	Sibsagar	17.70	15.5
17.	Dibrugarh	23.00	6
18.	Tinsukia	18.20	14
19.	Karbi-Anglong	11.60	23
20.	N.C. Hills	29.40	2
21.	Karimganj	23.60	5
22.	Hailakandi	17.70	15.5
23.	Cachar	24.60	3
	Assam	20.40	–
	C.V.	33.48	–

Source: Computed from District Profile : Assam 1991, Directorate of Census Operations, Assam.

The coefficient of variation (C.V.) for this indicator has been computed at 40.83% which indicates very large disparity in the establishment of primary and middle schools in the districts of Assam.

Table 5.4
Number of Primary and Middle Schools Per 10,000 Population in Districts of Assam

Sl No	*District*	*No of Primary & Middle Schools Per 10,000 Population*	*Rank*
1.	Dhubri	11.950	10
2.	Kokrajhar	11.970	9
3.	Bongaigaon	11.700	11
4.	Goalpara	13.450	7
5.	Barpeta	9.490	20
6.	Nalbari	9.570	19
7.	Kamrup	7.290	23
8.	Darrang	11.000	14
9.	Sonitpur	9.410	21
10.	Lakhimpur	18.160	3
11.	Dhemaji	19.420	2
12.	Marigaon	16.770	4
13.	Nagaon	14.480	5
14.	Golaghat	11.010	13
15.	Jorhat	10.590	15
16.	Sibsagar	10.570	15
17.	Dibrugarh	12.150	8
18.	Tinsukia	9.850	18
19.	Karbi-Anglong	14.220	6
20.	N.C. Hills	33.750	1
21.	Karimganj	11.550	12
22.	Hailakandi	10.510	17
23.	Cachar	9.120	22
	Assam	10.86	
	C.V.	40.83	

Source: Statement 3.1, Distribution of inhabited villages having different types of educational facilities in districts of Assam, 1991; Directorate of Census Operations, Assam.

5.3.5. Secondary Education

Most of the high schools in Assam suffer from lack of minimum facilities. Faced with discouraging scenario of the failure of a large percentage of students (about 70%) at the High School Leaving Certificate Examinations we have to go for radical changes in the secondary education system. Changes are necessary in the interest of making secondary education more meaningful for the students of whom only 25 or 30 per cent go for higher education.

Table 5.5 shows there are around 1.23 high schools per 10,000 population in the state. Only 10 districts out of 23 show a little bit better scenario than the state in this regard and in other 13 districts the number of high schools per 10,000 population is below the state figure. Lakhimpur district depicts the best picture with 2.67 high schools per 10,000 population followed by Jorhat (2.31), Sibsagar (1.65), Barpeta (1.62), Nalbari (1.56) and Dhemaji (1.56). The lowest rank is occupied by Karimganj with 0.58 high school per 10,000 population.

Hailakandi also depicts same scenario as that of Karimganj. Cachar occupied superior position over other two districts in Barak valley with 0.95 such schools per 10,000 population. The two hills districts of the state namely Karbi-Anglong and N.C. Hills also have almost one high school per 10,000 population. The high value of 40.05 of C.V. reflects greater imbalance in spread of high school education in the districts of Assam. The large scale failure and a dropout rate of 77% reflect poor quality of high school education leading to a colosal waste of human resources. The secondary education as of now is traditional in nature, providing skills and knowledge of a rather limited and specific nature. It does not increase in students competencies like ability to learn and relearn, to acquire knowledge on one's own, critical thinking and problem solving which are essence of modern living.

5.3.6. College Education

In Assam the access of higher education has no definite pattern. Increasing number of students and poor infrastructure have made institutions of higher education incapable of producing human resource as demanded by society. Deteriorating academic standard of colleges in the state gets reflected in poor pass percentage in higher secondary and degree level. Nearly 90% of the under graduate students get themselves enrolled in the courses in arts, science and commerce. A large section of students enroll themselves in colleges only for a degree without acquiring any specialized knowledge or skill. The standard of most of the colleges barring a few have become very low.

Table 5.5
Number of High Schools Per 10,000 Population in Districts of Assam

Sl. No.	*District*	*No. of High Schools Per 10,000 Population*	*Rank*
1.	Dhubri	0.900	19
2.	Kokrajhar	0.760	20
3.	Bongaigaon	1.077	13
4.	Goalpara	1.270	9
5.	Barpeta	1.620	4
6.	Nalbari	1.562	5
7.	Kamrup	1.240	10
8.	Darrang	1.100	12
9.	Sonitpur	1.040	14
10.	Lakhimpur	2.670	1
11.	Dhemaji	1.560	6
12.	Marigaon	1.370	8
13.	Nagaon	0.940	18
14.	Golaghat	1.470	7
15.	Jorhat	2.310	2
16.	Sibsagar	1.650	3
17.	Dibrugarh	1.120	11
18.	Tinsukia	0.690	21
19.	Karbi-Anglong	0.980	16
20.	N.C. Hills	0.990	15
21.	Karimganj	0.580	23
22.	Hailakandi	0.620	22
23.	Cachar	0.950	17
	Assam	1.230	–
	C.V.	40.05	

Source: Statement 3.1, Distribution of inhabited villages having different types of educational facilities in districts of Assam, 1991; Directorate of Census Operations, Assam.

Table 5.6
Number of Colleges Per Lakh Population in Districts of Assam

Sl No	District	No of Colleges Per Lakh Population	Rank
1.	Dhubri	0.150	23
2.	Kokrajhar	0.240	20
3.	Bongaigaon	0.241	19
4.	Goalpara	0.890	3
5.	Barpeta	0.930	2
6.	Nalbari	0.590	9
7.	Kamrup	0.540	10
8.	Darrang	0.760	4
9.	Sonitpur	0.210	21
10.	Lakhimpur	0.530	11
11.	Dhemaji	0.62	8
12.	Marigaon	0.310	16
13.	Nagaon	0.260	18
14.	Golaghat	0.720	5
15.	Jorhat	1.950	1
16.	Sibsagar	0.662	6
17.	Dibrugarh	0.380	15
18.	Tinsukia	0.200	22
19.	Karbi-Anglong	0.300	17
20.	N.C. Hills	0.660	7
21.	Karimganj	0.50	12.5
22.	Hailakandi	0.50	12.5
23.	Cachar	0.490	14
	Assam	0.500	–
	C.V.	69.94	–

Source: Statement 3.1, Distribution of inhabited villages having different types of educational facilities in the districts of Assam, 1991; Directorate of Census Operations, Assam.

Table 5.6 shows that there are 0.50 colleges per lakh population in the state. Jorhat, the most literate district of the state also tops the list of number of colleges per lakh population with 1.95. In all other 22 districts there is not even one college per lakh population.

Relatively in Barpeta (0.93), Goalpara (0.89), Darrang (0.76), Golaghat (0.72), Dibsagar (0.66), N.C. Hills (0.66), Dhemaji (0.62), Nalbari (0.59), Kamrup (0.54) and Lakhimpur (0.53) the scenario is better than that of the state. In all other districts the number of colleges per lakh population is less than that in the state. Dhubri occupies last rank with only 0.15 college per lakh population. Kokrajhar, Tinsukia, Sonitpur etc. also show lower figures than the state.

A very high value of C.V. of 69.94% also indicates high disparity in facilities for higher education in the districts of the state.

5.3.7. Health Care Units

'Health for all' is a world-wide social goal. The Constitution of India too has recognized this and has laid down in its directives that the state shall endeavour to raise the level of nutrition and standard of living, and to improve public health. Health plays a crucial role in the development of human capital and it is needless to say that economic development of a region mostly depends on the availability of qualitative manpower. In fact a large disparity in the health sector of different districts may affect economic development between regions notwithstanding the reduction of inter-district level disparity in the BIS sector. A better health care system of a district and the government's investment on this sector can well be understood from the indicators like number of hospitals/ dispensaries per lakh population, number of medical beds per 10,000 population, infant mortality rate per 1000 birth etc.

The state of health care in Assam is in bad condition. Number of hospital/primary health centres/dispensaries per lakh population is only 4.8 as shown in *Table 5.7.* A slightly better scenario than the state is revealed by 10 districts with N.C. Hills (9.9), Karbi-Anglong (8.1) and Nalbari (7.5) occupying the three first positions respectively. Barak valley is least privileged in this regard with Hailakandi (2.2) being ranked 23rd, Cachar (3.2) ranked 22nd and Karimganj (4.2) ranked 15th. The state of affairs are far from satisfactory in Dhubri, Dhemaji, Marigaon, Dibrugarh and Tinsukia. The large C.V. value of 35.62% also reveals higher disparity in health care system.

Table 5.7
Number of Hospitals/Primary Health Centres/Dispensaries Per Lakh Population in Districts of Assam

Sl. No.	*District*	*No of Hospitals/ Primary Health Centres/ Dispensaries Per Lakh Population*	*Rank*
1.	Dhubri	3.7	18
2.	Kokrajhar	7.1	4
3.	Bongaigaon	6.4	5
4.	Goalpara	3.7	18
5.	Barpeta	4.3	14
6.	Nalbari	7.5	3
7.	Kamrup	5.2	8
8.	Darrang	4.9	10
9.	Sonitpur	4.4	12.5
10.	Lakhimpur	4.8	11
11.	Dhemaji	4.1	16
12.	Marigaon	3.7	18
13.	Nagaon	5.1	9
14.	Golaghat	5.3	7
15.	Jorhat	6.2	6
16.	Sibsagar	4.4	12.5
17.	Dibrugarh	3.3	20
18.	Tinsukia	3.2	21.5
19.	Karbi-Anglong	8.1	2
20.	N.C. Hills	9.9	1
21.	Karimganj	4.2	15
22.	Hailakandi	2.2	23
23.	Cachar	3.2	21.5
	Assam	4.8	–
	C.V.	35.62	–

Source: Computed from *Statistical Hand Book*, Assam, 1997.

5.3.8. Health Care Facilities in Terms of Medical Beds

Table 5.8 shows that the number of medical beds in Assam per 10,000 population is only 5.74 compared to the national average of 7.16. The district of N.C. Hills again ranks first in this aspect with 14.98 medical beds per 10,000 population followed by Dibrugarh (13.38), Kamrup (12.43) and Sonitpur (11.77). Goalpara is the worst sufferer district with only 1.48 medical beds per 10,000 population. In Barak Valley except Cachar which ranks 5th with 8.11 beds, Karimganj and Hailakandi districts rank 21st and 22nd with 2.00 and 1.78 beds per 10,000 population respectively. Out of 23 districts of the state only 7 portray better picture in comparison to the state as a whole. The very large value of C.V. of 69.76 is indicative of the vast imbalance in this medical facility at district level in the state.

Table 5.8
Number of Medical Beds Per Lakh Population in Districts of Assam

Sl. No.	*District*	*No. of Medical Beds Per Lakh Population*	*Rank*
1.	Dhubri	4.130	13
2.	Kokrajhar	4.430	9
3.	Bongaigaon	2.930	18
4.	Goalpara	1.480	23
5.	Barpeta	2.220	20
6.	Nalbari	5.060	8
7.	Kamrup	12.430	3
8.	Darrang	3.250	16
9.	Sonitpur	11.770	4
10.	Lakhimpur	4.200	12
11.	Dhemaji	4.380	10
12.	Marigaon	2.500	19
13.	Nagaon	3.730	15
14.	Golaghat	4.250	11
15.	Jorhat	5.920	7
16.	Sibsagar	4.050	14
17.	Dibrugarh	13.380	2
18.	Tinsukia	3.020	17
19.	Karbi-Anglong	7.030	6
20.	N.C. Hills	14.980	1
21.	Karimganj	2.000	21
22.	Hailakandi	1.780	22
23.	Cachar	8.110	5
	Assam	5.740	
	C.V.	69.76	

Source: Computed from *Statistical Hand Book*, Assam, 1997.

Being denied of these much needed medical facilities people of the state are required to go outside the state for critical ailment and this involves huge expenditure. Therefore modernisation of the existing health care units should be the beginning of any proposed health care development programme.

5.3.9. Infant Mortality Rate

Another important indicator of health care development is infant mortality rate (IMR) per 1000 births. In Assam 92 infants out of 1000 births die according to 1991 census. As can be seen from *Table 5.9*, Dhubri district registers the highest IMR of 128 followed by Bongaigaon (122), Dhemaji (114) and Lakhimpur (112). On the other hand, IMR is the lowest in Jorhat district with 47 infant deaths per 1000 births. Dibrugah, Golaghat, Tinsukia and Sibsagar also register relatively lower IMR. In Barak Valley all the three districts namely Karimganj, Hailakandi and Cachar experience higher mortality than that of the state. In N.C. Hills IMR is higher than the state whereas in Karbi-Anglong it is lower. The C.V. value for this indicator is calculated at 23.54.

We find that the disparity relating to child care is less in comparison to disparities relating to the other two chosen health indicators namely number of hospitals/dispensaries/primary health centres per lakh population and number of medical beds per 10,000 population.

5.3.10. Transport and Communication

Economic development of an area more or less depends on the rapid means of transport and communication. A well developed transport and communication infrastructure generates multiple effects in the local and national economy. Assam is relatively batter placed in the overall road map of the country. Mobility, both in terms of travel and transportation may be fully ensured within the existing road system provided this is optimally maintained. The state government abruptly failed in maintaining the excellent road system of the state. Thus priority has to be given on this imperative task in any proposed plan and sufficient funds should be allocated for this purpose.

Table 5.9
Infant Mortality Rate Per 1000 Birth in Districts of Assam

Sl No	*District*	*Infant Mortality Rate Per 1000 of Birth*	*Rank*
1.	Dhubri	128	1
2.	Kokrajhar	78	15
3.	Bongaigaon	122	2
4.	Goalpara	106	8
5.	Barpeta	101	9
6.	Nalbari	96	13
7.	Kamrup	77	16.5
8.	Darrang	111	5.5
9.	Sonitpur	77	16.5
10.	Lakhimpur	112	4
11.	Dhemaji	114	3
12.	Marigaon	88	14
13.	Nagaon	97	11.5
14.	Golaghat	61	21
15.	Jorhat	47	23
16.	Sibsagar	75	19
17.	Dibrugarh	51	22
18.	Tinsukia	73	20
19.	Karbi-Anglong	76	18
20.	N.C. Hills	108	7
21.	Karimganj	111	5.5
22.	Hailakandi	99	10
23.	Cachar	97	11.5
	Assam	92	
	C.V.	23.54	

Source: Assam *State District Profile 1991*, Census of India, 1991.

It may be seen from Table 5.10 that although there is a wide variation among the districts with regard to road length in km per lakh population due to variation in population density, there is lesser variation in road length per 100 sq. km of land area. The C.V. value of the former is 104.68 per cent while it is only 28.10 per cent in case of the later.

Table 5.10
Road Length Per Lakh Population and Per 100 sq. km Area in Districts of Assam

Sl. No.	*District*	*Road Length Per Lakh Population*	*Rank*	*Road Length Per 100 sq. km Area*	*Rank*
1.	Dhubri	84	22	39.3	16
2.	Kokrajhar	128	15.5	40.6	12
3.	Bongaigaon	120	18	40.6	12
4.	Goalpara	155	7	40.6	12
5.	Barpeta	94	20	40.0	14
6.	Nalbari	153	8	68.8	2
7.	Kamrup	122	17	56.0	6
8.	Darrang	128	15.5	47.6	7
9.	Sonitpur	144	9	38.7	17
10.	Lakhimpur	135	12.5	44.5	8
11.	Dhemaji	192	4	28.4	22
12.	Marigaon	142	10	62.5	3.5
13.	Nagaon	135	12.5	62.5	3.5
14.	Golaghat	173	6	41.0	10
15.	Jorhat	190	5	58.0	5
16.	Sibsagar	206	3	70.1	1
17.	Dibrugarh	130	14	40.1	15
18.	Tinsukia	140	11	35.6	18
19.	Karbi-Anglong	474	2	30.1	21
20.	N.C. Hills	1050	1	32.4	20
21.	Karimganj	92	21	42.3	9
22.	Hailakandi	98	19	33.1	19
23.	Cachar	80	23	25.6	23
	Assam	148		42.2	
	C.V.	104.68		28.10	

Source: Computed from *Statistical Hand Book*, Assam, 1997.

In Assam there is 148 km of road per lakh population. The two hills district of the state namely N.C. Hills and Karbi-Anglong occupy top two ranks with regard to this indicator with 1050 km and 474 km per lakh population. Sibsagar ranks 3rd with 206 km, Cachar ranks 23rd with only 80 km, Dhubri ranks 22nd with only

84 km, Karimganj ranks 21st with only 92 km and Barpeta ranks 20th with only 94 km The range of variation is very high as indicated by the difference between N.C. Hills and Cachar district.

Again the highest road length per 100 sq. km of land is registered by Sibsagar district with 70.10 km followed by Nalbari (68.80 km), Marigaon and Nagaon each with 62.50 km and Jorhat (58 km). Cachar, in this respect too, occupies the last rank with only 25.6 km, Dhemaji (28.40 km) ranks 22nd and Karbi-Anglong (30.10 km) ranks 21st.

We observe that the range of disparity in districts of the state in this regard is relatively lower in comparison to road length per lakh population.

5.3.11. Electricfication of Villages

The modern economic development rests upon the increasing consumption of inanimated sources of energy. The availability of electricity in rural areas makes it possible to accelerate the pace of industrial and economic development. In so far as electrification of villages in the state of Assam is concerned, out of a total of 25,590 villages in the state, 18,999 villages are electrified up to 1996-97 and percentage of villages electrified comes out to be 74%. However, the state is facing acute power crisis. The C.V. of 23.49% indicates high disparity in rural electrification programme.

As shown in Table 5.11, Nalbari district tops the list in case of rural electrification with 97% of villages electrified followed by Sibsagar (92%), Bongaigaon and Darrang each (91%), Kokrajhar (90%), Kamrup (89%) and Barpeta, Nagaon Cachar each with 88%. Dhemaji district ranks last with only 28% of electrified villages. Karbi-Anglong (41%) ranks 22nd , N.C. Hills (45%) ranks 21st and Karimganj (57%) ranks 20th respectively.

A point to be noted is that, as is evident from tables 5.11 and 5.14, infrastructurally advanced districts like N.C. Hills and Jorhat have not been able to make much headway with regards to rural electrification. Whereas, Nalbari which ranks first in village electrification is also relatively sound infrastructurally.

Table 5.11
Percentage of Villages Electrified in Districts of Assam

Sl No	*District*	*% of Villages Electrified*	*Rank*
1.	Dhubri	78	14
2.	Kokrajhar	90	5
3.	Bongaigaon	91	3.5
4.	Goalpara	85	10.5
5.	Barpeta	88	8
6.	Nalbari	97	1
7.	Kamrup	89	6
8.	Darrang	91	3.5
9.	Sonitpur	81	13
10.	Lakhimpur	73	15.5
11.	Dhemaji	28	23
12.	Marigaon	73	15.5
13.	Nagaon	88	8
14.	Golaghat	61	19
15.	Jorhat	72	17
16.	Sibsagar	92	2
17.	Dibrugarh	83	12
18.	Tinsukia	71	18
19.	Karbi-Anglong	41	22
20.	N.C. Hills	45	21
21.	Karimganj	57	20
22.	Hailakandi	85	10.5
23.	Cachar	88	8
	Assam	74	
	C.V.	23.49	

Source: Computed from *Statistical Hand Book*, Assam, 1997.

5.3.12. Postal Services

In respect of postal services in Assam, the state has been recording steady growth. However, inspite of some improvement registered in the postal services in Assam in the past few years, the position of the state in this regard is found not much satisfactory in comparison to the position of India as a whole. According to

1991 census, there is a total of 3044 post offices in the state and thus the number of post offices serving per 10,000 population is 1.36 as shown in *Table 5.12.*

Table 5.12

Number of Post Offices per 10,000 of Population in districts of Assam

Sl No	*District*	*No. of Post Office per 10,000 of Population*	*Rank*
1.	Dhubri	0.990	20
2.	Kokrajhar	1.150	17
3.	Bongaigaon	1.350	11
4.	Goalpara	0.980	21
5.	Barpeta	1.340	12
6.	Nalbari	2.020	1
7.	Kamrup	0.930	22
8.	Darrang	1.050	18.5
9.	Sonitpur	1.282	14
10.	Lakhimpur	1.810	4
11.	Dhemaji	1.230	16
12.	Marigaon	1.280	15
13.	Nagaon	1.400	10
14.	Golaghat	1.530	7
15.	Jorhat	1.850	3
16.	Sibsagar	1.290	13
17.	Dibrugarh	1.522	8
18.	Tinsukia	1.050	18.5
19.	Karbi-Anglong	0.750	23
20.	N.C. Hills	1.520	9
21.	Karimganj	1.610	6
22.	Hailakandi	1.670	5
23.	Cachar	1.930	2
	Assam	1.36	
	C.V.	24.29	

Source: Statement – 3.IV, Distribution of inhibited villages having different types of Posts & Tele. Facilities in districts of Assam, 1991; Directorate of Census Operations, Assam.

Out of all the 23 districts in the state, Nalbari, Cachar, Jorhat and Lakhimpur occupy the first four positions respectively with regard to this service. In Nagaon, Golaghat, Dibrugarh, N.C. Hills, Karimganj and Hailakandi the scenario is slightly better than that of the state. Goalpara, Kamrup and Karbi-Anglong occupy last three ranks with less than one post office per 10,000 population. It is surprising to see from *Table 5.12* and *Table-6.14* that infrastructurally relatively better placed Kamrup district ranks 22nd in this regard whereas backward Cachar district occupies second rank.

The C.V. value shows 24% inequality in setting up post offices in 23 districts of the state.

5.3.13. Number of Banks per Lakh Population in Districts of Assam

Banking and other institutional financing facilities are an important part of economic infrastructure of a region. They play an important role by generating multiple effects in the modernization of a backward economy. So to say, organized financial institutions are one of the core indicators of development of basic infrastructural facilities in a backward region. Thus from this point of view an attempt is made to see the disparity in location of commercial banks in different districts of Assam.

Table 5.13 shows that up to December 1997, there is a total of 1241 numbers of commercial banks in Assam and around 5.45 banks serving per lakh of state population. The two hills districts namely N.C. Hills and Karbi-Anglong along with Kamrup in Brahmaputra Valley occupy the first three ranks with 10.61, 8.15 and 7.75 banks per lakh population respectively. In upper Assam Jorhat, Tinsukia, Dibrugarh and Sibsagar also depict better picture in comparison to the state in this regard. Dhubri (3.00), Dhemaji (3.34), Kokrajhar (3.37), Darrang (4.00), Hailakandi (4.01), Marigaon (4.38) and Nagaon (4.54) occupy lower ranks. The C.V. for number of Banks per lakh population in the districts of the state reveals around 31 per cent variation.

Table 5.13
Districtwise Distribution of the No. of Reporting Offices of Commercial Banks in Assam

Sl. No.	*District*	*No. of Reporting Office (Bank)*	*No. of Banks per Lakh Population*	*Rank*
1.	Dhubri	40	3.00	23
2.	Kokrajhar	26	3.37	21
3.	Bongaigaon	40	4.71	15
4.	Goalpara	38	5.69	10
5.	Barpeta	63	4.55	16
6.	Nalbari	51	5.02	14
7.	Kamrup	161	7.75	3
8.	Darrang	52	4.00	20
9.	Sonitpur	81	5.55	12
10.	Lakhimpur	48	6.65	6
11.	Dhemaji	17	3.34	22
12.	Marigaon	28	4.38	18
13.	Nagaon	88	4.54	17
14.	Golaghat	47	5.19	13
15.	Jorhat	60	6.77	5
16.	Sibsagar	57	6.17	8
17.	Dibrugarh	69	6.52	7
18.	Tinsukia	69	6.96	4
19.	Karbi-Anglong	54	8.15	2
20.	N.C. Hills	16	10.61	1
21.	Karimganj	47	5.92	9
22.	Hailakandi	20	4.01	19
23.	Cachar	69	5.59	11
	Assam	1241	5.45	–
	C.V.	–	30.96	–

Source: Calculated from *Statistical Hand Book*, Assam, 1997

5.4. BIS DISPARITY SCENARIO

It may be observed from *Table-6.14* that according to the Indexing Method 8 districts out of 23 in the state namely N.C. Hills, Jorhat, Kamrup, Lakhimpur, Dibrugarh, Karbi-Anglong, Sibsagar and Nalbari are reported to be relatively developed (RD) districts in descending order from BIS point of view. This method places both the hills districts – N.C. Hills and Karbi-Anglong together with Kamrup and Nalbari and in lower Assam and Jorhat, Dibrugarh and Sibsagar in upper assam as relatively developed. The rest 15 districts are found to be backward (B). The C.V. value of BISDI for all the district is calculated at 23.13% as shown in Table 5.14.

Table 5.14
Basic Infrastructure and Services (BIS) Ranking of Districts of Assam by Indexing Method and Deprivation Method

Sl. No.	*District*	*Indexing Method*			*Deprivation Method*		
		BISDI Value	*Rank*	*Status*	*BISDI Value*	*Value*	*Rank*
01	Dhubri	82.570	22	B	0.251	22	B
02	Kokrajhar	84.210	21	B	0.249	23	B
03	Bongaigaon	94.420	15	B	0.354	10	B
04	Goalpara	98.070	10.50	B	0.317	14	B
05	Barpeta	95.640	13	B	0.318	13	B
06	Nalbari	103.660	8	RD	0.477	4	B
07	Kamrup	132.640	3	RD	0.532	3	MD
08	Darrang	91.500	16.50	B	0.293	17	B
09	Sonitpur	95.500	14	B	0.314	15	B
10	Lakhimpur	113.210	4	RD	0.461	5	B
11	Dhemaji	91.500	16.50	B	0.264	20	B
12	Marigaon	90.280	18	B	0.305	16	B
13	Nagaon	98.640	9	B	0.379	8	B
14	Golaghat	96.920	12	B	0.324	11	B
15	Jorhat	140.210	2	RD	0.536	2	MD
16	Sibsagar	108.640	7	RD	0.427	6	B
17	Dibrugarh	110.420	5	RD	0.392	7	B
18	Tinsukia	85.710	20	B	0.254	21	B
19	Karbi Anglong	109.710	6	RD	0.286	18	B
20	N.C. Hills	194.350	1	RD	0.658	1	MD
21	Karimganj	89.140	19	B	0.321	12	B
22	Hailakandi	81.860	23	B	0.271	19	B
23	Cachar	98.070	10.50	B	0.376	9	B
	C.V.	23.13			28.87		

N.B. : (i) BISDI Implies Basic Infrastructure and Services Development Index and these values are taken from Table 5.15 and 5.16.

(ii) B refers to Backward, RD refers to Relatively Developed and MD refers to Moderately Developed.

(iii) While Indexing Method is a relative measure of development, Deprivation Method is an absolute measure of development.

On the other hand, Deprivation Method places only 3 districts as moderately developed. In descending order they are N.C. Hills, Jorhat and Kamrup. All the rest 20 districts are reported to be backward by this method. The C.V. value of BISDI is found to be 28.87% as shown in Table 5.14.

Both the methods place N.C. Hills in the first, Jorhat in the second and Kamrup in the third position so far as infrastructural development is concerned. Thus out of 23 districts of the state only those 3 districts should be regarded as relatively or moderately developed in respect to BIS.

The reason for N.C. Hills being ranked first in respect to BIS by both the methods may possibly be the concentration of large population of the district around the district head-quarters of Haflong Township which is relatively well developed with respect to most of the 14 BIS indicators we have chosen. The reason for Jorhat being placed in the 2nd position is due to a good network of high schools and colleges, highest literacy in the state, better urbanization, good share of workers in the tertiary sector, good roadways and road transport facilities and better postal services in the district in comparison to other counterparts in the state.

Kamrup being placed at the third position is perhaps due to the capital city of Guwahati, higher literacy, highest urbanisation, highest share of work force in the tertiary sector, good medical facilities, good amount of rural electrification and a very good banking network.

REFERENCES

Medhi, S. B. (1978). *Transport System and Economic Development in Assam* – Publication Board of Assam, p. 1.

Meher, Rajkishor (1999). *"Development Disparities in a Backward Region (A District Level Analysis)"*, APH Publishing Corporation, New Delhi.

Mehta, V. (2000). "Three weakest links in economic reforms" – *The Assam Tribune*, April 21.

Prasad, S. (2000). "Steady growth in infrastructure" – *The Assam Tribune*, May 25.

Saxena, K. K. and Sahoo, S. (1998). *"Infrastructure and economic development: A case study of Kanpur City" – Indian Jurnal of Regional Science*, 30(1).

Shukla, N and Dhagat, S. (1999). *"Disparities of economic development in India – A factor analysis approach." Indian Journal of Regional Science*, 31(1).

Table 5.15

Development Indicators and Indices of Basic Infrastructure and Services (BIS) in Districts of Assam (By Indexing Method)

Sl. No.	District	% of Literacy	% of Urban Population	% of Territory sector workers	No. of Primary and Middle Schools per 10,000 population	No. of High schools per 10,000 population	No. of Colleges per lakh Population	No. of Hospitals/Dispensaries per 10000 population
		X1	X2	X3	X4	X5	X6	X7
01	Dhubri	38.31 (72)	12.16 (110)	18.30 (90)	11.95 (110)	0.90 (73)	0.15 (30)	0.37 (77)
02	Kokrajhar	40.57 (77)	6.34 (57)	13.00 (64)	11.97 (110)	0.76 (62)	0.24 (48)	0.71 (148)
03	Bongaigaon	49.06 (93)	9.15 (83)	20.40 (100)	11.70 (107)	1.08 (88)	0.24 (48)	0.64 (133)
04	Goalpara	46.81 (89)	7.80 (70)	19.90 (98)	13.45 (124)	1.27 (103)	0.89 (178)	0.37 (77)
05	Barpeta	43.24 (82)	7.02 (63)	18.40 (90)	9.49 (87)	1.62 (132)	0.93 (186)	0.43 (90)
06	Nalbari	55.99 (106)	2.31 (21)	22.00 (108)	9.57 (88)	1.56 (127)	0.59 (118)	0.75 (156)
07	Kamrup	65.04 (123)	32.76 (295)	42.50 (208)	7.29 (67)	1.24 (101)	0.54 (108)	0.52 (108)
08	Darrang	42.00 (79)	4.93 (44)	12.90 (63)	11.00 (101)	1.10 (89)	0.76 (152)	0.49 (102)
09	Sonitpur	48.14 (91)	7.30 (66)	18.30 (90)	9.41 (87)	1.04 (85)	0.21 (42)	0.44 (92)
10	Lakhimpur	58.96 (111)	6.54 (59)	16.20 (79)	18.16 (167)	2.67 (217)	0.53 (106)	0.48 (100)

11	Dhemaji	53.84	1.86	12.20	19.42	1.56	0.62	0.41
		(102)	(17)	(60)	(179)	(127)	(124)	(85)
12	Marigaon	47.99	5.16	13.10	16.77	1.37	0.31	0.37
		(91)	(47)	(64)	(154)	(111)	(62)	(77)
13	Nagaon	54.74	10.87	19.90	14.48	0.94	0.26	0.51
		(103)	(98)	(98)	(133)	(76)	(52)	(106)
14	Golaghat	58.54	5.90	15.10	11.01	1.47	0.72	0.53
		(111)	(53)	(74)	(101)	(120)	(144)	(110)
15	Jorhat	65.51	15.27	24.30	10.59	2.31	1.95	0.62
		(124)	(138)	(119)	(98)	(188)	(390)	(129)
16	Sibsagar	64.46	7.23	17.70	10.57	1.65	0.66	0.44
		(122)	(65)	(87)	(98)	(134)	(132)	(92)
17	Dibrugarh	58.32	17.61	23.00	12.15	1.12	0.38	0.33
		(110)	(159)	(113)	(112)	(91)	(76)	(69)
18	Tinsukia	50.28	16.49	18.20	9.85	0.69	0.20	0.32
		(95)	(149)	(89)	(91)	(56)	(40)	(67)
19	Karbi Anglong	45.57	10.63	11.60	14.22	0.98	0.30	0.81
		(86)	(96)	(57)	(131)	(80)	(60)	(169)
20	N.C. Hills	57.76	22.87	29.40	33.75	0.99	0.66	0.99
		(109)	(206)	(144)	(311)	(80)	(132)	(206)
21	Karimganj	54.71	7.30	23.60	11.55	0.58	0.50	0.42
		(103)	(66)	(116)	(106)	(47)	(100)	(87)
22	Hailakandi	53.07	7.60	17.70	10.51	0.62	0.50	0.22
		(100)	(69)	(87)	(98)	(50)	(100)	(46)
23	Cachar	59.19	9.81	24.60	9.12	0.95	0.49	0.32
		(112)	(88)	(121)	(84)	(77)	(98)	(67)
	Assam	52.89	11.09	20.40	10.86	1.23	0.50	0.48
		(100)	(100)	(100)	(100)	(100)	(100)	(100)
	C.V.	14.56	66.95	33.48	40.83	40.05	67.45	35.62

(contd...)

Table 5.15 Contd...

Sl. No.	District	No. of Medical Beds per 10000 population	Infant Mortality per 1000 Births	Road Length Per 100 sq.km. area	Road Length per Lakh population	% of Villages electrified	No. of Post Offices per 10000 population	No. of Banks per lakh population	BIS Development Index
		X8	X9	X10	X11	X12	X13	X14	
01	Dhubri	4.13 (72)	128 (139)	39.30 (93)	84 (57)	78 (105)	0.99 (73)	3.00 (55)	82.57
02	Kokrajhar	4.43 (77)	78 (85)	40.60 (96)	128 (86)	90 (122)	1.15 (85)	3.37 (62)	84.21
03	Bongaigaon	2.93 (51)	122 (133)	40.60 (96)	120 (81)	91 (123)	1.35 (100)	4.71 (86)	94.42
04	Goalpara	1.48 (26)	106 (115)	40.60 (96)	155 (105)	85 (115)	0.98 (73)	5.69 (104)	98.07
05	Barpeta	2.22 (39)	101 (110)	40.60 (95)	94 (64)	88 (119)	1.34 (99)	4.55 (83)	95.64
06	Nalbari	5.06 (88)	96 (104)	68.80 (163)	153 (103)	97 (131)	2.02 (150)	5.02 (92)	103.66
07	Kamrup	12.43 (217)	77 (84)	56.00 (133)	122 (82)	89 (120)	0.93 (69)	7.75 (142)	132.64
08	Darrang	3.25 (57)	111 (121)	47.60 (113)	128 (86)	91 (123)	1.05 (78)	4.00 (73)	91.50
09	Sonitpur	11.77 (205)	77 (84)	38.70 (92)	144 (97)	81 (109)	1.28 (95)	5.55 (102)	95.50
10	Lakhimpur	4.20 (73)	112 (122)	44.50 (105)	135 (91)	73 (99)	1.81 (134)	6.65 (122)	113.21
11	Dhemaji	4.38 (76)	114 (124)	28.40 (67)	192 (130)	28 (38)	1.23 (91)	3.34 (61)	91.50
12	Marigaon	2.5 (44)	88 (96)	62.50 (148)	142 (96)	73 (99)	1.28 (95)	4.38 (80)	90.28

13	Nagaon	3.73	97	62.50	135	88	1.40	4.54	98.64
		(65)	(105)	(148)	(91)	(119)	(104)	(83)	
14	Golaghat	4.25	61	41.00	173	61	1.53	5.19	96.92
		(74)	(66)	(97)	(117)	(82)	(113)	(95)	
15	Jorhat	5.92	47	58.00	190	72	1.85	6.77	140.21
		(103)	(51)	(137)	(128)	(97)	(137)	(124)	
16	Sibsagar	4.05	75	70.10	206	92	1.29	6.17	108.64
		(71)	(82)	(166)	(139)	(124)	(96)	(113)	
17	Dibrugarh	13.38	51	40.00	130	83	1.52	6.52	110.42
		(233)	(55)	(95)	(88)	(112)	(113)	(120)	
18	Tinsukia	3.02	73	35.60	140	71	1.05	6.96	85.71
		(53)	(79)	(84)	(95)	(96)	(78)	(128)	
19	Karbi Anglong	7.03	76	30.10	474	41	0.75	8.15	109.71
		(122)	(83)	(71)	(320)	(55)	(56)	(150)	
20	N.C. Hills	14.98	108	32.40	1050	45	1.52	10.61	194.35
		(261)	(117)	(77)	(709)	(61)	(113)	(195)	
21	Karimganj	2	111	42.30	92	57	1.61	5.92	89.14
		(35)	(121)	(100)	(62)	(77)	(119)	(109)	
22	Hailakandi	1.78	99	33.10	98	85	1.67	4.01	81.86
		(31)	(108)	(78)	(66)	(115)	(124)	(74)	
23	Cachar	8.11	97	25.60	80	88	1.93	5.59	98.07
		(141)	(105)	(61)	(54)	(119)	(143)	(103)	
	Assam	5.74	92	42.20	148.00	74	1.35	5.45	
		(100)	(100)	(100)	(100)	(100)	(100)	(100)	(100)
	C.V.	69.76	23.54	28.10	104.68	23.49	24.29	30.96	

N.B. : Figures in parentheses refer to the values of indices computed on the basis of state average as100.

Sources :
(i) Statistical Hand Book of Assam 1997, Directorate of Economics and Statistics, Govt. of Assam.
(ii) Statement 3.1, "Distribution of inhabited villages having different types of educational facilities in district of Assam, 1991, Directorate of census operations, Assam.
(iii) *Economic Survey of Assam*,1997-98

Table 5.16
Development Indices for Basis Infrastructure and Services (BIS) in Districts of Assam (by Deprivation Method)

Sl. No.	District	X1	X2	X3	X4	X5	X6	X7	X8	X9	X10	X11	X12	X13	X14	Total	Average Deprivation Index	BIS Dev-lopment Index
01	Dhubri	1.00	0.66	0.78	0.82	0.85	1.00	0.81	0.80	0.00	0.69	0.99	0.28	0.81	1.00	10.49	0.749	0.251
02	Kokrajhar	0.92	0.85	0.95	0.82	0.91	0.95	0.36	0.78	0.62	0.66	0.95	0.10	0.69	0.95	10.51	0.751	0.249
03	Bongaigaon	0.60	0.76	0.72	0.83	0.76	0.95	0.45	0.89	0.07	0.66	0.96	0.09	0.53	0.78	9.05	0.646	0.354
04	Goalpara	0.69	0.81	0.73	0.77	0.67	0.59	0.81	1.00	0.27	0.66	0.92	0.17	0.82	0.65	9.56	0.683	0.317
05	Barpeta	0.82	0.83	0.78	0.92	0.50	0.57	0.72	0.95	0.33	0.68	0.98	0.13	0.54	0.80	9.55	0.682	0.318
06	Nalbari	0.35	0.99	0.66	0.91	0.53	0.76	0.31	0.73	0.40	0.03	0.92	0.00	0.00	0.73	7.32	0.523	0.477
07	Kamrup	0.02	0.00	0.00	1.00	0.68	0.78	0.61	0.19	0.63	0.32	0.96	0.12	0.86	0.38	6.55	0.469	0.532
08	Darrang	0.86	0.90	0.96	0.86	0.75	0.66	0.65	0.87	0.21	0.51	0.95	0.09	0.76	0.87	9.90	0.707	0.293
09	Sonitpur	0.64	0.82	0.78	0.92	0.78	0.97	0.71	0.24	0.63	0.71	0.93	0.23	0.58	0.66	9.60	0.686	0.314
10	Lakhimpur	0.24	0.85	0.85	0.59	0.00	0.79	0.66	0.80	0.20	0.58	0.94	0.35	0.17	0.52	7.54	0.539	0.461
11	Dhemaji	0.43	1.00	0.98	0.54	0.53	0.74	0.75	0.76	0.17	0.94	0.88	1.00	0.62	0.96	10.30	0.736	0.264
12	Marigaon	0.64	0.89	0.95	0.64	0.62	0.91	0.81	0.92	0.49	0.17	0.94	0.35	0.58	0.82	9.73	0.695	0.305
13	Nagaon	0.40	0.71	0.73	0.73	0.83	0.94	0.62	0.83	0.38	0.17	0.94	0.13	0.49	0.80	8.70	0.621	0.379
14	Golaghat	0.26	0.87	0.87	0.86	0.57	0.68	0.60	0.80	0.83	0.65	0.90	0.52	0.34	0.71	9.46	0.676	0.324
15	Jorhat	0.00	0.57	0.59	0.86	0.17	0.00	0.48	0.67	1.00	0.27	0.89	0.36	0.13	0.50	6.49	0.464	0.536
16	Sibsagar	0.04	0.83	0.80	0.88	0.49	0.72	0.71	0.81	0.65	0.00	0.87	0.07	0.57	0.58	8.02	0.573	0.427
17	Dibrugarh	0.26	0.49	0.63	0.82	0.75	0.87	0.86	0.12	0.95	0.68	0.95	0.20	0.39	0.54	8.51	0.608	0.392
18	Tinsukia	0.56	0.53	0.79	0.90	0.95	0.97	0.87	0.86	0.68	0.78	0.94	0.38	0.76	0.48	10.45	0.746	0.254
19	Karbi Anglong	0.73	0.72	1.00	0.74	0.81	0.92	0.23	0.59	0.64	0.90	0.59	0.81	1.00	0.32	10.00	0.714	0.286
20	N.C. Hills	0.29	0.32	0.42	0.00	0.80	0.72	0.00	0.00	0.25	0.85	0.00	0.75	0.39	0.00	4.79	0.342	0.658
21	Karimganj	0.40	0.82	0.61	0.84	1.00	0.81	0.74	0.96	0.21	0.62	0.99	0.57	0.32	0.62	9.51	0.679	0.321
22	Hailakandi	0.46	0.81	0.80	0.88	0.98	0.81	1.00	0.98	0.36	0.83	0.98	0.17	0.28	0.87	10.21	0.729	0.271
23	Cachar	0.23	0.74	0.58	0.93	0.82	0.81	0.87	0.51	0.38	1.00	1.00	0.13	0.07	0.66	8.73	0.624	0.376

N.B.: Calculated from the values of 14 BIS indicators given in Table 5.15 using the formula for Deprivation Method.

6

Inter-District Variation in Overall Economic Development in Assam

6.1 DISPARITIES AS PER INDEXING METHOD AND DEPRIVATION METHOD

Overall development means aggregate development in agriculture, industry and basic services and infrastructure sectors. In Chapter 3 we have noticed that both the Indexing and Deprivation Methods classified Barpeta, Nalbari, Darrang, Marigaon and Nagaon as relatively or moderately developed districts in respect of agricultural development and other 18 districts as backward. In Chapter 4 we have found that both the methods classified only Tinsukia, Dibrigarh, and Kamrup as relatively or moderately developed districts in respect of industrial development and remaining 20 districts as backward. Again, in Chapter 5 we have found that both the methods classified Kamrup, Jorhat and N.C. Hills as relatively or moderately development districts with regard to basic services and infrastructural development and the remaining 20 districts as backward. From the foregoing analysis we have observed that only Kamrup district scores over all other districts as it is relatively or moderately development in respect of two aspects – industry and basic infrastructure and services.

Table 6.1, which contains indices of overall development by both Indexing and Deprivation Methods, shows that Indexing Method has Classified 10 districts out of 23 as relatively developed in respect of overall economic development. These districts in descending order of overall development are N.C. Hills, Kamrup, Jorhat, Dibrugarh, Bongaigaon, Sibsagar, Tinsukia, Nagaon, Sonitpur and Marigaon. All other 13 districts are categorised as backward.

On the other hand, Deprivation Method has classified only three districts namely. Kamrup, N.C. Hills and Jorhat (Jorhat just below and very close to the Border Line and N.C. Hills on the Boarder Line as shown by Deprivation Method) as moderately developed districts with regard to overall economic development and the rest 20 districts as backward.

Table 6.1
Overall Development Index (ODI) values for districts of Assam (By Indexing Method and Deprivation Method)

Sl No	District	Indexing Method			Deprivation Method		
		ODI	Rank	Status	ODI	Rank	Status
1.	Dhubri	82.3243	21	B	0.2840	22	B
2.	Kokrajhar	79.3226	22	B	0.3160	19	B
3.	Bongaigaon	115.0000	5	RD	0.3740	8	B
4.	Goalpara	90.3621	16	B	0.3164	18	B
5.	Barpeta	92.1048	13	B	0.3580	12	B
6.	Nalbari	97.7420	11	B	0.4413	5	B
7.	Kamrup	136.3002	2	RD	0.5168	1	MD
8.	Darrang	89.9464	17	B	0.3274	17	B
9.	Sonitpur	102.9914	9	RD	0.3425	13	B
10.	Lakhimpur	91.6350	14	B	0.3723	9	B
11.	Dhemaji	73.9347	23	B	0.2187	23	B
12.	Marigaon	101.5880	10	RD	0.3693	10	B
13.	Nagaon	105.3548	8	RD	0.4386	6	B
14.	Golaghat	92.8887	12	B	0.3308	15	B
15.	Jorhat	127.5598	3	RD	0.4689 ≅ 0.50	3	B
16.	Sibsagar	108.6450	6	RD	0.4448	4	B
17.	Dibrugarh	120.9012	4	RD	0.4128	7	B
18.	Tinsukia	107.845	7	RD	0.3325	14	B
19.	Karbi-Anglong	91.0158	15	B	0.3030	20	B
20.	N.C. Hills	144.5153	1	RD	0.4988 ≅ 0.50	2	MD
21.	Karimganj	89.8615	18	B	0.3640	11	B
22.	Hailakandi	82.8477	20	B	0.2888	21	B
23.	Cachar	89.2974	19	B	0.3306	16	B
	C.V.	17.69			19.61		

Note:(i) ODI values are computed on the basis of all the 25 indicators of development, which includes 7 for Agriculture, 4 for Industry and 14 for Basic infrastructure and service.

(ii) * Border line means Overall Development Index value of 0.50 by Deprivation Method.

We also observe from *Table 6.1* that both the methods have classified only Kamrup, N.C. Hills and Jorhat, as relatively or moderately developed districts with respect to overall economic development and the rest 20 districts as backward. Dhemaji is adjudged by both the methods as the most backward district in the state. Dhubri, Kokrajhar, Hailakandi, Karimganj, Cachar, Goalpara and Karbi-Anglong are classified as having lower ranks in respect of overall development.

The C.Vs of ODI values by both the methods show less than 20 per cent variation. Thus the disparity in overall development among the districts of Assam cannot be asserted as that prominent. A few infrastructural development indicators and industrial development indicators are mostly responsible for the prevailing inter-district development disparities in Assam as revealed by Indexing and Deprivation Methods.

6.2 DISPARITIES AS PER PRINCIPAL COMPONENT METHOD

Following the method of Principal Component Analysis we have given as input the data matrix of order 23 × 25 as given in Table 6.2 and then run principal component analysis programme using SPSS[1] software. The output are (i) the correlation matrix as given in *Table 6.3,* (ii) the initial statistics as given in *Table 6.4,* (iii) the scree plot[2], (iv) the final statistics as given in *Table 6.5,* (v) the matrix of factor loadings[3] before and after VARIMAX Rotation[4] as given in *Table 6.6* and (vi) the factor scores[5] as given in *Table 6.7.*

In Table 6.4 of initial statistics, 25 eigen values for the 25 factors, percentage of variation explained by each factor and cumulative percentage of variations are presented. As principal component analysis is mainly concerned with data condensation, retaining all the 25 factors or principal components seems to be meaningless. The question is how many factors should be retained to represent the original variables (25 in our study). There are two ways to answer this question – (i) To retain those factors whose corresponding eigen values are greater than unity (**Mahmood and Raza**, 1998) and (ii) to plot a scree plot. In *Table 6.4* there are seven eigen values greater than unity and this suggests retaining of 7 factors to represent the input variables. We observe that

Table 6.2
Values of 25 Indicators of Economic Development for Districts of Assam

District	Agri Indicators							Industrial Indicators				BIS Indicators			
	X1	X2	x3	x4	x5	x6	x7	x8	x9	x10	x11	x12	x13	x14	x15
Dhubri	60.573	86.982	9.524	153.061	787.400	36.341	19.448	5.900	1.108	1.116	20.436	38.310	12.160	18.300	11.950
Kokrajhar	34.505	79.630	24.483	168.600	823.600	30.863	8.655	3.000	1.412	0.828	15.659	40.570	6.340	13.000	11.970
Bongaigaon	48.400	80.165	10.109	155.670	774.400	39.626	16.847	4.600	4.639	38.208	13.147	49.060	9.150	20.400	11.700
Goalpara	49.457	86.813	14.480	129.114	869.600	41.299	20.853	5.000	0.372	2.380	16.474	46.810	7.800	19.900	13.450
Barpeta	62.424	89.320	30.166	175.540	801.400	41.257	14.606	5.200	0.312	1.452	9.553	43.240	7.020	18.400	9.490
Nalbari	79.808	90.361	11.870	132.000	916.000	54.827	18.868	6.500	0.579	3.283	8.418	55.990	2.310	22.000	9.570
Kamrup	54.036	74.689	18.156	123.333	873.500	42.729	27.810	12.200	3.833	8.130	104.718	65.040	32.760	42.500	7.290
Darrang	72.989	81.890	24.192	129.327	790.000	79.025	20.877	3.200	1.275	2.266	2.125	42.000	4.930	12.900	11.000
Sonitpur	35.526	88.888	30.428	139.881	845.800	29.221	12.127	3.900	2.703	18.696	25.544	48.140	7.300	18.300	9.410
Lakhimpur	45.957	87.963	10.902	172.632	726.200	30.211	1.317	3.300	0.952	1.702	12.296	58.960	6.540	16.200	18.160
Dhemaji	39.198	53.543	7.751	141.176	876.400	24.518	1.833	2.300	0.122	3.252	2.780	53.840	1.860	12.200	19.420
Marigaon	72.327	83.478	16.339	137.500	888.600	60.362	69.977	4.700	1.659	2.737	5.281	47.990	5.160	13.100	16.770
Nagaon	64.964	89.513	36.195	160.669	854.000	65.184	25.419	5.700	1.289	2.144	37.066	54.740	10.870	19.900	14.480
Golaghat	46.045	73.619	13.387	140.000	916.200	40.899	10.404	4.200	3.390	1.453	43.689	58.540	5.900	15.100	11.010
Jorhat	89.123	70.857	9.775	130.645	813.400	36.381	17.327	6.900	5.632	1.251	63.837	65.510	15.270	24.300	10.590
Sibsagar	67.308	80.571	11.099	113.475	1000.250	27.505	15.125	7.000	5.978	0.869	68.215	64.460	7.230	17.700	10.570
Dibrugarh	51.622	72.000	8.880	132.539	877.600	31.720	19.059	8.300	10.612	5.625	86.956	58.320	17.610	23.000	12.150
Tinsukia	55.409	45.714	5.483	138.541	825.200	31.973	20.766	9.900	13.122	2.298	87.862	50.280	16.490	18.200	9.850
Karbi Anglong	12.585	100.000	16.823	139.231	954.600	56.615	1.397	3.600	1.107	2.822	3.641	45.570	10.630	11.600	14.220
N.C. Hills	5.726	100.000	17.843	135.714	856.800	21.753	1.894	7.700	1.892	12.314	3.273	57.760	22.870	29.400	33.750
Karimganj	48.619	69.318	4.741	173.770	927.000	63.768	19.367	7.600	2.998	1.009	22.111	54.710	7.300	23.600	11.550
Hailakandi	42.857	80.702	7.872	134.783	812.500	57.263	20.225	5.300	2.982	0.981	18.085	53.070	7.600	17.700	10.510
Cachar	40.476	73.203	4.801	124.107	872.000	39.865	13.661	6.400	2.487	1.451	28.262	59.190	9.810	24.600	9.120

District	x16	x17	x18	x19	x20	x21	x22	x23	x24	x25
Dhubri	0.900	0.150	0.370	4.130	128.000	39.300	84.000	78.000	0.990	3.000
Kokrajhar	0.760	0.240	0.710	4.430	78.000	40.600	128.000	90.000	1.150	3.370
Bongaigaon	1.077	0.240	0.640	2.930	122.000	40.600	120.000	91.000	1.350	4.710
Goalpara	1.270	0.890	0.370	1.480	106.000	40.600	155.000	85.000	0.980	5.690
Barpeta	1.620	0.930	0.430	2.220	101.000	40.000	94.000	88.000	1.340	4.550
Nalbari	1.560	0.590	0.750	5.060	96.000	68.800	153.000	97.000	2.020	5.020
Kamrup	1.240	0.540	0.520	12.430	77.000	56.000	122.000	89.000	0.930	7.750
Darrang	1.100	0.760	0.490	3.250	111.000	47.600	128.000	91.000	1.050	4.000
Sonitpur	1.040	0.210	0.440	11.770	77.000	38.700	144.000	81.000	1.280	5.550
Lakhimpur	2.670	0.530	0.480	4.200	112.000	44.500	135.000	73.000	1.810	6.650
Dhemaji	1.560	0.620	0.410	4.380	114.000	28.400	192.000	28.000	1.230	3.340
Marigaon	1.370	0.310	0.370	2.500	88.000	62.500	142.000	73.000	1.280	4.380
Nagaon	0.940	0.260	0.510	3.730	97.000	62.500	135.000	88.000	1.400	4.540
Golaghat	1.470	0.720	0.530	4.250	61.000	41.000	173.000	61.000	1.530	5.190
Jorhat	2.310	1.950	0.620	5.920	47.000	58.000	190.000	72.000	1.850	6.770
Sibsagar	1.650	0.660	0.440	4.050	75.000	70.100	206.000	92.000	1.290	6.170
Dibrugarh	1.120	0.380	0.330	13.380	51.000	40.000	130.000	83.000	1.520	6.520
Tinsukia	0.690	0.200	0.320	3.020	73.000	35.600	140.000	71.000	1.050	6.960
Karbi Anglong	0.980	0.300	0.810	7.030	76.000	30.100	474.000	41.000	0.750	8.150
N.C. Hills	0.990	0.660	0.990	14.980	108.000	32.400	1050.000	45.000	1.520	10.610
Karimganj	0.580	0.500	0.420	2.000	111.000	42.300	92.000	57.000	1.610	5.920
Hailakandi	0.620	0.500	0.220	1.780	99.000	33.100	98.000	85.000	1.970	4.010
Cachar	0.950	0.490	0.320	8.110	97.000	25.600	80.000	88.000	1.930	5.590

Table 6.3
Correlation matrix

	V-01	V-02	V-03	V-04	V-05	V-06	V-07	V-08	V-09	V-10	V-11	V-12	V-13	V-14	V-15	V-16	V-17	V-18	V-19	V-20	V-21	V-22	V-23	V-24	V-25
V-01	1.0000																								
V-02	-0.2214	1.0000																							
V-03	-0.0048	0.5145	1.0000																						
V-04	-0.1187	0.1154	0.2632	1.0000																					
V-05	-0.0922	-0.0001	-0.1287	-0.4490	1.0000																				
V-06	0.3411	0.2010	0.2173	0.0553	0.0778	1.0000																			
V-07	0.5419	-0.0597	0.0624	-0.1627	0.0789	0.4595	1.0000																		
V-08	0.1651	-0.2709	-0.2533	-0.3272	0.2047	-0.1079	0.2251	1.0000																	
V-09	0.1388	-0.5940	-0.3871	-0.2849	0.0693	-0.2764	0.0899	0.5931	1.0000																
V-10	-0.2302	0.1295	0.0725	0.0411	-0.2384	-0.2012	-0.0631	-0.0202	0.1065	1.0000															
V-11	0.2667	-0.4968	-0.1909	-0.3786	0.1862	-0.2615	0.1250	0.7732	0.7815	-0.0767	1.0000														
V-12	0.1297	-0.2317	-0.3431	-0.4136	0.3286	-0.2460	-0.0824	0.5062	0.3292	-0.0489	0.5603	1.0000													
V-13	-0.1729	-0.0457	-0.0206	-0.2661	-0.0339	-0.2448	0.0204	0.7999	0.4188	0.1532	0.6518	0.3850	1.0000												
V-14	0.0155	-0.0128	-0.0865	-0.2542	0.0454	-0.1491	0.0546	0.8241	0.2014	0.1965	0.5407	0.5644	0.8175	1.0000											
V-15	-0.5148	0.2949	0.0293	0.0890	-0.0476	-0.2771	-0.2048	-0.1601	-0.2457	0.0929	-0.4073	0.0459	0.1144	-0.0270	1.0000										
V-16	0.3731	0.0737	-0.0463	-0.0015	-0.1721	-0.2723	-0.1204	-0.1825	-0.1485	-0.1215	0.0183	0.4204	-0.1367	-0.0382	0.0836	1.0000									
V-17	0.4033	-0.0657	-0.0868	-0.2229	-0.0345	-0.0443	-0.1027	0.0539	-0.0465	-0.2465	0.1025	0.4100	0.0467	0.1797	-0.0140	0.5931	1.0000								
V-18	-0.3379	0.4965	0.2567	0.0615	0.1207	-0.0969	-0.3704	-0.0728	-0.2639	0.2762	-0.2694	0.0452	0.1841	0.1328	0.4896	0.1044	0.1232	1.0000							
V-19	-0.4214	0.1780	0.1054	-0.3487	0.1381	-0.4144	-0.2359	0.4003	0.2056	0.2552	0.3348	0.3741	0.6600	0.5710	0.3000	-0.0466	-0.0560	0.3614	1.0000						
V-20	-0.1363	0.2296	-0.0238	0.3808	-0.3717	0.1826	-0.0696	-0.3052	-0.5670	0.2046	-0.6575	-0.4277	-0.2879	-0.1107	0.3016	-0.1482-	0.2914	0.0306	-0.3513	1.0000					
V-21	0.7345	0.1592	0.2246	-0.1771	0.2514	0.2800	0.5041	0.2296	0.0082	-0.1205	0.2581	0.3237	-0.0212	0.1553	-0.2210	0.3742	0.2203	0.0936	-0.1512	-0.2226	1.0000				
V-22	-0.5965	0.4086	0.0782	-0.1651	0.1857	-0.2666	-0.3322	0.0771	-0.0967	0.1476	-0.2147	0.1308	0.3506	0.1727	0.8296	-0.0529	0.0778	0.7161	0.5219	0.0271	-0.2081	1.0000			
V-23	0.5390	0.1600	0.2482	-0.0861	-0.2283	0.2077	0.3338	0.1881	0.1010	0.0984	0.2362	-0.0546	-0.0074	0.1952	-0.6002	-0.0195	-0.0446	-0.2556	-0.1452	-0.0428	0.4725	-0.5326	1.0000		
V-24	0.1985	-0.0168	-0.3149	0.0309	-0.0986	-0.0054	-0.0725	0.0232	0.0012	-0.0771	-0.0766	0.5133	-0.2123	0.1397	0.0202	0.2900	0.3165	-0.0531	0.0014	-0.0431	0.1127	-0.0653	0.1559	1.0000	
V-25	-0.4115	0.1836	-0.1077	-0.2792	0.2469	-0.2752	-0.2520	0.5202	0.3048	0.1194	0.3165	0.5080	0.6576	0.5291	0.4272	0.1057	0.1814	0.4824	0.6310	-0.3148	-0.0664	0.7147	-0.3223	-0.0008	1.0000

though the cumulative percentage of variation explained by these 7 factors is around 80 per cent, the contribution of the four factors after the first three is not so significant. These four factors jointly contribute to explain around 27 per cent of variation whereas the first three factors explain little more than 53 per cent of total variation. Again, the cumulative contribution of the last 18 factors is only 20 per cent. So retaining these 18 factors will not do any good. First seven factors are good enough to represent the 25 original variables.

Table 6.4
Initial Statistics

Variable	*Communality*	*Factor*	*Eigen value*	*Pct of Var*	*Cum Pct*
V-01	1	1	5.7193	22.9	22.9
V-02	1	2	4.8839	19.5	42.4
V-03	1	3	2.7170	10.9	53.3
V-04	1	4	2.4517	9.8	63.1
V-05	1	5	1.8123	7.2	70.3
V-06	1	6	1.3700	5.5	75.8
V-07	1	7	1.0681	4.3	80.1
V-08	1	8	0.9501	3.8	83.9
V-09	1	9	0.7727	3.1	87
V-10	1	10	0.6928	2.8	89.8
V-11	1	11	0.6743	2.7	92.4
V-12	1	12	0.5053	2	94.5
V-13	1	13	0.4024	1.6	96.1
V-14	1	14	0.3072	1.2	97.3
V-15	1	15	0.2807	1.1	98.4
V-16	1	16	0.1658	0.7	99.1
V-17	1	17	0.1120	0.4	99.5
V-18	1	18	0.0632	0.3	99.8
V-19	1	19	0.0285	0.1	99.9
V-20	1	20	0.0106	0	100
V-21	1	21	0.0089	0	100
V-22	1	22	0.0030	0	100
V-23	1	23	0.0000	0	100
V-24	1	24	0.0000	0	100
V-25	1	25	0.0000	0	100

On the other hand the scree plot suggests to retain only the first fhree factors as an elbow occurs at factor number 3. Thus the first three factors effectively summarize the total variance. For our analysis we prefer to be guided by the scree plot.

Table 6.5
Final Statistics

Variable	*Communality*	*Factor*	*Eigen value*	*Pct of Var*	*Cum Pct*
V-01	0.86304	1	5.7193	22.9	22.9
V-02	0.49027	2	4.88386	19.5	42.4
V-03	0.15064	3	2.717	10.9	53.3
V-04	0.31007				
V-05	0.09852				
V-06	0.27362				
V-07	0.31178				
V-08	0.76894				
V-09	0.70096				
V-10	0.11668				
V-11	0.90368				
V-12	0.71586				
V-13	0.71163				
V-14	0.56863				
V-15	0.65946				
V-16	0.5216				
V-17	0.50082				
V-18	0.63895				
V-19	0.66543				
V-20	0.42041				
V-21	0.66304				
V-22	0.85902				
V-23	0.38101				
V-24	0.20739				
V-25	0.81872				

In *Table 6.5* of the final statistics we observe that the communality, which is the amount of a variable's variance that is explained or accounted for by the factors, for variables 1, 8 , 9,

11, 12, 13, 22 and 25 are very high. Therefore, their variation is represented fairly completely by the three factors we have retained. For the remaining variables communalities are relatively lower indicating lesser representation of their respective variations.

Table 6.6
VARIMAX converged in 6 iterations

	Factor Matrix			*Rotated Factor Matrix*		
	Factor 1	*Factor 2*	*Factor 3*	*Factor 1*	*Factor 2*	*Factor 3*
V-01	-0.0608	-0.8359	0.4008	0.0493	-0.7387	0.5612
V-02	-0.2344	0.4640	0.4691	-0.4023	0.4717	0.8255
V-03	-0.2717	0.1532	0.2310	-0.3328	0.1230	0.1574
V-04	-0.5245	0.1646	-0.0886	-0.5247	0.0151	-0.7857
V-05	0.3014	-0.0123	0.0867	0.2782	0.0763	0.1236]
V-06	-0.3925	-0.3126	0.1481	-0.3373	-0.3652	0.8627
V-07	-0.0543	-0.5547	0.0346	0.0583	-0.5356	0.1466
V-08	0.8224	-0.2592	-0.1596	0.8733	-0.0791	0.0022
V-09	0.6246	-0.3531	-0.4316	0.7484	-0.2655	-0.2652
V-10	0.0693	0.2765	-0.1883	0.0405	0.2460	-0.2335
V-11	0.7898	-0.4833	-0.2150	0.8984	-0.3107	-0.0071
V-12	0.7426	-0.1423	0.3797	0.6810	0.1114	0.4896
V-13	0.8139	0.1383	-0.1736	0.7841	0.2954	-0.0981
V-14	0.7514	-0.0179	0.0606	0.7172	0.1741	0.1548
V-15	0.0491	0.7890	0.1856	-0.1497	0.7980	0.0156
V-16	0.0672	-0.0994	0.7122	-0.0346	0.0510	0.7196
V-17	0.2347	-0.1522	0.6501	0.1482	0.0295	0.6914
V-18	0.1504	0.6673	0.4136	-0.0650	0.7477	0.2751
V-19	0.6850	0.4420	-0.0292	0.5719	0.5804	-0.0396
V-20	-0.5784	0.2784	-0.0918	-0.5999	0.1101	-0.2200
V-21	0.1245	-0.5147	0.6185	0.1236	-0.3484	0.7255
V-22	0.3347	0.8427	0.1919	0.1131	0.9188	0.0451
V-23	-0.0535	-0.6053	0.1086	0.0572	-0.5703	0.2292
V-24	0.0849	-0.1506	0.4213	0.0423	-0.0466	0.4510
V-25	0.7514	0.4841	0.1409	0.5982	0.6674	0.1242

In *Table 6.6* the factor loadings for the three unrotated factors are given in the first half (left side of the table). From these factor loadings the interpretation of the factors are somewhat difficult. Here the use of varimax rotation has greatly improved the interpretability of the factors. In the rotated factor matrix we observe that for the first factor higher factor loadings correspond to variables 8, 9, 11, 13 and 14. Variables 8, 9 and 11 are indicators of industrial development. Variable 13 is an indicator of urbanization and variable 14 is an indicator of tertiary sector workforce. Now urbanization and tertiary sectors are direct consequences of industrialization. Therefore, factor 1 may be regarded as Industrial Factor. We also observe that for the second factor higher factor loadings in the rotated factor matrix corresponds to variables 1, 15, 18, 22 and 23. Except variable 1 all these variables are indicators of infrastructural development. Variable 1 is *'per cent of cultivable land to total land area'* which can be viewed as an indicator for agricultural infrastructure. So factor 2 may be regarded as Infrastructural Factor. Lastly, the higher factor loadings for the third factor are related to variable 2, 4 and 6 which are all indicators of agricultural development. Therefore factor 3 may be regarded as agricultural factor.

We also note that Industrial Factors explains around 23 per cent, Infrastructural Factor explains nearly 19 per cent and Agricultural Factor explains around 11 per cent total variation respectively.

We observe from *Table 6.8* that the Principal Component Method classifies 6 districts of the state as moderately developed (MD), 6 districts as developing (D), 6 districts as backward (B) and the remaining 5 districts as very backward (VB). The moderately developed districts are Kamrup, Jorhat, Bongaigaon, Nagaon, Sonitpur and N.C. Hills respectively in descending order. This method has placed N.C. Hills in the 6th rank in contrast to Indexing Method and Deprivation Method which place this district in the first and second position respectively. The ranking of Kamrup district by this method is the same as that by Deprivation Method i.e. both Principal Component Method and Deprivation Method rank Kamrup in the first posittion.

Table 6.7
Factor Scores

Fac 3-1	*Fac 3-2*	*Fac 3-3*
-0.076	0.022	-0.466
-0.991	0.576	0.511
0.155	1.118	0.632
-0.338	-0.244	-0.010
-0.413	0.532	0.490
-0.397	0.806	1.296
3.092	0.621	0.165
-0.774	0.394	0.520
-0.302	1.213	1.161
-0.440	-0.333	0.110
-1.517	-1.578	-1.522
-0.517	-0.107	0.145
0.153	0.606	1.123
-0.844	-0.082	-0.426
0.741	0.228	-0.419
-0.141	0.700	0.022
1.095	0.735	-0.859
1.041	0.030	-2.578
-0.862	-1.653	0.904
1.724	-3.113	1.762
0.029	-0.908	-1.111
-0.476	0.214	-0.760
0.057	0.225	-0.690

The earlier two methods place Jorhat in the 3rd position but Principal Component Method places Jorhat in the 2nd position. Bongaigaon being ranked 5th and 8th respectively by Indexing and Deprivation Methods is ranked 3rd by Principal Component Method. The districts of Nagaon and Sonitpur are better placed in 4th and 5th positions respectively by Principal Component Method whereas these two districts are ranked 8th and 6th and 9th and 13th respectively by Indexing and Deprivation Methods.

We have presented the ODI ranks and status of each of the 23 districts in Table 6.9 for easy viewing of the picture of "overall economic development" as portrayed by the three methods we have used. We observe from this table that all the three methods place Kamrup, Jorhat and N.C. Hills as relatively or moderately developed and thus these districts are considered as the leading districts in the state with Kamrup in the first place in overall economic development so far as our 25 select indicators pertaining to Agriculture, Industry and BIS are concerned. Among the remaining 20 districts, some are developing, some are backward and some are very backward in respect of overall development.

Table 6.8
Overall Development Index (ODI) Values for districts of Assam (By Principal Component Method using Varimax Rotation)

Sl No.	*District*	*ODI (By Principal Component Method)*	*Rank*	*Status*
1.	Dhubri	-0.520	15	B
2.	Kokrajhar	-0.037	12	D
3.	Bongaigaon	1.905	3	MD
4.	Goalpara	-0.592	16	B
5.	Barpeta	0.609	8	D
6.	Nalbari	0.550	10	D
7.	Kamrup	3.878	1	MD
8.	Darrang	0.140	11	D
9.	Sonitpur	1.705	5	MD
10.	Lakhimpur	-0.663	17	B
11.	Dhemaji	-4.617	23	VB
12.	Marigaon	-0.479	14	B
13.	Nagaon	1.882	4	MD
14.	Golaghat	-1.352	19	VB
15.	Jorhat	2.072	2	MD
16.	Sibsagar	0.581	9	D
17.	Dibrugarh	0.921	7	D
18.	Tinsukia	-1.507	20	VB
19.	Karbi-Anglong	-1.611	21	VB
20.	N.C. Hills	0.981	6	MD
21.	Karimganj	-1.990	22	VB
22.	Hailakandi	-1.022	18	B
23.	Cachar	-0.408	13	B

N.B. – (i) V.B refers to very backward, B refers to backward, D refers to developing and MD refers to moderately developed.
(ii) ODI value for each district is the sum of three factors scorewhich are given in Table 5.7.

Table 6.9
Ranking and status of districts of Assam by Indexing, Deprivation and Principal Component Methods

Sl No	*District*	*Indexing Method*		*Deprivation Method*		*Principal Component Method*	
		Rank	*Status*	*Rank*	*Status*	*Rank*	*Status*
1.	Dhubri	21	B	22	B	15	B
2.	Kokrajhar	22	B	19	B	12	D
3.	Bongaigaon	5	RD	8	B	3	MD
4.	Goalpara	16	B	18	B	16	B
5.	Barpeta	13	B	12	B	8	D
6.	Nalbari	11	B	5	B	10	D
7.	Kamrup	2	RD	1	MD	1	MD
8.	Darrang	17	B	17	B	11	D
9.	Sonitpur	9	RD	13	B	5	MD
10.	Lakhimpur	14	B	9	B	17	B
11.	Dhemaji	23	B	23	B	23	VB
12.	Marigaon	10	RD	10	B	14	B
13.	Nagaon	8	RD	6	B	4	MD
14.	Golaghat	12	B	15	B	19	VB
15.	Jorhat	3	RD	3	MD	2	MD
16.	Sibsagar	6	RD	4	B	9	D
17.	Dibrugarh	4	RD	7	B	7	D
18.	Tinsukia	7	RD	14	B	20	VB
19.	Karbi-Anglong	15	B	20	B	21	VB
20.	N.C. Hills	1	RD	2	MD	6	MD
21.	Karimganj	18	B	11	B	22	VB
22.	Hailakandi	20	B	21	B	18	B
23.	Cachar	19	B	16	B	13	B

FOOTNOTES

1. SPSS stands for Statistical Package for Social Sciences.
2. Scree plot is a useful visual aid to determining an appropriate number of principal components. It is a plot (or graph) of eigen values (l_i) versus i – the magnitude of an eigen value versus its number. To determine the appropriate number of components, we look for a elbow (bend) in the scree plot. The number of components is taken to be the point at which the remaining eigen values are relatively small and all about the same size. (Johnson and Wichern, p. 475)
3. Factor loadings are the correlations between the factors and the original variables. They provide an indication of which original variables are correlated with each factor and the extent of the correlation (Aaker and Day, p. 547)
4. Factor analysis is complicated somewhat by the fact that it is possible to generate several factor analysis solutions for any data set. Each solution is termed a particular factor rotation and is generated by a factor rotation scheme. Each time the factors are rotated the pattern of loadings changes as does the interpretation of the factors. When Principal Components are used, the interpretation of the factors can be difficult. The use of 'Varimax Rotation' can improve greatly the interpretability. Varimax rotation scheme searches for a set of factor loadings such that each factor has some loadings close to zero and some loadings close to –1 or +1. (**Aaker and Day**, PP. 549-550).
5. One out put of most factors analysis programmes is values for each factor for all original variables. These values are termed factor scores (**Aaker and Day**, P. 547)

REFERENCES

Aaker, David A and Day, George S. (1990): "*Marketing Research*" (4th Edition) – John Wiley & Sons.

Johnson, Richard A. and Dean W. Wichern (1998): "*Applied Multivariate Statistical Analysis*" (4th Edition) – Prentice-Hall International, Inc., 1998.

Raza, M and Mahmod, A. (1998): "*Statistical Methods in Geographical Studies*" (4th edition), Rajesh Publications, New Delhi, p. 162.

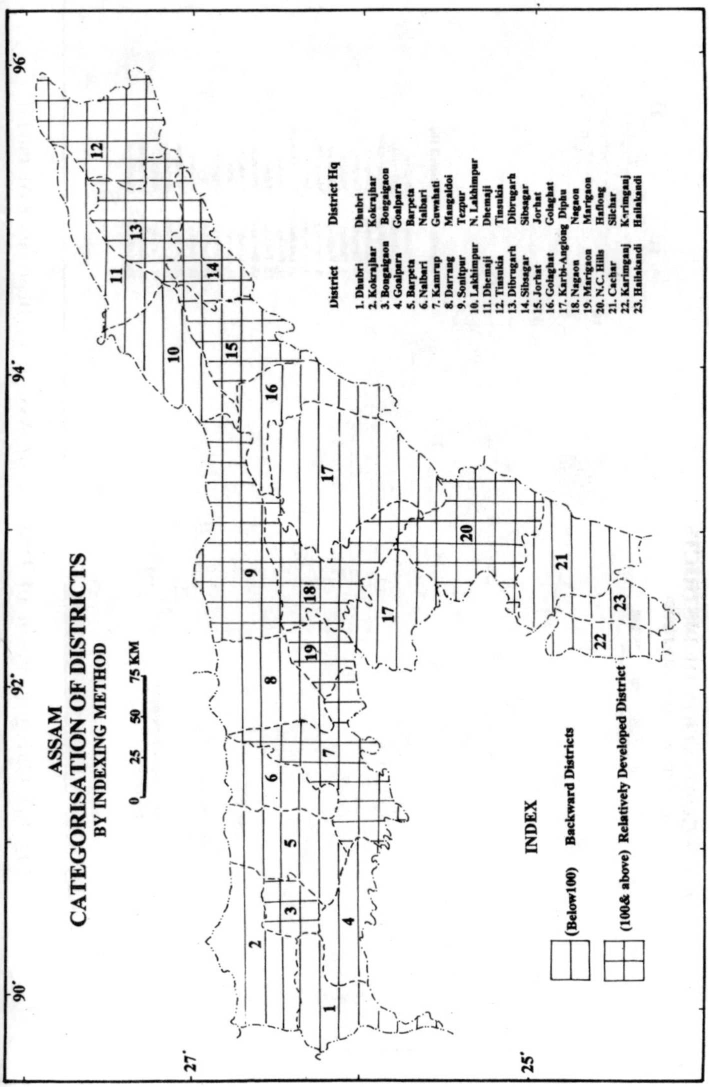

Fig 6.1 Categorisation of Districts of Assam by Indexing Method

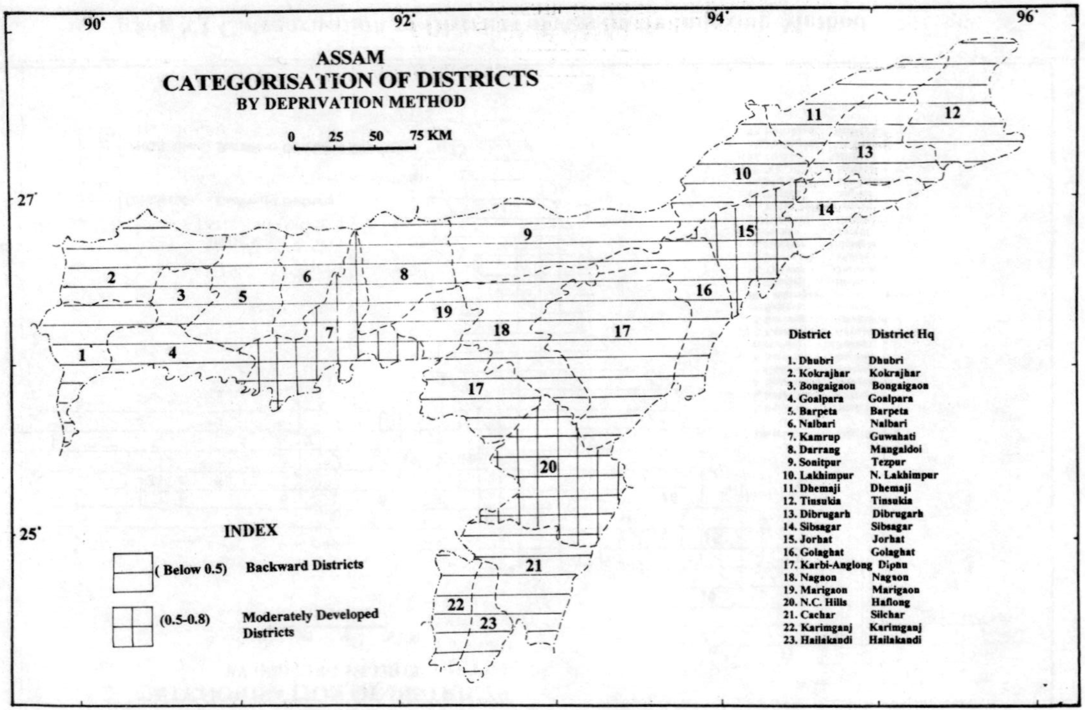

Fig 6.2 Categorisation of District of Assam by Deprivation Method

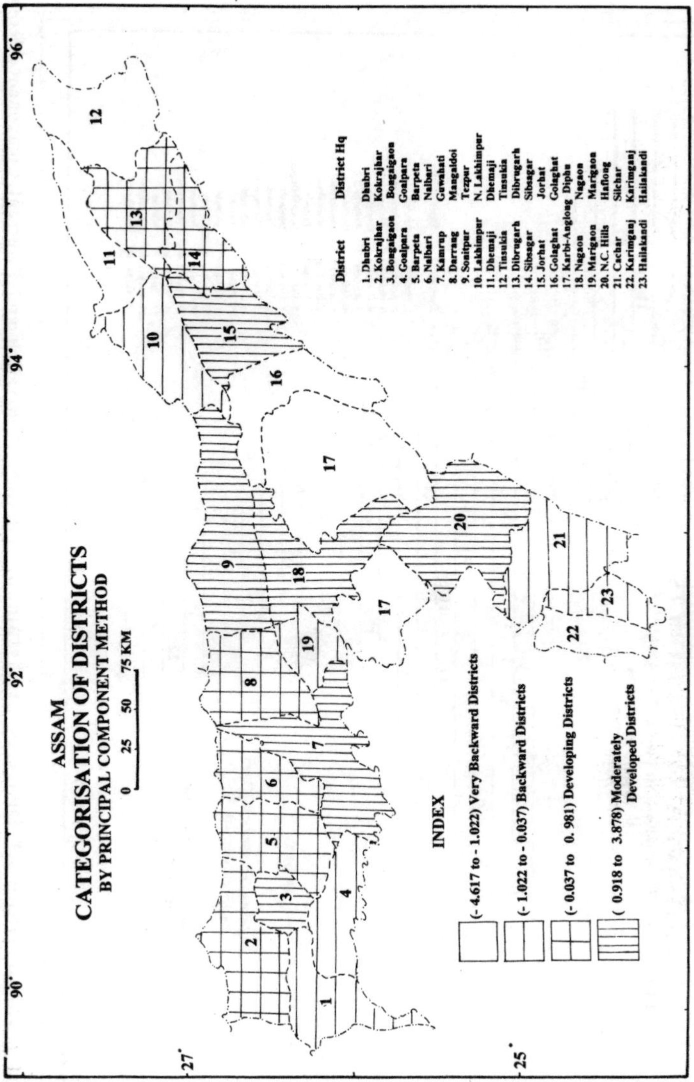

Fig 6.3 Categorisation of District of Assam by Principal Component Method

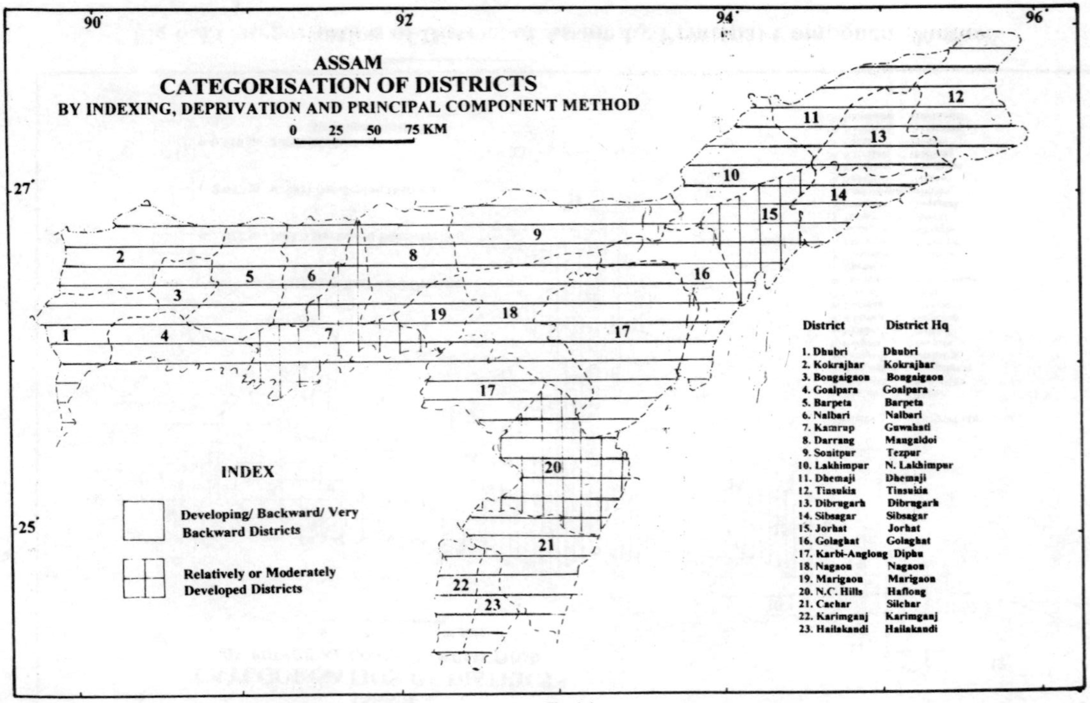

Fig 6.4 Categorisation of Districts of Assam by Indexing, Deprivation and Principal Component Method

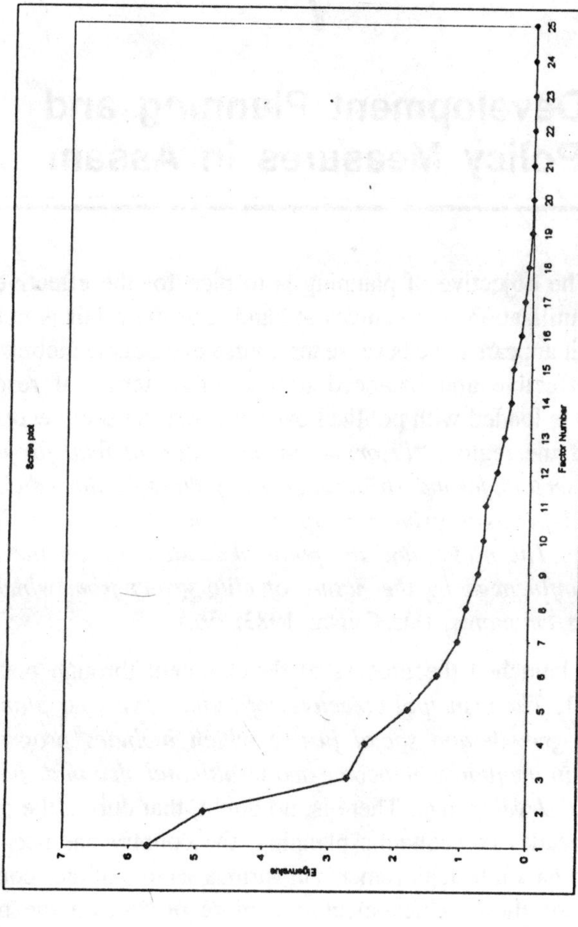

Fig 6.5 Scree plot

7

Development Planning and Policy Measures in Assam

7.1 The objective of planning is to plan for the effective and balanced utilization of resources at hand. But the affair is not that simple as it appears to be because the course of resource mobilization and its effective and balanced utilization in terms of resource allocation is loaded with political overtone and the socio economic climate of the region. "*Priorities in allocation of fund for urban and rural sectors, for industrialization, agriculture, health, education, etc. are dependent primarily upon the policy of the political leadership. The policy and the political leadership, on the other hand, is influenced by the nature of elite group from which the leadership emanates.* (DasGupta, 1983: 56.)

India launched the process of development through planning since 1951. *The principal objectives of India's five year plans are economic growth and social justice which includes progressive reduction in inequality in income and wealth and also in disparities in regional development.* There is, no doubt, that during the period of five decades of economic planning, the country has been able to make remarkable achievements in various sectors of the economy. But most of these achievements are more or less on the macro level and when we come down to the micro level or to be specific, to the state or district level or to levels further down, much is yet to be done to achieve a meaningful economic development based on social justice. One of the glaring failures of Indian Planning is the non-fulfilment of the objective of balanced regional development. The problem has rather aggravated over the years. The widening disparity in the regional development constitutes an important factor causing poverty and deprivation for an increasingly large section of people and thus generating social tension and political unrest. Because of the working of long term forces-historical, geographical, political, sociological and economic, some regions of the country have achieved faster and higher rates of growth, while some other regions have registered a slow and tardy growth rate. The states of North-Eastern Region are typical cases of the latter type of regions. It is not only that the whole region has remained at the stage of relative backwardness in spite of five decades of economic planning, but also there are glaring inter-state differences in economic development in the region as well as inter-district disparities in economic development within a state.

The North Eastern Council (N.E.C) emerges as an effective regional planning authority looking after the balanced development of all the constituent units of the north eastern region. But only blanket measure for all the units will not bring about economic development for all the states of the region and all the districts within a state. A package of measures specific for each area should be there so that the state as a whole might develop evenly.

In a vast agricultural country like India, there are naturally different levels of economic development which can be identified as economically backward regions, districts, sub-divisions, blocks and villages. These units can plan separately to achieve the balanced economic growth. "*For large scale participation of people in planning exercise it is necessary to draft and implement the plan from below (local level). Each state plan should be divided into different district, sub-division, block and panchayat level units and each unit should be allowed to fix their target in order to achieve the desired goal*". (Dutta, 1983: 142.)

A historical review of the planning process in India shows that there has been attempts in the past to draw up development plans for districts and blocks as well as production plans for villages. During the formulation of the 5th Five-Year Plan also it was recognized that a more overview of problems of states or the application of generalized solutions is unlikely to lead to the desired results in areas with significantly different resource endowments, infrastructure, settlement pattern and production relations. The

Planning Commission thus accepted the principle of multilevel planning by constituting State Planning Board and District Planning Cells (sub-divisional level in Assam) to plan from below. "*But for future action, it may be made clear that there can be no meaningful district planning unless there is some scope for decision making at district level.* (Reddy, 1979: 149.)

In the state, local planning for balanced development failed due to lack of commitment on the part of departmental heads and absence of local level co-ordination among the different departments. So it is necessary to set up inter-departmental development committees at district and sub-division level under the leadership of a senior officer of the planning department to guide, scrutinize and later finalize the plans.

The planners, both at the state and central level streamlined the investment on a national pattern, without giving rational consideration to the local needs and aspirations of the people, living under varieties of physical, ecological and social situations. The plans ought to have delivered the goods to the districts in accordance with the level of socio-economic development. The socio-economic differences are the root of the differences in the level of development. "*The success of a plan does not depend upon the quantum of investment alone, but to a greater extent on the acceptance of the schemes by the people for whom it is meant and their unconditional participation. This is the area where lacuna of the present planning process lies, the ideology enshrined in the planning principle does not motivate the people in general to participate in the development process.*" (Barthakur, 1983: 165.)

"An important development taking place in Assam is decentralization of the planning process. A two-tier *Panchayati Raj* system came into force under Assam Panchayati Raj Act. 1972. A three-tier system has now been provided under the Act of 1986 which consists of *mahakuma parishad*, *anchalik panchayat* and *gram panchayat*. The origanizational set up consists besically of sub-divisional planning and development councils in the plains districts and core groups at the district level. The core group prepares plan and puts them up before the sub divisional planning and development councils. These plans then go to the appropriate departments". (Raman, 1991)

Although the organizational set up of the planning process seems to be very sound yet the success will depend on the sincere implementation of the programmes at various levels.

7.2 AGRICULTURAL POLICY MEASURES

The economy of Assam is mainly dependent on agriculture. About 70 per cent of the total population of the state are getting their means of livelyhood from agricultural sector. As per 1991 census, 64 per cent of the total workforce in Assam are agricultural workers.

Since the Third Five-Year Plan onwards, Green Revolution or New Agricultural strategy was adopted in India in a restricted manner. It is only since eighties that Assam started to experience the adoption of new agricultural strategy with the growing use of HYV seeds, chemical fertilizers, modern implements etc. to a limited extent only. The following are some of the impacts of Green Revolution on the agriculture of Assam.

7.2.1 Area under HYV Paddy

In rice (HYV) the replacement rate is kept low in the initial years because the farmers generally keep seed from the best part of their plots and harvest the desired variety which is stored after proper drying. Although late, but due to adoption of new agricultural policy, the area under HYV paddy in Assam gradually increased from 2.87 iakh hectares in 1975-76 to 11.44 lakh hectares in 1993-94 and further to 12.47 lakh hectares in 1997-98 which amounts to 45 per cent of net sown area of the state.

7.2.2 Consumption of Chemical Fertilizer

With the adoption of new agricultural strategy, the consumption of fertilizer by the agricultural sector of the state is gradually on increasing trend. Total consumption of fertilizer in Assam has thus gradually increased from a mere 3.48 thousand tonnes in 1975-76 to 43.17 thousand tonnes in 1993-94. In 1997-98, total consumption of fertilizer is 71.25 thousand tonnes for both *Rabi* and *Kharif* crops which accounts for consumption of almost 18 kg per hectare. Some new statistics reveals that during 1998-99 it was 21.1 kg per hectare against the target of 35 kg per hectare whereas consumption during 1999-2000 was 29.3 against the target of 40 kg per hectare. With a view to achieve the target of 45 kg per hectare during 2000-01, the government has laid emphasis up on availability of fertilizer at any point of time. All the manufacturers are requested to stock pile of fertilizer at their different buffer points so that no district/sub-division suffer from scarcity of fertilizer in the peak season of crop cultivation. Moreover all the District Agriculture Officers (DAO) are instructed to gear up the extension machineries to keep strict vigil on availability of fertilizer at different whole sellers/retailers.

Assam State Agricultural Marketing Board (ASAMB) has been permitted by the government to deal in fertilizer business in the state in addition to the state agencies like STATFED and Assam Agro-Industries Development Corporation Ltd. The ASAMB will handle fertilizer business through their various regulated market committees. *[Seminar Papers on Green Revolution in Assam, 2000]*.

7.2.3 Yield Rate

With the introduction of new agricultural strategy to a limited range along with the adoption of hybrid seeds, chemical fertilizers and expansion of irrigation facilities, the average yield per hactare of some principal crops started to show some positive results. The average yield per hectare of winter rice has increased from 1046 kg in 1960-61 to 1472 kg. in 1994-95. The average yield of wheat per hectare in Assam has also increased from 824 kg. In 1960-61 to 1290 kg in 1994-95 and further to 1332 kg in 1996-97. The average yield per hectare of potato has increased from 4784 kg in 1960-61 to 7854 kgs in 1994-95. Other important crops which recorded rise in productivity includes jute, sugarcane and rape and mustard.

7.2.4 Increase in Production

With the adoption of the new strategy, total production of foodgrain in the state of Assam gradually increased from 16.79 lakh tonnes in 1960-61 to 34.90 lakh tonnes in 1994-95 and 35.77 lakh tonnes in 1997-98. During 1997-98 the production of foodgrains shows a very marginal increase of 1.3 per cent over the previous year.

7.2.5 Multiple Cropping System

With the adoption of the new strategy, the farmers in the state started to adopt multiple cropping system in agricultural operations. This has resulted increase in agricultural production and has also enlarged the employment opportunities for the farm labourers. With the expansion of irrigation facilities within the state, more and more areas can be brought under the multiple cropping system, which would go a long way to benefit the farmers of the state.

7.2.6 Irrigation

Investment to large scale irrigation system over the years in the state have not shown much contributing results. Given the increasing difficulty and time needed to raise rice yields, a major thrust for cost effective expansion of irrigated area and generating technology for higher rice yields has been given during the current plan period. The target set is 10 lakh hectares of assured irrigation by installation of quick maturing irrigation project with coverage of 2 to 2.2 hectares per unit of Shallow Tube-wells (STW) and LLP. In order to achieve the target, assured irrigation facilities need to be increased from the present level of 2.24 lakh hectares by an additional area of 7.76 lakh hectares so as to reach the targeted total of 10 lakh hectares by the end of 9th Five-Year Plan.

The period spanning between independence till 1995-96 records an incipient number of 61,428 of STW installed throughout the state. The year after i.e. 1996-97 marked the watershed in the history of STW in the state when a thrust was given to sinking STW in a large scale as a mean of providing assured irrigation to the farming community. Financial assistance was availed of from the World Bank and NABARD with the result that an additional number of 62,250 STW were installed till March, 2000. Another 70,000 STW under NABARD are expected to be installed by May 2000 and 15,000 under World Bank by March 2001 during which time a total number of 1,47,250 STW would have been installed providing assured irrigation to 2,94,500 hectares. The irrigation network so provided is vital for growing *Rabi* crops, specially

Summer Rice and will pave the way for increased rice production in the state.

7.2.7 Intra-State Imbalance

"The adoption of the new strategy of green revolution has been widening the agricultural disparities between different district of the state of Assam. The districts like Marigaon, Nagaon, Barpeta, Nalbari and Darrang have been progressing at a quicker pace in respect of modernization as compared to other districts like Dhemaji, N.C. Hills, Cachar, Lakhimpur etc. leading to alerming disparities between different districts of the state." **Dhar, 1998: 129**.)

Adoption of modern technology or method is known as modernization of agriculture or transfer of technology in agriculture. Transfer of technology in agriculture in the state is progressing at a very slow pace. Adoption of the strategy of green revolution could not make much headway in Assam even at this later stage. There are certain major obstacles responsible for the slow pace of technology transfer in agriculture in the state. Some of them are – absence of sufficient assured irrigation, small size of agricultural holdings, limited use of HYV seeds, scanty use of chemical fertilizer, lack of adequate finance, natural problems like flood, lack of agricultural research and last but not the least – lack of motivation on the part of farmers and educated youths.

7.2.8 Land Reform in Assam

Land is one of the basic inputs for production in agriculture and allied activities. Thus to remodel the existing agrarian structure, reform of the present land system is an important step. The economy of Assam is totally dependent on agriculture. The land tenure system in Assam was not at all satisfactory. The system of land holding stood in a way of agricultural development of the state. Thus the Government of Assam introduced various land reform measures in the state during different years since independence. The main purpose of such land reforms would be to alter the pattern of land ownership and bring about such a structural change in the rural society as to ensure the fruits of production are equitably enjoyed by those who toil in the agricultural land. Some of these measures include – Abolition of intermediary tenures, Protection to *Adhiars*,

Preparation of Tenants' and *Adhiars*' Records of Rights, Protection to tribal people, Consolidation of holdings and Land ceiling etc. But due to faults in legislation, lack of political will, bureaucratic hurdles and lack of people's co-operation the response from land reform programme in Assam which was started with good spirit and enthusiasm was lost in the mid-stream.

Globalization of the economy and economic reforms introduced in the country have also widened the scope of development of agriculture sector along with the development of industry and trade. Assam being an agricultural state can reap the maximum benefit exporting various agricultural, horticultural and floricultural products to different countries. For this some modifications of land reform in view of ongoing economic reform are the urgent need of the hour.

7.2.9 Programmes for increasing agricultural production and productivity (1995-96)

The department of agriculture have taken up 48 state plan schemes, 20 Central Sector Schemes and 7 Centrally-sponsored Schemes providing thrust on -

(a) Irrigation and water management,

(b) Machanisation,

(c) Quality Input supply,

(d) Training and transfer of technology.

Centrally-sponsored schemes

1. National pulse development programme,
2. Special Jute development programme (100%),
3. Oilseed production programme (75% 25%),
4. Integrated cereal development programme (75% 25%),
5. NWDPRA (100%),
6. Control of pest and diseases (50% 50%),
7. I. P. M. (Integrated Pest Management) (100%).

Central Sector Schemes:

1. Minikit demonstration of wheat,
2. Minikit demonstration of Maize,
3. Promotion of agricultural Mechanisation,
4. Integrated programme for development of spices,
5. Development of horticulture in temperate region,
6. Development of Arecanut,
7. Establishment of nutritional garden,
8. Integrated development of tropical and arid zones fruits,
9. Mushroom cultivation,
10. Transfer of technology through fruits and vegetable growers,
11. Betelvine cultivation,
12. Production and supply of vegetable seeds,
13. Root and tuber crops,
14. Commercial floriculture,
15. Use of plastic in agriculture,
16. Fertilizer subsidy to small and marginal farmers,
17. Assistance to fertilizer promotion,
18. Strengthening of quality control laboratory,
19. Balance and integrated use of fertilizer,
20. I. P. R. D. (II) rice minikit.

7.2.10 Major Schemes at a Glance

1. **Integrated Cereals Development Programme in Rice-based Cropping System Areas (ICDP-Rice):**

In order to boost up production of rice, a centrally sponsored ICDP–Rice scheme is in implementation in 75 Nos. of Development

Blocks in the state. The programme during 1995-96 is proposed to be taken up with the following components –

(i) Field demonstration on cropping system approach with assistance limited to Rs. 2,000.00 per acre.

(ii) Demonstration on IPM approach with assistance limited to Rs. 6,000.00 per demonstration or 40 hectares.

(iii) Technology transfer through training of farmers including women

(iv) Varietal replacement and propogation of new germplasm incentative at Rs. 200.00 per Qtls of HYV paddy seeds.

(v) Awards to GPs for maximum productivity

(vi) Incentive on improved Bullock drawn and hand operated farm implements at 50% limited to Rs. 1500.00 per implement per farmer

GOI share – Rs. 147.21 lakhs (1995-96

State share – *Rs. 28.47 lakhs*

Total – *Rs. 175.68 lakhs*

2. Oilseed production programme

This is a Centrally-sponsored scheme implementing presently in 19 districts. In the state, rape and mustard occupies on an average 92 per cent of total oilseeds areas followed by linseed 3 per cent and sesamum 5 per cent. In order to boost up oilseeds production, greater efforts are laid on groundnut and sunflower during *Rabi* / Pre-*Kharif* and Nizer in the Rabi season. The major components are as follows:

(i) Subsidy on seeds @ Rs. 300 per qtl.

(ii) Free distribution of input kit for rape and mustard, groundnut, sunflower.

(iii) Opening of new retail outlet @ Rs. 5000 each

(iv) Large size demonstration on rape and mustard and sesamum cultivation

(v) Distribution of micronutrients @ Rs. 100 per hactare

(vi) Farmers training

Total scheme - Rs. 325.25 lakhs (1995-96)

GOI Share - Rs. 243.94 lakhs

State Share - Rs. 81.31 lakhs

3. National Pulse Development Programme

This is a central sector scheme and implementing solely to narrow the gap of production and requirement. The major components are as below:

(i) Subsidy on certified seeds @ Rs. 300 per qtl.

(ii) Assistance for production and purchase of breeder seeds and foundation seeds @ Rs. 400 per qtl.

(iii) Free minikit seed distribution – summer green gram and *rajmah.*

(iv) Organization of demonstration (10 hactare) 100% subsidy. (pea, *rajmah*, black gram etc.)

Total Scheme - Rs. 27.00 lakhs (1995-96)

GOI - Rs. 20.00 lakhs

State seeds - Rs. 7.00 lakhs

4. Special Jute Development Programme

Jute is an important fibre crop in Assam. Considering the potentiality, government of India introduced a special Jute Development Programme with 100 per cent subsidy. The components are given below:

(i) Seed Subsidy @ Rs. 600. per Qtl

(ii) Implements subsidy

(iii) *Katcha* retting tank – 80 nos.

(iv) Fungal culture Pkt – 40,000 nos.

(v) demonstration

5. Ramie Crop

Along with jute crop, government of India also introduced a programme for the extensive cultivation of Ramie crop and accordingly components are fixed as follows:

(i) Rhizome subsidy – 80 Qtls

(ii) Demonstration – 20 ha

(iii) Minikit distribution

(iv) Decorticator – 20 nos.

(v) Deguming unit – 1 nos.

Total Scheme	-	Jute:	Rs. 45,73,000.00
(1995-96)	-	Ramie:	Rs. 39,81,000.00
Total	-		Rs. 85,54,000.00

6. Promotion of Agricultural Mechanisation

The state agricultural department also implemented a Central Sector Scheme on Promotion of Agricultural Mechanisation and provided subsidy to the farmers to the maximum of Rs. 30,000 for the purchase of tractors below 18 HP and their matching implements.

7. Farm Machinery Training Programme

In view of making available trained manpower for operation, maintenance and management of agricultural machinery, the state department of agriculture have 18. Farm Machinery Training Centres where regular training is imparted.

8. Horticulture Development

Horticulture crops presently occupy around 5 lakh hectares or 13% of the gross cropped area in order of 23% fruit crops, 16% nut crops, 31% vegetables, 15% tuber crops and 15% spices crops. The departments of agriculture has already undertaken promotional activities to boost up production of fruits, vegetables and spices.

Promotional steps proposed are:

(a) assistance to growers and entrepreneurs, for quality materials,

(b) assistance for market development and promotion,

(c) assistance to promote quality,

(d) training facilities for upgradetion for technical skills,

(e) information for improvement of post harvest handling.

Besides State Plan Schemes, the department is implementing 11. Central sector schemes and providing assistance to growers and entrepreneurs to boost-up horticultural production.

9. Floriculture

Assam is the treasure house of various flowers, ornamental plants, orchids etc. Flowers like gladiolus, rose, marigold, ornamental plants and orchids have great potential and market demand.

Emphasis has been given and identified some pockets for production of flowers commercially. It is proposed to provide assistance for planting materials and other inputs. More stress has been given on training for production technology. The department is implementing a Central Sector Scheme "Commercial Floriculture" for development of floriculture in the state.

10. Medicinal Plants

The state has abundant rich varieties of medicinal plants and herbs. Efforts have been under way to identify selected pockets for extensive cultivation of medicinal plants and herbs. Assistance and incentives are proposed to help development of entrepreneurs.

Employment Generation

Stress has been given on Self-Employment to the educated unemployed youth through several departmental schemes so as to reduce the pressure of growing unemployment. The department has been creating employment avenues for the year 1994-95 as follows:

i) Indirect/Self-Employment	36,025 nos.
ii) Target for 1995-96	50,000 Nos.

PROGRAMME COMPONENTS OF TSP AND SCCP SCHEMES (1995-96)

Scheme	*T.S.P*	*S.C.C.P*
1. **Multiple cropping**	a) Seed, fertilizer, . pesticides etc at 100% subsidy for multiple cropping	a) Seed, fertilizer pesticides etc at 100% subsidy for at 100% subsidy for
	b) Plant protections sprayer at 95% subsidy	b) Plant protections sprayer at 95% subsidy
	c) Seed bin at 100% subsidy	c) Seed bin at 100% subsidy
2. **50% subsidy sale of fertilizer**	Distribution of fertilizer at 50% subsidy to the maximum benefit Rs. 154 per benificiary for 3 bigha land	Nil
3. **Integrated Horticulture Development**	Distribution of inputs for for Horticultural crop and maintenance of progency orchard	Distribution of inputs for horticultural crop to the benificiary
4. **Agril marketing**	a) distribution of paddle thresher at 95% subsidy	distribution of paddle thresher at 95% subsidy (948 benificiary)
	b) Thella/ boat with Rs. 1400/- subsidy each (1299 beneficiary)	b) Thella/ boat with Rs. 1400/- subsidy each (948 benificiary)
	c) Sale counter of fertilizer to provide inputs for an amount of Rs 5424/- per beneficiary (1299 beneficiary).	c) Sale counter of fertilizer to provide inputs for an amount of Rs 5424/- (948 benificiary)
5. **Integrated agril engineering Div.**	a) Distribution of 524 sets of Paddle Thresher, Paddy Weeder, M. B. Plough at 75% subsidy,	Nil
	b) Tractorisation of farmers, land at 50% subsidy hiring rate,	b) Tractorisation of farmers, land at 50% subsidy hiring rate,
	c) 25 . Medium HP Tractor with a subsidy of	33 Medium HP Tractor with 75,000/-

(contd...)

Scheme	T.S.P	S.C.C.P
	Rs. 75,000/- each, 45 Nos. Power tillers with a subsidy of Rs. 30,000/- each and 5 HP Power Pump with a subsidy of Rs. 5,000/- each.	subsidy, 33 Nos. power tillers with 30,000/- subsidy and 187 nos. power sets with Rs. 5000/- subsidy each.
	d) Three agril growth centres at Jonai, Goalpara & Dimoria to be set up to provide customer hire service facilities to S T farmer.	3 nos. growth centres at Boko, Marigaon and Mangaldois
6. **Promotion of technology**	a) Training an modern method of cultivation to the ST farmerof by providing stipend,	a) Training an modern method cultivation to the ST farmer by providing stipend,
	b) To conduct the outside the state tour and inside the state tour for farmer	
7. **Inputs distribution in flood prone area**	Nil	a) Distribution of paddy seeds with the subsidy of Rs. 200/- per Qtl seed.
		b) Distribution of wheat seeds with the subsidy of Rs. 250/- per Qtl.

Agricultural Marketing and Quality Control

The State government has drawn up schemes for strengthening regulation and development of rural markets by creating infrastructural facilities, grading and standardisation of agricultural commodities, setting up of cold storage and assistance for marketing of fruits and vegetables.

(a) Scheme for Development of Regular Markets

Fifteen of principal markets and 19 of sub-markets have been established to regulate marketing of about 20 notified agriculture commodities providing facilities like godowns, auction platform etc.

(b) Scheme for Marketing of Fruits and Vegetables

A decentralized scheme providing subsidized transport facility to farmer groups/PPS to carry surplus produce to the terminal/ consumer market to safeguard remunerative prices. The year wise achievements are as follows:

Year	*Fruits/vegetables Carried in tonns*	*Growers benefited*
1991-92	1491	2500 Nos.
1992-93	2700	6000 Nos.
1993-94	6286	8575 Nos.
1994-95	9500	11,000 Nos.

(c) Scheme for Quality Control and Agmark Grading

Agmark laboratories have been established in Guwahati, Tezpur, Nagaon, Jorhat, Dibrugarh, Silchar and Barpeta Road with the programme of agmarking mustard oil, spices, honey etc. The progress of four years are as follows:

1991-92	268 tonns
1991-93	282 tonns
1993-94	305 tonns
1994-95	418 tonns
1995-96 (target)	1705 tonns

(d) Scheme for Jute grading and bailing

Two months training on jute grading and bailing is imparted at Howli jute grading and bailing training Centre.

The progress of four years are as follows:

Year	*Nos. trained*
1991-92	68
1991-93	57
1993-94	23
1994-95	95

(e) India International Trade Fair at New-Delhi

The marketing wing of the department of agriculture participated in the IITF at New Delhi since past few years with a view to develop working of indigenous agriculture products in the international market.

For the first time, 8 entrepreneurs participated in the fair with Govt. assistance. Products like Joha rice, Bora rice, Kamal rice, Ginger, Pine apple, spices etc. displayed by them received tremendous response from the visitors. Marketing linkage of mushroom, ginger, rice etc. had been established for future trading.

7.3 INDUSTRIAL POLICY MEASURES

The manufacturing sector of Assam is very poor in its size and its contribution to state income is also very poor. Being industrially poor, the state's economy cannot expect sufficient income out of this sector. Thus the per cent of income derived from manufacturing sector out of total state income remained at a poor level as the economy of the state is mainly agrarian in nature.

During the British period the industrial development in Assam was very poor. After independence, although planning started in Assam along with other states of the country, the aim of the state plan was tilted towards the development of agricultural sector neglecting the industrial sector.

During the first decade of planning the industrial sector practically remained stagnant. It was during the third plan that industrial development programmes were accelerated to provide much needed boost to this sector. A favourable climate for investment in industries had been created with expansion of infrastructural facilities. During the fourth plan, the pace of industrialization in the state was geared up with the establishment of a number of resource-based industries mostly in the public sector located in some of the relatively badkward areas of Assam. These include Assam Co-operative Jute Mill at Silghat, Assam Alkali Allied and Chemicals Ltd. at Jogighopa, Ashok Paper Mill at Jogighopa. Some existing industries of the state were also expanded during this plan period. During 19 years of planning till fourth plan the number of registered factories in Assam increased from 911 in 1951 to 1588 in 1969 and employment increased from 65.1 thousand to 79.4 thousand over the same period in such factories. During the fifth plan some important industries were commissioned which included Bokajan Cement Factory, Assam Petro-Chemicals Complex at Namrup and Cachar Sugar Mills Ltd. Bongaigaon Refinery and Petro-Chemicals Ltd. (BRPL) is among the factories registered during 1978 with highest number of 1000 employees.

The state government is not only patronizing establishment of industries in the private sector but has also, increasingly involved itself in undertaking many industrial ventures of its own. Due to these efforts, a few important resource and demand-based industries have come up in the state in the recent past and a few more are in the offing.

Industrial development till the end of the Sixth Plan in Assam were not at all satisfactory considering the degree of economic problems faced by the state. Tea and oil industries are still dominating the economy of the state. But for proper industrial and economic development of the state industrial diversification based on the basis of natural resources is the best way.

7.3.1 Industrial Policy of Assam, 1986

In December, 1986 the new industrial policy of Assam was announced by the government for serving the local interests. This policy aimed at encouraging growth and production of all industries based on local resources, local demands, local scarcity conditions and local environment. In this new policy the State government attached priority to speedy industrial development of the state as well as generation of adequate employment opportunities through self-employment in industrial sector.

7.3.2 Industrial Policy of Assam, 1991

After the announcement of new industrial policy in July 1991 by the Rao Government at the Centre, the government of Assam has also announced its new industrial policy keeping conformity with the Central Policy. While framing the new policy, although the State government has followed the central policy directions, it has duly considered the local issues and problems faced by the state. The new industrial policy (1991) had set certain definite policy guidelines and objectives to meet its requirements of industrial opportunities. The new policy had been formulated with the experience of the 1986 policy and keeping in view the shortcomings of the 1986 policy which have come to notice so that the genuine aspirations of the people could be met within a time frame, through economic and industrial development of the state. The new policy aimed at encouraging growth and promotion of all industries based on local scarcity condition, local environment and to the extent possible by utilizing locally available raw materials. The first and foremost objective of this policy was to wipe-out regional disparity and ensure balanced regional development through rapid promotion of Khadi and village industry, cottage industry, tiny, small and ancillary industries throughout the state on the basis of techno-economic surveys.

7.3.3 Industrial Policy of Assam, 1997

Industrial Policy Resolutions, 1997

The Industrial Policy 1997 has been formulated with the experience of implementation of Industrial Policies declared by government of Assam in 1982, 1986 and 1991. Before formulating the policy, views and opinions of large cross section of academicians, industrialists, businessman, prominent personalities, Industries Associations and individuals having interest in industrial development in the state were obtained through advertisement in prominent newspapers. The response was overwhelming and a number of suggestions have been considered. Besides, recommendations made in the seminar on Industrial Policy held on 30th July, 1996 and also the broad recommendation made by the Advisory Committee on industries on 5th August, 1996 have also been considered for the purpose.

The Goal of the Industrial Policy

The Industrial Policy will be to provide an effective thrust to expeditious promotion and growth of all industries with a view to creating a strong industrial base and employment opportunities in various directions:

The basic thrust of the new industrial policy is to:

1. Create necessary conditions for maximum possible utilization of locally available raw materials and human resources for industrialization.
2. Offer competitive advantages to investors from both within and outside the region as well as foreign investors setting up industries within the state.
3. Ensure that advantages offered by the State and Central Government's incentives packages are reaped by every one in time.
4. Give special attention to the following areas in the process of industrialization:

   (i) Development of local skill and entrepreneurial abilities.

   (ii) Development of women entrepreneurs.

   (iii) Creation of maximum employment opportunities for local people.

   (iv) Development of food processing industry.

   (v) Growth of export oriented units.

   (vi) Promotion of rural non-farm sector.

   (vii) Balanced regional development within the state by giving special attention to the less developed areas and the hill districts.

   (viii) Revival of sick units

   (ix) Development and promotion of village and small scale service and business enterprises (SSSBEs)

   (x) Establishment of medium and large scale mother industries in public, private, joint and assisted sector to create an industrial base, offering large scale opportunities in multiple directions through backward and forward linkages.

BROAD MEASURES TO ACHIEVE THE GOAL AND OBJECTIVES OF THE INDUSTRIAL POLICY

1. Take effective steps to provide basic infrastructural facilities.
2. Provide an attractive incentive package offering competitive advantages.
3. Take up with Central Government for providing an incentive package to facilitate flow of fund from within and outside the country to the state to enable major projects to be setup as nucleus of growth without sacrificing competitiveness in national and global market.
4. Set-up a responsive industrial network.
5. Maintain close interaction with those engaged in development and production of hydrocarbon resources
   (i) For enhancing the resource base
   (ii) For creating conditions for utilization of their end-products within the state.
6. Initiate interaction with major industrial houses within and outside the country as well as those operating within the state for taking up new industrial projects in the state.
7. Create an environment conducive to generation of investor's confidence and smooth implementation of the projects
8. Ensure a preferential treatment to local entrepreneurs under various schemes of IDBI/SIDBI/NEDFI and other financial institutions and banks.
9. Ensure all possible assistance to tea industry including small tea growers for further growth as well as for shifting of their Head Offices to meet socio-economic objectives and also to other related agencies/institutes like Guwahati Tea Auction Centre, Inland Container Depot etc. in their efforts for growth and expansion.
10. Take up with major industries like Tea, Oil, Coal, Paper for providing all required help and for taking result oriented

action for setting up ancillary units relevant to these industries.

11. Take up with major United Nations Development Programme (UNDP) & National Centre for Jute Diversification (NCJD) to provide financial and technical assistance to all entrepreneurs of Assam to setup diversified jute industries in the state.

12. Take up with Central Government for intensification of exploration activities to enhance the production of hydrocarbon resources to which the industrial development of Assam is closely linked.

APPROACH TO INDUSTRIAL DEVELOPMENT

The Government of Assam has identified the following priorities to facilitate setting up of industries in the state.

Infrastructure

Adequate infrastructure are considered to be the pre-requisite for industrial development. Lack of infrastructure in North East is one of the main reasons for poor growth of industries in the state of Assam. Therefore, Government of Assam proposes to give top most priority to development of infrastructural facilities in the state to promote setting up of industries. The state has a shortage of developed land for industrial purposes. The Assam Industrial Development Corporation Limited (AIDC) has been allotted Government land at a number of places for development as Industrial Areas. The state Government would provide adequate fund to the AIDC Ltd. for development of these areas. The state Government has also a proposal for setting up of three Growth Centres within next five years. The state Government also proposes to implement the scheme Integrated Infrastructure Development (IID) centres which are at different stages of clearance from the authorities. The State Government will continue its policy of construction of industrial esatae and making available industrial sheds, and commercial sheds at subsidized rents to Small and Tiny sector industries. The existing industrial estates will be revived and industrial sheds etc. which are being occupied by industries already closed down will be got vacated and allotted to new entrepreneurs. The Government will also make a study on the working of the existing/ proposed industrial estates/industrial areas/ commercial estates/ growth centres of the state. A common rules and procedures will be adopted for allotment of land/sheds/fixation of rent/recovery of outstanding dues/vacation of defaulting industries to ensure proper functioning.

Power

The total power available in the state at present is around 315 MW which is less than peak demand of 375-400 MW, but the off-peak demand is around 270 MW only. Therefore there is surplus power during off-peak time. The Government, with help of Assam State Electricity Board and North Eastern Power Corporation Ltd. would take steps to increase the availability of the power during the next five years by facilitating completion of the power generation projects under implementation in the state. Such projects are Kathalguri Gas Based Power Project, Amuguri Gas based Power Project, Karbi-Anglong Hydor Electric power project and Lower Kopili Hydro Electric Power project. Once these projects are commissioned within the next few years the state of Assam as well as North Eastern Region will be a power surplus area. The Government will also take up with Assam State Electricity Board for priority connections to the industries to be set up in the state and for ensuring the supply of quality power to industries. The Industries Department of Govt. of Assam will impress upon the Government of Assam to declare a power policy for encouraging captive power generation units by the industries. The Government in its package of incentives will also provide subsidy for the generating sets apart from subsidy on power tariffs.

Communication

Surface Communication

The length of National Highway in the State of Assam is over 2000 km and that of State Highway is over 2100 km. The major towns in the state are connected by National Highways. During the next five years, the Government would give priority for development of the roads leading to the industrial areas. The conversion of Metre Gauge railway line from Lumding to Dibrugarh is likely to be completed soon. The third railway cum road bridge at Jogighopa, Goalpara is likely to be completed by end of 1997. The State Government has already taken up with Government of India for the conversion of existing Meter Gauge Railway line from Lumding to Badarpur and from Rangia to Murkangselek to Broad Gauge. The Government would also give top most priority to construction of the 4th bridge over river Brahmaputra at Bogibeel near Dibrugarh. To remove the transport bottleneck, the State Government has also taken up with Government of India for upgradation of existing Broad Gauge railway line up to Guwahati from single track to double tracks

Air Communication

In view of the high priority given by Government to the export oriented units, the State Government already pursuing with Government of India to declare Guwahati Airport as an International Airport at least for giving custom clearance facilities to the industrial units at Guwahati itself.

Waterways

The matter of developing the Brahmaputra River way which has already been declared as National Waterways, will be taken up with Government of India for economic movement of the cargo through the river ways.

Tele-communication

The present tele-communication net-work in the state is fast growing in comparison to other parts of the country and no problems faced presently by the industries in getting telephone and other tele-communication facilities by them.

Finance

The regional offices of all leading financial institutions and banks in the country are located in the state and, therefore, it is expected that entrepreneurs will not face any problem in the matter of getting finance for their projects. In addition to regional offices of Industrial Development Bank of India (IDBI), Industrial Finance Corporation of India, Small Industries Development Bank of India (SIDBI) which are already located in the state, recently the Government of India has setup the North Eastern Development Finance Corporation Ltd. (NEDFI) especially for financing the industrial projects in the North Eastern Region. Therefore, these institutions would be able to make the finance available to the entrepreneurs for setting up of industries. There are more than 1200 bank branches in the state in addition to the regional offices of all the leading nationalized banks. The Government is, however aware about the slow rate of flow of credit to the local entrepreneurs and the problems they are facing in getting term loan and working capital. To help the entrepreneurs to sort out their problems with the financial institutions and banks, services of the officers of the District Industries Centre will be made available to them to liaise on their behalf with fnancial institutions and banks. The industries department will take effective steps for recovery of outstanding dues payable to the banks and financial institutions by the borrowers.

STRENGTHENING DISTRICT INDUSTRIES CENTRES

There are 23 District Industries Centres (DIC) in the state and the Government recognises the vital roles to be played by the DICs for development of SSI and tiny sector industries. The Government would strengthen the DICs of Bongaigaon, Morigaon, Golaghat, Tinsukia, Dhemaji and Hailakandi and these will be upgraded to full fledged DIC at the earliest. Each DIC will have a *Udyog Sahayak Cell* to guide the entrepreneurs in the matter of setting up industries including selection of industries/entrepreneurs, preparation of project report and arrangement of finance for projects. There will also be a women cell in each DIC to give special attention to the women entrepreneurs. Steps would be taken to prepare viable project profiles for each DIC and make them available to the entrepreneurs. The data bank will also be created in each DIC for the benefit of the entrepreneurs. The District Advisory Committee is to be reconstituted for monitoring the working of the District Industries Centres.

Categories of Industries

Small, Tiny and Ancillary Industries

Keeping in view the employment potentiality in the small scale sector, the state Government would give top most priority towards setting up of industries in the small scale sector. Additional incentives would be given for the small scale and tiny sector. The Assam Preferential Store Purchase Act, 1989 is already in force to give marketing support to these industries. The raw materials bank in Assam Small Industries Development Corporation Ltd. (ASIDC Ltd.) would be revived and strengthened. The State Government will take up with the Central Public Sector Undertakings the matter of giving ancillary status to the industries wherever possible. There are more than 25000 number of small scale and tiny sector registered units (both of SIDO and non-SIDO) in the state. According to the last SSI census, generally 45% of the units are either closed or untraceable. The State Government will prepare a status report in the units to study in detail the reasons for the high mortality of the unit in the small sector and will take appropriate steps for rehabilitation of sick units.

Large and Medium Industries

The Government will encourage environment friendly industries and projects in the state. The AIDC Ltd. has identified several viable projects for the coming years. On selective basis Government will also participate by way of equity participation in the projects. The Government will constitute a High Level Committee under the Chairmanship of Commissioner/Secretary Industries to monitor the implementation of industrial entrepreneur memorandum (IEM) and Letter of Intent (LI)/Industrial Licence (IL) issued by the Government of India from time to time.

Handloom and Handicraft Industries

The State of Assam is traditionally known for its rich handloom and handicraft products and the Government will ensure promotion of this sector through various development schemes. The Government will take all possible steps for getting financial and technical assistance from the Government of India for implementation of various schemes. The State Government will conduct a survey on various handicraft products and registration of handicraft unit willl be done by DICs of Assam. The Government will strengthen the Handicraft Research and Design Centre, Cottage Industries Training Institute and Cottage Industries Museum for the development of Handicraft Industries in the state. All possible measures will be taken to assist the craftsman, artisans of various crafts and also the Non-Government Organizations (NGO)/Co-operative Societies for development of Handicraft Industries in the state. The Government will take necessary measures to export the Handicraft products to outside the country and will also participate in exhibitions at various parts of the country to give exposure to the Handicraft products.

Rural Non-Farm Sector

The Rural Non-Farm Sector (RNFS) has a tremendous scope for development in the state. In a. recently conducted sruvey, NABARD has identified 10 sectors for development which includes sectoral schemes like agriculture, fish rearing and processing, rural retail trade, sericulture and silk textile, fibre products, construction, small plantation products, handloom, handicraft, mainly cane, bamboo and wood products. These activities are to be developed for creation of additional employment in the rural areas. The development department like agriculture, handloom and textile, sericulture, fishery, veterinary, panchayat and rural development etc. are to be associated to implement these schemes within a definite time frame.

Agro and Food Processing Industries

The economy of Assam is predominantly an agrarian economy. There is ample scope for development particularly in the rural areas for processing of cereals, fruits, vegetables, milk, meat and other agricultural products like jute, ramie etc. The Government will encourage development of agro and food processing industries by providing possible basic infrastructure to the industries. The Government of Assam will encourage setting up of fruit processing, vegetables processing, aquaculture, horticulture based projects in the state. Apart from that, Government will take necessary action to motivate the investors for commercial exploitation and setting up of projects on medicinal herbs, aromatic plants, rubber plantation and processing, small tea garden etc. The Government of Assam is very much aware about the viability of setting up of industries like diversified jute products and ramie based industries in Assam by prospective entrepreneurs. The Government of Assam will provide necessary support for setting up of such units in the state.

Industrial Sickness

Revival of industries in the SSI and tiny sector is a major problem in the state. The Government of Assam feels that the potentially viable sick SSI and tiny units are to be identified through an intensive survey as the revival process is a complex one since the reasons leading to sickness are manifold and most of the units are too tiny in nature. To facilitate revival of sick units Government will provide meaningful assistance. The Government will suitably amend the Assam Industrial Relief Undertaking (Special Provision) Act. 1984. The units declared as relief undertaking under the provision of the act will be provided assistance under the policy.

NRI and Foreign Direct Investment

The State Government will actively promote foreign direct investment in the projects that involve and improve infrastructure like power, roads, social and health care facilities. To accelerate the process of implementation and reduce the time required for obtaining permission and clearance a high power co-ordination committee will be setup. The Government has declared AIDC Ltd. as a nodal agency for co-ordinating NRI and Foreign investment.

Export

In the coming year Assam has a tremendous potential for exporting various products manufactured locally to the East and South East Asian countries due to its strategic location. The first traditional route was opened at Moreh in Manipur with a possibility of a second border point being open at Chamhai. The internal waterways net-work connect it to Bangladesh, giving its access to the parts of Chittagong (Bangladesh) and Calcutta (India). Both the waterways and land routes could be made available to investors for export to East and South East Asia.

The Government of Assam is already pursuing with the Government of India to declare Guwahati Airport as an International Airport with all clearance facilities. The Government of Assam in association with the Government of India is setting up an Export Promotion Industrial Park (EPIP) at Amingaon to facilitate export units. The Government of Assam will also provide additional incentive to the Export Oriented Units under the policy.

Human Resource Development

Lack of skilled man power is one of the most important factors for industrial backwardness of the state of Assam. The Government will ensure development of skills among the local people and up-gradation of skill on a continuous basis. For this purpose the Government will review the performance of out-dated training programme and new technology suitable to the present context will be adopted. Government will give top most priority on technical training in reputed organization/Institutes for skill development. Apart from that, emphasis will also be given for development of managerial capability to the local youths through incentives to Entrepreneurship Development Programme (EDP).

Public Sector Policy

The State Government is aware of the fact that most of the State Government Public Sector Units (PSU) are running at losses. The Government will take/adopt a policy for revival of such PSUs and wherever necessary the Government will not hesitate in involving the private sector participation for such revival.

Women Entrepreneur

Women constitute half of the population of the state and they have been entering in every field of economic activity now a days. The Government of Assam is aware of the fact that the women entrepreneurs should get due priority for their economic development as well as to meet ends of social justice. To encourage the women entrepreneurs as well as for generation of employment among the women, the Government will give preference to them while allotting industrial sheds, developed plots in Industrial Area/Estate/Growth Centre to the extent of 30%. The Government will also open a women cell in each and every DIC to cater to the need of the women entrepreneurs in addition to women cell already functioning in the Directorate of Industries. Apart from that Government will also provide additional incentives to the women entrepreneurs for setting up of industries.

Electronic Industry

In the Electronic sector Government of Assam will declare the Assam Electronics Development Corporation Ltd. (AEDC Ltd.) as a Nodal Agency for over all development of electronic Industries of the state. The AEDC Ltd. will prepare a detail action plan for setting up of Software Technology Park, Optical Fibre project and other viable projects including skill development, raw material assistance to the other small units. The Government will provide necessary incentives to these units under the policy.

Plastic Based Industries

Plastics are fast replacing the conventional metal and wood item in our day to day life. Their uses have been more pronounced in industrial sectors. The Government of Assam has attached considerable importance for development of this sector. All possible efforts will be mobilized for development of this sector providing necessary incentives under the policy.

Gas Cracker and Refinery Downstream Industries

In a bid to tap the vast resource of oil and gas the fourth oil refinery at Numaligarh has already been sanctioned and works are going on. The much awaited Gas Cracker project is also in the way. The State Government will take necessary measures to establish feasible down stream/ancillary industries to the state based on these two mega projects.

Congenial Atmosphere For Industrial Development

The Government of Assam recognizes the fact that the prevailing situation in the state has slowed down the pace of industrial development. Therefore, the Government of Assam would strive to uhser in a congenial atmosphere in the state by maintenance of law and order. Special attention will be given for security to the industries to be set up in the state.

Package of Incentives

Incentives

The incentives under the 1997 scheme shall be available for eligible units of the following categories:

1. SSI units
2. Tiny unit
3. Small Scale Service and Business Enterprises (SSSBEs)
4. Sick Units/Relief Undertaking Units subject to a maximum period of 3 years
5. Units set up by women entrepreneurs
6. Large and medium sector units
7. Export-oriented Units
8. Units undergoing Expansion/Diversification/Modernisation

The incentives under 1997 Scheme are as follows:

1. Power subsidy
2. State Capital Investment Subsidy
3. Sale Tax Exemption
4. Subsidy on Generating Set
5. Equity Participation in the assisted sector
6. Contribution to Feasibility study cost
7. Miscellaneous subsidy comprising of drawl of power line subsidy, subsidy on fees for procurement of NRDC technology, study on pollution control measures and quality control measure.
8. Subsidy on infrastructure facilities.

9. Manpower development subsidy
10. Special incentives for pioneer unit
11. Special incentives for Export-oriented Unit comprising of additional SCIS and special incentives for getting ISO 9000 and BIS 14000 series.
12. Special package of incentives for women entrepreneurs, physically handicapped persons and agro-food processing industries.

PROCEDURE FOR IMPLEMENTATION AND MONITORING

Udyog Sahayak Cell

In order to provide various information and facilities and to ensure proper delivery of all services, a separate wing known as *Udyog Sahayak* is already functioning in DIC, AIDC Ltd. and Directorate of Industries.

The primary objectives of *Udyog Sahayak* is to provide various facilities to the entrepreneurs and to ensure expeditious identification of entrepreneurs and projects, guidance for registration, processing of eligibility certificates, monitoring of proposals financed by the financial institutions, disbursement of incentives, follow-up for rapid implementation of the projects etc.

Functions of Udyog Sahayak

All administrative departments shall refer all issues related to the implementation of the 1997 Industrial Policy to the Udyog Sahaik and keep the *Udyog Sahayak* apprised of all actions taken in this regard. Accordingly, all administrative departments shall issue instruction to all Heads of Departments/Officers/Corporations/ Boards under their administrative control to co-ordinate effectively with the *Udyog Sahayak* in the implementation of the 1997 Industrial Policy. The *Udyog Sahayak* will perform the following function:

(i) Proper and adequate publicity of the Industrial Policy of 1997 as well as render all assistance to the entrepreneurs to avail the benefits of the incentives scheme.

(ii) Identification of prospective entrepreneurs, building up of a data bank to guide and motivate the potential entrepreneurs and also to prepare viable projects profiles in different categories on investment.

(iii) Enlistment of application and issuance eligibility certificates under industrial policies.

(iv) Co-ordination with the connected agencies/administrative departments, including processing and forwarding of financial proposals.

(v) Proper and effective implementation of all incentives schemes and issuance of sanctions thereof.

(vi) To refer all relevant issues to the Government on Committees framed thereunder to any matter connected with implementation of the policy.

REFERENCES

Barthakur, M. (1985). "Formulation of Planning and development strategies for N. E. India – the land of seven sisters" – in: Alam K. (ed) *Planning in North East India*, Omsons publications, Guwahti.

Das Gupta, P. K. (1985). "Social dimensions of planning with reference to North-East India" – in Alam K. (ed) *op. cit*, Guwahti.

Dhar, P. K. (1988) *The Economy of Assam*, Kalyani Publishers, New Delhi.

Dutta Kartick Ch. (1985) "Need for local level planning for economic development – A case study of Sibsagar sub-division planning" in: Alam K. (ed), *op cit.*

Reddy, Y. V. (1979). "Multilevel planning in India" , Viking Publishing House, New Delhi.

Seminar papers on Green Revolution in Assam, June 2000, organized by Government of Assam with RBI, NABARD and Public Sector Banks.

8

Summary of Findings and Conclusion

8.1 MAJOR FINDINGS OF THE STUDY AND CONCLUSION

One of the main objectives of planning in India is the attainment of an egalitarian socio-economic order with balanced development of regions. The reduction of regional development disparity both at the inter-state and intrastate level is given much importance by the Indian planners. In our study we have made an attempt with the help of quantitative tools and techniques to analyse the inter district development disparities in Assam having 23 districts at present. An analysis of the disparities in different sectors of the state economy such as agriculture, industry and basic infrastructure and services (BIS) at the inter-district level has been attempted through secondary statistics. An overall inter-district disparities has also been analysed taking cognisance of disparities at inter-district level in all the three sectors namely Agriculture, Industry and BIS.

In the introductory chapter (Chapter 1) we have outlined in detail the objectives of the study, rationale of the study, hypotheses encountered, sources of data, methodology of study with a detail discussion on the construction of composite indices we have used in our analysis, limitations of the study and the chapterisation scheme. Besides we have made a review of the existing literature relating to the overall development in the state of Assam.

In Chapter 2 entitled "Eco-Geographical Profile of Assam and its Districts", we have presented the economical and geographical profile of the state of Assam and its districts. Under geographical profile we have presented location and boundaries of the state, the physiography of the state and its natural resource base. Under economic profile we have given an outline of agriculture, industry and BIS separately. Under agricultural economy we have discussed land use pattern, yield rate of crops, consumption of fertilizer, irrigation facilities, agricultural implements used by the cultivators and tea plantation in Assam.

Under Industrial Profile we have made a discussion on registered factories, small industries and large and medium scale industries in the state.

Under Infrastructural profile of the state a discussion is made on transport and communication system of the state, postal and telecommunication services, power, co-operative movement in the state, banking services and socio-economic environment.

Under District Profile of Assam we have discussed location and boundaries; natural geography; population and habitation; natural resources; agriculture and industry and transportation of each district. We have also presented in tabular form information relating to population, area, density, sex-ratio, literacy rate, number of sub-divisions and blocks, length of road under PWD, ranking positions in terms of poulation and literacy rate of each district.

Chapter 3 entitled "Spatial Disparities in Agricultural Development in Assam" is devoted to an empirical study in inter-district disparities in agricultural development in the state of Assam. We have first of all given a brief description relating to the state of agriculture in Assam, agro-climatic sub-zones of Assam, agricultural development in crop production in Assam where the various crops include rice, wheat, pulses, oil seeds, jute and mesta, sugarcane, potato, spices and fruits like banana, pineapple, orange, lemon, jackfruit, guava mango etc. We have also made a review of some works done on disparities in agricultural development.

In our empirical work we have made an alalysis of inter-district development disparities in agricultural sector in Assam with secondary data collected from various sources. The indicators choosen for the purpose of our study are – (i) percentage of cultivable land to total land area, (ii) percentage of area sown to total cultivable area, (iii) percentage of irrigation potential created to net sown area, (iv) cropping intensity, v) average yield of food grains per hectare, (vi) percentage of high yielding variety area under paddy to net sown area and (vii) consumption of fertiliser per hectare of total cropped area. We have ranked all the 23 districts in terms of each of the seven chosen indicators. We have also calculated the co-efficient of variation (C.V) in respect of each indicator which reflects the degree of heterogeneity among the districts in terms of the indicator under study.

Agricultural Development Indices (ADI) for different districts of Assam by Indexing Method have been calculated and the districts have been ranked. As per this method, Marigaon district ranks first in terms of agricultural development followed by Nagaon, Darrang, Barpeta, Nalbari etc.

The agricultural development indices (ADI) for different districts have also been calculated by using the Deprivation Method. As per this method, Nagaon district tops the list in terms of agricultural development followed by Marigaon, Barpeta, Darrang, Nalbari etc. We find a very little difference or no difference between the ranks of the same district assigned on the basis of Indexing Method and Deprivation Method.

The results based on both the methods are displayed in a systematic way in tabular form showing the development status of various agro-climatic sub-zones of Assam. We have found that the entire Upper Brahmaputra Valley (North) comprising Lakhimpur, Dhemaji and Sonitpur districts is backward so far as agricultural development is concerned. So far as the Upper Brahmaputra Valley (South) sub-zone (which consists of five districts, namely. Tinsukia, Dibrugarh, Sibsagar, Jorhat and Golaghat) is concerned, while Indexing Method shows only Jorhat district as relatively developed and others as backward, the Deprivation Method shows only Sibsagar district as moderately developed and others as backward. Hence we conclude the entire sub-zone as backward in terms of agricultural development. We find that out of eight agricultural sub-zones of the state only the Central Brahmaputra Valley comprising Nagaon and Marigaon districts and Lower Brahmaputra Valley (North-West) comprising Nalbari, Barpeta and Darrang districts are relatively or moderately developed sub-zones and all other 6 agricultural sub-zones comprising 18 districts are backward. Since Deprivation Method is an absolute measure of development and no district is categorized as developed on the basis of this method, hence we conclude that there is not a single district in Assam which may be called agriculturally developed in absolute sense.

Chapter 4 entitled "Levels of Industrial Development in Assam" is devoted to an empirical study of inter-district disparities in industrial development in Assam. In this chapter, first we have given a description of industrial features of the state of Assam, industrial potential of Assam and a review of some works done on disparities in industrial development.

We have then made an alalysis of inter-district development disparities in industrial sector in Assam with secondary data collected from different sources. The indicators selected for our study are: (i) percentage of secondary sector workers to total workforce, (ii) percentage of registered factory workers to total workforce, (iii) number of registered factories per 100 sq. km. area and (iv) maximum horse-power installed per industrial worker in registered factories. We have ranked each of the 23 districts of the state in terms of all the four chosen indicators. We have then calculated the coefficient of variation (C.V.) in respect of each indicator to reflect the degree of inequality among the districts of the state in terms of indicators under study.

Industrial Development Indices (IDI) for all the 23 districts of the state have been calculated by Indexing Method and the districts have been ranked on the basis of IDI values. As per this method 8 districts out of 23 are categorised as relatively developed and the rest 15 are shown as backward. Bongaigaon ranks first in industrial development followed respectively by Tinsukia, Dibrugarh, Kamrup, Sonitpur, Sibsagar, Jorhat and N.C. Hills respectively.

We have also calculated IDI values for districts of Assam by applying Deprivation Method. This method places only 3 districts of the state namely Tinsukia, Kamrup and Dibrugarh as moderately developed in industrial sector and the rest 20 districts as backward. This method, being an absolute measure of development, classifies no districts as developed and thus we conclude that in the state there is even not a single district which may be termed industrially developed in absolute term.

The C.V. for IDI values by both Indexing Method and Deprivation Method are calculated at 70% and 73% respectively indicating significant imbalances in industrial development in the districts of the state.

Chapter-V is entitled as "Inter District Developmental Disparities in Basic Infrastructure and Services (BIS) in Assam". In this chapter, we have discussed at the beginning the role of infrastructure in economic development of a region citing some examples. Then we have made a review of works done on developmental disparities in BIS. After this we have made an attempt to analyse inter-district developmental disparities in the state of Assam with secondary data collected from varius sources. The 14 select indicators for this analysis are – (i) percentage of literacy, (ii) percentage of urban population, (iii) percentage of tertiary sector workers, (iv) number of primary and middle schools per 10,000 population, (v) number of high schools per 10,000 of population, (vi) number of colleges per lakh population, (vii) number of hospitals/dispensaries per 10,000 population, (viii) number of medical beds per 10,000 population, (ix) infant mortality per 1000 births, (x) road length per 100 sq. km. area, (xi) road length per lakh population, (xii) percentage of villages electrified, (xiii) number of post offices per 10,000 population and (xiv) number of banks per lakh population. We have then ranked all the 23 districts of the state in terms of all the 14 chosen indicators of BIS and have also calculated the C.V. in respect of each indicator for reflecting disparities among the districts of the state.

We have also calculated Basic Infrastructure and Services Development Indices (BISDI) for all the 23 districts of the state using Indexing Method and Deprivation Method and the districts have been ranked on the basis of BISDI values by both the methods. According to the Indexing Method 8 districts out of 23 in the state namely N.C. Hills, Jorhat, Kamrup, Lakhimpur, Dibrugarh, Karbi-Anglong, Sibsagar and Nalbari are classified as relatively development districts in BIS sector and the remaining 15 districts are reported to be backward. The co-efficient of variation (C.V.) of BISDI by Indexing Method has been calculated at 23%.

Deprivation Method has classified only 3 districts namely, N.C. Hills, Jorhat and Kamrup as moderately developed in respect of

BIS and the rest 20 districts as backward. The C.V. of BISDI by this method has been found to be around 29 per cent. Deprivation Method being an absolute measure of development, classified no districts of the state as developed and hence we conclude that not a single district in the state is developed in respect of BIS in absolute sense.

Chapter 6 entitled "Inter-District Variation in Overall Economic Development" is devoted to an empirical study of inter-district disparities in overall economic development in the state of Assam covering all the three sectors of state economy viz. Agriculture, Industry and BIS with all the chosen 25 indicators (7 for agriculture,4 for industry and 14 for BIS). Here we have calculated Overall Development Indices (ODI) for all the 23 districts of Assam by using Indexing Method, Deprivation Method and Principal Component Method on the basis of the 25 select indicators of development.

Indexing Method has classified 10 districts out of 23 as relatively developed in respect of overall economic development. These 10 districts are respectively N.C. Hills, Kamrup, Jorhat, Dibrugarh, Bongaigaon, Sibsagar, Tinsukia, Nagaon, Sonitpur and Marigaon. The rest 13 districts are categorized as backward with Dhemaji placed in the 23rd position.

Deprivation Method has classified only 3 districts viz. Kamrup, N.C. Hills and Jorhat as moderately developed districts with regard to overall economic development and the remaining 20 districts as backward. No district in the state is found to be developed by this method in absolute sense.

On the other hand, Principal Component Method had classified six districts of the state as moderately developed. These are respectively Kamrup, Jorhat, Bongaigaon, Nagaon, Sonitpur and N.C. Hills in descending order. Out of the remaining 17 districts, 6 districts are classified as developing, 6 districts as backward and 5 districts as very backward. The developing districts are respectively Dibrugarh, Barpeta, Sibsagar, Nalbari, Darrang and Kokrajhar. The backward districts are Cachar, Marigaon, Dhubri, Goalpara, Lakhimpur and Hailakandi. The very backward districts are Golaghat, Tinsukia, Karbi-Anglong, Karimganj and Dhemaji.

Dhemaji is placed in 23rd position by all the three methods we have used. Only three districts namely Kamrup, N.C. Hills and Jorhat are calassified as developed – relatively or moderately by all the three methods. So these three districts in the state with Kamrup in the first position (as classified by Principal Component Method and Deprivation Method) have been considered to be the leading districts in the state so far as overall economic development is concerned on the basis of the 25 select indicators of development. Of the remaining 20 districts, some are developing, some are backward and some are very backward in respect of overall economic development. We have also found that there exists only a little difference in ranking positions of some districts by the three methods we considered. Some districts have been assigned the same rank by all the three methods.

From our study we have come to the conclusion that inter-district disparity in agricultural development in the state is not so singnificant. Out of the seven agricultural development indicators we have chosen, consumption of fertilizer, irrigation facilities and area under HYV paddy are mostly responsible for agricultural heterogeneity in the districts of Assam. It is expected that proper policy from government's side will be able to iron out the agricultural development disparities in districts of the state.

From the empirical analysis of our study relating to industrial sector we have come to the conclusion that inter-district disparities in industrial development in the state is alarming. All the four indicators of industrial development we have chosen, depict very high heterogenity in respect of industrial development in districts of the state of Assam and this points to the fact that inter-district imbalances in industrial development is one of the main forces behind overall economic development disparities in districts of the state.

Our empirical work on BIS sector involving 14 select indicators brings to light the fact that out of these 14 indicators only a few, namely - road length per lakh population, number of medical beds per lakh population and number of colleges per lakh population are mostly responsible for the existing inter-district heterogeneity in respect of BIS sector development. Thus we like to conclude /that concrete efforts on the part of policy-makers to develop transportation, health care and educational networks would certainly be able to wipe out inter-district inequalities in development of BIS sector.

As all the three methods viz. Indexing Method, Deprivation Method and Principal Component Method we have chosen for our quantitative analysis of inter-district development disparities in the state of Assam are telling almost the same story with a little variation, regarding the three sectors of state economy namely, Agriculture, Industry and BIS, we have confidently drawn the above conclusions.

Economic stagnation distorts social equilibrium. It results in chaos and also anarchy at all levels of society. For breaking the economic impass a stable and sustainable economic re-engineering process is urgently required which will build Assam a land of prosperity wiping out prevailing disparities. Change for better future can only originate from change in the mindest of people and policy makers. The mind set of our people and planners has to be radically changed if the mission of building a better future for Assam with balanced development is to succeeded.

REFERENCES

Assam Beyond, 2000 by Assam Prakalpa, *The Tribune Press*, Guwahati.

Insurgence to resurgence – A Blueprint of Economic Development of Assam, North East Chamber of Commerce & Industries Guwahati, 2000.

Seminar papers on Green Revolution in Assam, June-2000, Organised by Government of Asssm with RBI, NABARD and Public Sector Banks.

Goswami A., (1985), "Contents of economic development of North-East India" in: Alam K. (ed) *Planning in North East India*, Omsons Publication, Guwahati.

BIBLIOGRAPHY

RESEARCH PAPERS/ARTICLES

Anuradha, A and Rao, A.V.V.S.K,: "An Analysis of Inter-State Industrial Disparities in India, 1970-71 – 1985-86" – *Indian Journal of Regional Science*, Vol. XXIX, No. 1, 1995.

Baishya, P.: "Handlooms and Handicrafts of Assam – A 21st Century Poerspective", presented at Seminar on *Assam Beyond 2000*, 1998.

Barthakur M.,: "Formulation of Planning and development strategies for N. E. India – the land & seven sisters", in: Alam K. (ed) P*lanning in North East India*, Omsons publications, Guwahti. 1985.

Barua, G.: "Information Technology in Assam Beyond 2000", presented at *seminar on Assam Beyond* 2000, 1998.

Baruah, R. K.: "Stepping up Development in Assam", *Financial Express*, 2 September, 1990, PP. 4 –1.

Baruah, Tapanlal.: "Role of AIDC Ltd. in Promotion of Industries in Assam. *Assam Information*, Vol. 42 June–August, 1990, PP. 19 – 24.

Bhatia, S. S., (1966): "Spatial variations, changes and trends in agricultural efficiency in U.P. 1953-63", *Indian Journal Agricultural Economics*, Vol. 207, no. 4, Oct-Dec.

Barman, A. K.: "Agriculture in Assam: New twist needed", *The Assam Tribune*, Feb – 18, 2000.

Barman, K. K.: "Rejuvenating the economy of Assam", *The Assam Tribune*, March 30, 2000.

Bezbarua, A. K.: "IT vision for Assam – Building the virtuous cycle", presented at *Seminar on Assam Beyond 2000*, 1998.

Bezbaruah, M. P.: Assam Economy – The Past Trends and Some Future Projections", presented at *seminar on Assam Beyond 2000*, 1998.

Bhagat, L. N.: "Inter-Regional Disparity in Agricultural Infrastructure – A case study in Bihar", *Indian Journal of Agricultural Economics*, Vol. XXXVII, No. 1, January–March 1983.

Bhuyan, Padmalochan and Das, N.C.: "Financing of rural development programmes: A case study in Assam", In Mathur, T. N. and Garg, Subhash, (eds). *Strategies and practices of rural development in India*, Jaipur, Arihant, 1991.

Bhaumik, Kirit: "Assam: Focus on agrarian aspects", *Yojana*, 15 June 1991, PP. 28,30.

Bhowmick, Pradip Kumar: "Rural Development Through Voluntary Action – A Study in Assam", *Bulletin of the Cultural Research Institute*, 18(3–4), 1992, pp. 65-67.

Bhuyan, Kabita.: "Credit utilization pattern of IRDP beneficiaries of Darrang district, Assam", *Journal of North East India Council*, 21(1) April 1997, pp. 58-63.

Bhuyan, Sanjib.: "Marketing agricultural produce and development of the tribal economy in Assam: Overview", *Journal of the North Eastern Council*, 11(4) October–December 1990. pp. 14-17.

Borthakur, D. N.: "Floods in Assam – Causes and Cure With Particular Reference to Ecology and Environment", *Assam Beyond 2000*, 1998.

Bose, A. N.: "Regional Planning in India in the current phase of globalisation", *Indian Journal of Regional Science*, Vol. XXXI, No. 1, 1999.

Chattopadyaya, B and Raja Moonis: "Regional Development, Analytical framework and Indicators" – *Indian Journal of Regional Science*, Vol. VII, No. 1, 1975.

Choudhury, A.: "Higher Education – General", presented at seminar on *Assam Beyond 2000*, 1999.

Das Gupta P. K.,: "Social dimensions of planning with reference to North-East India", in: Alam K. (ed), *Planning in North East India,* Omsons publications, Guwahti. 1985.

Das Gupta, B: "Socio-Economic classification of Districts – A Statistical Approach" – *Economic and Political Weekly*, April 14, 1971.

Das, Samirkumar.: "Immigration and agricultural modernization: The case of Assam (1979-83)", *Socialist Perspective* 20 (3-4) December 1992 – March 1993, pp. 165-175.

Dash, Tapsh R. and Sudhir, V.: "Performance of Handloom Cooperatives in Assam – An Economic Study", *Asian Economic Review*, 37(2), August 1995 pp. 312-17.

De, Ranabijoy: "Sickness in small industry: A case study", *Assam Economic Journal,* Vol. 8, 1991, PP. 54-64.

Don, H. and Others: "Potential welfare effects of spreading agricultural protection to developing countries in the Asian pacific region", *Indian Journal of Agricultural Economics*, 45(4) October-December 1990, PP. 495-502.

Dutta Kartick Ch.,: "Need for local level planning for economic development – A case study of Sibsagar sub-division planning" - in: Alam K. (ed), *Planning incentives North East India*, Omsons publications, Guwahti. 1985.

Dadibhavi, R. V.: "Disparities in development of North-Karnataka", *Indian Journal of Regional Science*, Vol. XXX, No. 2, 1998.

Dutta, S. K. and Mukhopadhyay, F.: "Industrial Disparity in India: A Test of Convergence" – *Indian Journal of Regional Science*, Vol. XXXI, No. 1, 1999.

Goswami A.,: "Contents of economic development for North-East India" in: Alam K. (ed), *Planning in North East India*, Omsons Publications, Guwahati. 1985.

Goswami, Atul and Goswami, Homeswar: "Some disquieting trends of urbanisation in Assam", *Assam Economic Journal*, Vol. 8 1991, pp. 95-99.

Goswami, P. C.: "Population growth, food grains requirement and problem of food grains supply by 2001 A.D. in Assam", *Assam Economic Journal*, Vol. 10, 1994, pp. 1-10.

Goswami, P. C.: "Land Utilisation and its Econòmic Implictions (With special reference to Assam)" in: Thakur, K (ed), *Profile of a Development Strategy for India's North-East*, SPAN Publications Pvt. Ltd., Guwahati, 1988, p. 25.

Goswami, T. C.: "The cause of low consumption of tertilizers in Assam", *The North-East Times*, June 14, 2000.

Goswami, S. N. and Patgiri, A. K.: "Optimum production under risk and uncertainty in Rani block of Assam", *Indian Journal of Economics*, 73(4) April 1993, pp. 463-472.

Gogoi, J. K.: "Human resource development in agricultural sector", *The Assam Tribune*, April 3, 1999.

Gupta, S. P.: "College education in Assam", *University News*, 30(18) 4 May 1992, pp. 9-12.

Hazarika, Haren Kumar.: "Resource Mobilization for Industrialization in Assam", *Assam Information*, Vol. 42 October 1990, pp. 15-17.

Hotteling, H.: "Analysis of Complex Statistical Variable into Principal Component", *Journal of Educational Psychology* (1933), Vol. 24, pp. 407-441.

Hussain, T.: "Impact of industrial policy", *Assam Information*, Vol. 42 June-August 1990, PP. 12-15.

Joshi, B. M.: "Infrastructure and Regional Imbalances in U.P.- An Inter-District Analysis" – *Indian Journal of Regional Science*, Vol. XIX, No. , 1987.

Joshi, B. M.: "Inter-State Disparities and Economic Development" *Yojna*, Vol. 31, No. 4, March 1 – 15, 1987.

Joshi, S.: "Regional Disparities in Industrial Development in India", *Indian Jurnal of Regional Science*, Vol. XXIX, No. 1, 1997.

Kabita, B. and Barman, R.: "Accessibility: A challenge to rural development: A study in the lower Kulasi Basin of Assam", *North Eastern Geographer*, 26(1-2) 1995, pp. 33-39.

Kar, Bimal K.: "Socio-Economic Well-Being of Different Population Groups of Assam", *North Eastern Geographer* 27 (1-2), 1996, pp. 26-36.

Kaur, Dhian, Ghuman, B. S.: "Inter-District Disparities in Punjab – Implications for planning" – *Indian Journal of Regional Science*, Vol. XXVII, No. 1&2, 1995.

Kellong, C. F.(1963): "Interactions in Agriculture Development, Science, Technology and Development", *World Food Congress*, Washington, D. C.

Kanagadurai, B. and Chandra, J.: "Relation between Regional Development and Infrastructural Facilities", *Indian Journal of Regional Science*, Vol. XXVI, No. 1, 1994.

Kaur, P. and **Sethi, K.**: "Inter district variation in agricultural productivity in Punjab" – *Indian Journal of Regional Science*, Vol. XXVII, No. 1 & 2, 1995.

Kumar, S.: "Inter-State Variations in Productivity in Indian Manufacturing Sector: A Translog Index Approch." - *Indian Journal of Regional Science*, Vol. XXXI, No. 2, 1999.

Lalitha, N.: "Sate level reforms to promote Industrialization: A case study of Gujarata", *Indian Journal of Regional Science*, Vol. XXX, No. 1, 1998.

Madhab, Jayanta (2001): "New Economic Policy and Regional Disparities", in: Atul Goswami (ed), *Regional Disparities in India*, Akansha Publishing House, New Delhi.

Mahanty, G.: "Regional Development in Andhra Pradesh: A District Level Analysis" – *Indian Journal of Regional Science*, Vol. XXXI, No. 2, 1999.

Mathur, O. P.: "The problem of Inter-Regional Disparities", *Indian Journal of Regional Science*, Vol. VII, 1973.

Mazumdar, N. N.: "Contribution of SBI in the industrial development of Assam", *Assam Information*, Vol. 42 October 1990, P 37-41.

Mehta, V.: "Wanted: An agricultural policy", *The Assam Tribune*, March 2, 1999.

Mehta, V.: "Three Weakest Links in Economic Reforms", *The Assam Tribune*, April 21, 2000.

Mehta, V.: "Service Sector needs a big boost", *The Assam Tribune*, April 21, 2000.

Mitra, Ashok (1965): "Levels of Regional Development in India", Government of India.

Mitra, Mrinal K. and Mishra, S. K.: "Forward and backward linkages of rural in debetedness: A study of four tribal villages in Assam", *Man and Life*, 16(1-2) January – June 1990, pp. 37-41.

Meher, R. K.: "Industrialization drive and the functioning of small scale industries in Orissa", *Indian Journal of Regional Science*, Vol. XXV, No. 2, 1993.

Medhi, S.: "North-East needs a dynamic approach", *The Assam Tribune*, March 27, 1993.

Murugaiah, V. (1997): "Economic Disparities in Karnataka – A micro level study", *Indian Journal of Regional Science*, Vol. XXIX, No. 1.

Nath, V. (1970): "Regional Development in Indian Planning", *Economic and Political Weekly*, Annual Number, January 1970, pp. 242-260.

Nayak, P.: "Socio-economic dynamics in South Assam", Yojana 41(3) March 1997, PP. 29-30.

Neog, P. C. and Kalita, D. R.: "Diversification of small farms in flood affected areas of Assam", *Assam Economic Journal*, Vol. 10, 1994, pp. 20-25.

Nizami, Fareed A.: "Lamentable Educational Condition in Assam", *Educational Review*, 97(10) October 1991, pp. 174-75.

Pal, M. N.: "Regional Disparities in the Levels of Development in India" – *Indian Journal of Regional Science*, Vol. VII, No. 1, 1975.

Pradhan, G.: "Inter-District Analysis of Orissa: Industrial Estates" – *The Economic Times*, Aug, 24 1984.

Prasad, H. P.: "Roots of Uneven Regional Growth in India", *Economic and Political Weekly*, Vol. XXII, No. 33, 1988.

Pal, M. N.: "A method of regional analysis of economic development with special reference to South India", in Misra, R. P. (ed), *Contributions to Indian Geopraphy.*

Prasad, S.: "Steady Growth of Infrastructure", *The Assam Tribune*, May 25, 2000.

Purkayastha, G. and Chakraborty, A.: "Rural Economy in Assam", *The Assam Tribune*, March 12, 1999.

Prakash, S., Mohapatra, A. C. and Goel, N. P.: "Sectorial linkage and strategies of development in north-east region", *Indian Journal of Regional Science*, Vol. XXX, No. 2, 1998.

"Proper implementation of N.E. Industrial Policy Urged", *The Assam Tribune*, June 13 & 14, 2001.

Rahman, R. and Singh, S.: "Regional Disparities in Agricultural Growth in Assam", *North Eastern Geographer* 26(1-2) 1995, pp. 24-32.

Raman, C. V.: "Role of planning in Assam's development", *Yojana* 35(6) 15 April, 1991, p. 23.

Rao, H.: "Identification of Backward Regions and the Trends in Regional Disparities in India", *Artha Viganana*, Vol. 19, No. 2, 1977.

Rao, S. K.: "A Note on Measuring Economic Distance Between Regions in India" – *Economic and Political Weekly*, April, 28, 1978.

Rao, S. K.: "Inter Regional Variation in Agricultural Growth, 1952-53 to 1964-65 – A tentative study in Relation to Agriculture", *Economic and Political Weekly.*

Raza, M. and Singh, J.: "Food Production in India – The Regional Dimension", in: Mishra, R.P. (ed.) *Contributions to Indian Geography.*

Reddy, G. J. and Reddy, N. B. K.: "Regional Disparities in Industrial Development in Andhra Pradesh" – *India Journal of Regional Science*, Vol. XXVI, No. 1, 1994.

Raza, M and Singh, J.: "Food Production in India: The Regional Dimension" – in: Mishra, R.P. (ed.) *Contributions to Indian Geography*, PP. 258-259.

Sahai, Baldeo: "Expanding oil industry in Assam", *Democratic World*, 2 September 1990, PP. 13-14.

Sahoo, S.: "Determinants of Regional Productivity Disparities in Organised Factory Sector in Oirssa: An Econometric Analysis", *Indian Journal of Regional Science*, Vol. XXVII, No. 1&2, 1995.

Saikia, K.: "Assam Agenda – A Development Strategy for Assam Beyond 2000 A.D.", presented at *seminar on Assam Beyond 2000*, 1998.

Sarin, K. K.: "Road network in Assam developing a vital link", Yojana, 15 May 1991, P. 23.

Sarma, D.: "The impact of attitude on development", *The Assam Tribune*, April 20, 2000.

Sarma, Nandita: "Higher education in Assam: A quantitative study of Gauhati University", *University News*, 32(13) 28 March, 1994, PP. 11-13.

Sarmah, J. N.: "Problems of Economic Development in Assam", *Economic and Political Weekly*, Vol. 1, No. 7, 1996.

Saxena, K. K. and Sahoo, S: "Infrastructure and Economic Development – A Case-Study of Kanpur City", *Indian Journal of Regional Science*, Vol. XXX, No. 1, 1998.

Sen, B. K.: "Capital structure: plywood industry of Assam", *Indian Journal of Economics*, 74(1) July 1993, pp. 105-23.

Sen, Badal Kumar: "Creditorship and ownership scenario in the financial markets: A case study of plywood industry of Assam", *Assam Economic Journal*, Vol. 10, 1994, pp. 67-73.

Saikia, S.: "Marketing Strategy for SSI products", *The Assam Tribune*, July 7, 1999.

Shridharan, L.: 'District Planning: Some Basic Issues", *Indian Journal of Regional Science*, Vol. XXII, No. 2, 1991.

Sarma, A.: "Remedies for a dying economy", *The Assam Tribune*, March 23, 1999.

Shaban, A and Bhole, L. M.: "Development and Disparities in Maharastra – A spatiotemporal analysis", *Indian Journal of Regional Science*, Vol. XXXI, No. 1, 1999.

Shah, Narrottam: "Levels of Economic Development in Districts of Maharashtra – Approach in the Problems of Key Statistics" – Centre for Monitoring Indian Economy, June, 1982.

Sharma, Archana: "Co-operatives in rural economy: The case of Assam", *Indian Journal of Agricultural Economics*, 51(4) October-December 1996.

Sharma, Chandan Kumar: "Poverty and Inequality – A case of Assam", *Economic and Political Weekly*, 30(7-8) 18 February 1995, PP. 403-404.

Shukla, N and Dhagat, S.: "Disparities of Economic Development in India – A Factor Analysis Approach", *Indian Journal of Regional Science*, Vol. XXXI, No. 1, 1999.

Sidhu, Hina: "Industrial Development in Gujarat: Inter District Variation", *Indian Journal of Regional Science*, Vol. XXVII, No. 1 & 2, 1995.

Singhal, C. S.: "District rural development agencies in Assam: A study", *Kurukshetra* 43(6) March 1995, PP. 39-42.

Srivastava, S. C.: "Status of Micro Level Data in North-East India", *NIRD, NERC*, 1996.

Schwartzberg, J. E.: "Three approaches to the mapping of economic development in India", in: R.P.Misra (ed) *Contributions to Indian Geography*.

Subramanian, M. S.: "Inter-State variations in the development of family health in India – A texonomic approach", *Indian Journal of Regional Science*, Vol. XXVII, No. 1 & 2, 1995.

Tyagi Sadhna: "Levels of Agricultural Development in Aligarh District" – *Indian Journal of Regional Science*, Vol. XXVI, No. 1, 1994.

Verma, B. N. and **Das H.C.L.**: "Regional Pattern of Agriclutural Development in India (1891-1976): An Institutional Approach", *Indian Journal of Regional Science*, Vol. XXVII, No. 1 & 2, 1995.

Williamson, I. G.: "Regional Inequalities and the Process of National Growth", *Economic Development and Cultural Change*, Vol. 13, No. 4, Part – II, July, 1965.

BOOKS

A, Koutsoyiannis: "*Theory of Ecnometrics*", ELBS, 1996.

Aaker, David A and Day, George S.: "*Marketing Research" (4th Edition)* – John Wiley & Sons, 1990.

Alam, K. (ed): "*Planning in North-East India*", Omsons Publications, Guwahati, 1984.

Boyd, H. W., Westfall, R and Stasch, S. F.: "Marketing Research – Text and Cases", (6th ed), Richard D. Irwin, Inc., Homewood, Illinois, 1986.

Bhat, L. S., Kundu, A. and Sharma, A. N. (et all): "*Micro Level Planning – A Case Study of Karnal Area, Haryana, India*, K. B. Publications, New Delhi, 1976.

Chand, Mahesh and Puri, V.: "*Regional Planning in India*", Allied Publishers Pvt. Ltd., 1983.

Chaudhury, P. (1972): "*Readings in Indian Agricultural Development*", George Allen Unwin Ltd., London.

Development Issues of North-East India – Essays in Honour of P. C. Goswami, Lawyer's Book Stall, Guwahati, 1992.

Deka, P. and Bhagabati, A.: "*Geography – Economic and Regional*", Willey Eastern, Guwahati, 1992.

Dhar, P. K.: "*The Economy of Assam*", Kalyani Publishers, New Delhi, 1998.

Dutta, S. K.: *Co-operative societies and rural development (a politico-economic study)*, Mittal, New Delhi, 1991, P 206.

Falcon, W. (1970): *The green revolution: Generation of problems*, Mimco.

Ganguli, B. N. and Gupta, Debendra B. (1976): *Levels of Living in India – An Inter-State Profile*, S. Chand & Co. Ltd, New Delh.

Goswami A. (ed): *Regional disparities in India*, Akansha Publishing House, New Delhi, 2001.

Goswami, P. C.: *The Economic Development of Assam*, Kalyani Publishers, New Delhi, 1988.

Hirschman, A. O. (1961): *The Strategy of Economic Development*, Yale University Press, New Haven.

Inter-State Disparities in Development in India in Regional Structure of Development and Growth in India, Vol. 1, Ahish Publishing House, 1985.

Johnson, Richard A. and Dean, W. W.: *Applied Multivariable Statistical Analysis (4th ed)*, Prentice Hall International, Incorporated. 1998.

Joshi, B. M.: *Infrastructure and Economic Development in India*, Ashish Publishing House, New Delhi, 1993.

Kindleberger, C. P.: *Economic Development*, McGraw Hill Book Co. INC. New York, 1965.

Leibenstein, H.: *Economic Backwardness and Economic Growth Studies in Theory of Economic Development*, John Wiley & Sons INC., New York, 1957.

Medhi, S. B.: *Transport System and Economic Development in Assam*, Publication Board of Assam, 1978.

Meher, Rajkishor: *Development Disparities in a Backward Region (A District Level Analysis)*, A.P.H. Publishing Corp., New Delhi, 1999.

Mishra, G. P. (ed): *Regional Structue of Development and Growth in India*, Ashish Publishing House, New Delhi,

Mollett, J. A. (1984): *Planning for Agricultural Development*, St. Martin's Press, New York,.

Mukherjee, A.: *Methodology and Database for Decentralized Planning*, Heritage Publishers, New Delhi, 1991.

Misra, R. P. (ed): *Regional Planning – Concepts, techniques, policies and case studies*, Prasaranga, The University of Mysore, 1969.

Mishra, R. P., Sundaram, K. V. & Pradash Rao, V. S. L.: *Regional Development Planning in India – A New Strategy*, Vikash, Delhi, 1974.

Myint, H.: *The Economics of the Devloping Countries*, B. I. Publications, New Delhi, 1973.

Needleman, L. (ed): *Regional Analysis*, Penguine Modern Economic Readings, England, 1968.

Raza, M and Mahmod, A: *Statistical Methods in Geographical Studies* (4th edition), Rajesh Publications, New Delhi, 1998.

Reddy, Y. V.,(1979): *Multilevel planning in India*, Viking Publishing House, New Delhi.

Schumpeter, Joseph A: *The Theory of Economic Development*, Oxford Universith Press, New Delhi, 1961.

Sen, S. R.: *The Strategy for Agricultural Development and Other Essays on Economic Policy and Planning*, Asia Publishing House, New Delhi, 1966.

Shrivastava, S. C. (1999): *Levels and structure of development – An inter-district study of north-east India*, National Institute of Rural Development, Hyderabad.

Singh, R. L. (ed): *India – A Regional Geography*, National Geographic Society of India, Varanasi, 1999.

Taher, M. and Ahmed, P.: *Geography of North-East India*, El-Dorado Publications, Guwahati, 1998.

Thakur, P. (ed): *Profile of a Development Strategy for India's North-East*, Span Publications Pvt. Ltd., Guwahati, 1988.

Tewari, R. T. (1986): *Economic Infrastructure and Regional Development in India*, Working Paper No. 67, Giri Institute of Development Studies, Lucknow.

Verma, R. K.: *Development Infrastructure for Rural Economy,* Printwell, Jaipur (India), 1996.

THESIS

Bora, Devendra Nath: "Problems and prospects of sugar industry in Assam: A case study of Assam Cooperative Sugar Mills Ltd.", Borua Bamungaon, (Unpublished) Ph.D. Thesis submitted in Gauhati University, 1990.

Chaoudhury, Sunanda Kumar: "A study on the agricultural development of Karbi Anglong since independence", (Unpublished) Ph.D. Thesis submitted in Gauhati University, 1985.

Choudhury, B.: "Spatio-Temporal Dynamism in the Agricultural Development in Assam – An Econometric Approach", Ph. D. Thesis (unpublished) submitted in Gauhati University, 1994.

Choudhury, M. K (1993): " Inter-District Disparity in Industrial Development of Assam: An Econometric Approach", (Unpublished) Ph. D. thesis submitted in Gauhati University.

Goswami, Ajit Pavan: "Educational development and economic growth in Assam, 1961-70 to 1974-75: An empirical investigation", 1990. Ph.D. Thesis suabmitted in Dibrugarh University.

Sarma, Basanta Kumar: "Role of industrial estates in the promotion of small industrial undertakings in Assam", (Unpublished) Ph.D. Thesis submitted in Gauhati University, 1990. Govt. of Assam Publications

Government of Assam Publications.

Agricultural Development in Assam, Dept. of Agriculture, Govt. Assam

Basic Statistics Relating to Community Development Blocks in Assam, 1977-78.

Basic Agricultural Statistics, Assam, 1997-98, Directorate of Agriculture, Govt. of Assam.

Development and Planning – Five Year Plan Documents (From 1st to 8th Plans)

Directorate of Information and Public Relation – Assam Information, June – 1995, Vol. 47(41), Feb 1990; Vol. 43, April 1, 1991.

Economic Survey of Assam, 1997-98

Statistical Handbook of Assam, 1995, 1997

"Seminar papers on Green Revolution in Assam", June-2000, Organised by Government of Assam with RBI, NABARD and Public Sector Banks.

GOVT. OF INDIA PUBLICATIONS

Annual Survey of Industries – Provisional Results for Factory Sector, 1996-97, C.S.O., Government of India.

Census of India 1991 Assam – Town Directory, Part – IX – A.

Census of India 1991, Series 4 – Assam, Part III – B Series – Economic Tables.

Census of India, 1991 – Assam State District Profile 1991.

Census of India: Census Reports 1951,1961,1971,1981.

Features of the New Industrial Polity & Other Concessions for the North-Eastern Region.

Government of India, Identification of Backward areas, Planning Commission, 1969.

Government of India (1976): *Report on National Commission on Agriculture*, New Delhi.

Government of India (1973): *Report of the Task-Force on Agrarian Relations in India*, New Delhi.

Government of India, Planning Commission – *Approach Paper to the Ninth Five Year Plan* (1997-2002).

Planning Commission, Government of India, Second Five Year Plan, 1956.

Statistical Pocket Book, India, 1985.

REPORTS

Assam Beyond 2000, *ASOM PRAKALPA, The Tribune Press,* Guwahati, 2000.

Databank, by NEDFi, NIC and NEC.

India's Agricultural Sector – A Compendium of Statistics, September 1995, CMIE Pvt. Ltd.

District profiles of states, CMIE Pvt. Ltd., 1993.

Insurgence to Resurgence – A Blueprint for Economic Development of Assam, NECCI, Guwahati, 2000.

Report of Advisory Committee on Industry, Assam, Vol. 1 & 2, Aug 1996.

Report on the second all India Census of Small Scale Industrial Units (Registered Up to 31.03.1988), Assam, Vol. 1, Government of India.

Regional Resource Database for North Eastern Region, Prepared by NEDFi Corp. Ltd., NIC (Assam State Unit) and NEC.

Report on Environment Analysis (Comprehensive Business plan for NEDFI – Vol. 1), Prepared by: Tata Consultancy Services, Feb, 1996.

Survey of Indian Agriculture, 2000, The Hindu.

United Nations, *Report on International Definitions and Measurement of Standards and Levels of Living*, 1954.

Index